Books by Antony Jay

MANAGEMENT AND MACHIAVELLI
THE ENGLISH (with David Frost)
THE NEW ORATORY
CORPORATION MAN

CORPORATION MAN

CORPORATION
MAN *by Antony Jay*

Who he is, what he does,
why his ancient tribal
impulses dominate the life
of the modern corporation

Random House, New York

Who sees the variety
and not the unity,
wanders on from death
to death.
        Katha Upanishad

Contents

Preface

ANYONE who tries to force a crystal to yield up the innermost secrets of its structure encounters an intriguing problem: the only available method is x-ray diffraction, but this provides two-dimensional photographs, whereas the atoms are arranged three-dimensionally in the crystal. From one single picture you cannot possibly tell how the individual atoms are arranged: you have to take more and more, until finally you are able to deduce the shape of reality from the shadowy images. Eight atoms arranged in a simple cube may surrender their secret after three or four diffraction photographs; the double helix of the DNA molecule took years of work by some of the world's leading scientists.

I use this parallel because this book is an attempt to explain the central reality of the modern corporation, and yet I always mistrust those writers who claim to have done so. Each seems to come up with a new complete explanation. The corporation is an economic unit. The corporation is a complex of personal relationships. The corporation is an organization chart. The corporation is a concept, a pyramid, a state, a monster, a game, a jungle, a battlefield, a way of life. How can all these truths be true, and what on earth is the point of my adding another unsubstantiated assertion to a list that is too long already?

That is why I started with crystallography. The point is that none of these generalizations can be the whole truth because the complexity of the corporation, as of the crystal, is three-dimensional: but any or all of them can be valuable two-dimensional diffraction photographs which help us to build up more and more understanding of the elements that compose the complex three-dimensional whole and of their relationship to each other. Some of these photographs are so close in angle to previous ones that they tell us hardly anything we did not know already. Others, by taking an unfamiliar or unexpected angle, can be a revelation. For me the original idea of *Management and Machiavelli*, the concept of business corporations being the same as political states, came like a diffraction photograph from a new angle, exposing all sorts of new elements and relationships which had been concealed in all the other plates I had looked at. Nevertheless, when I had finished the book I had a feeling that there was still something lurking inside that corporate crystal, some even more revealing picture to be taken, if only I could find the angle to look from.

I believe that I have now found the angle, and this book is the picture which it has revealed. It makes sense—at least for me—of a great many elements of the modern corporation that did not previously fit together. But I want to emphasize that this book is not the full and sole truth about the nature of the corporation which has somehow been concealed from all previous writers. It is just one more photograph, even if it is taken from a new angle, and it does not make sense unless it is looked at in conjunction with the other familiar pictures which we have all been looking at for some time. The most I would claim is that none of the others make sense either, unless looked at in conjunction with this one.

CORPORATION MAN

I

The Evolution
of Corporation Man

O N E of the most important discoveries of my working life was made between 8:30 a.m. and 6:00 p.m. on Thursday, April 9th, 1964.

On Wednesday, April 8th, I left the British Broadcasting Corporation, which I had joined more or less straight from university and military service nine years earlier. At BBC I had been a trainee, a production assistant, a producer, a program editor, a head of department. But at 8:30 a.m. on April 9th I was just me, sitting at my desk at home with a number of writing assignments which I had prudently contracted before giving in my notice. The discovery I had made by 6:00 p.m., to express it the way it appeared at the time, was the enormous amount of work that could be done in a day. Nine years in a great corporation had obliterated the memory of how much time there was if you had no telephone calls, correspondence, minutes, routine meetings,

departmental meetings, budget reviews, requests for authorization, annual interviews, policy documents, appointments
with visitors, and all the rest of that endless succession of
events and non-events that compose the manager's day, and
his year, and his life.

But the discovery can be expressed in the opposite way:
that the corporation day is absurdly, ludicrously short. Only
a week before I left I had spent a whole morning at a meeting with the head of my group, my three fellow departmental
heads, and the group administrative officer. Our problem
had what the Caliph in *Hassan* called "the monstrous beauty
of the hindquarters of an elephant." In the past year we had
recruited a large number of trainee producers to prepare for
the opening of the BBC's second channel. In a few more
months, when we thought the trainees were ready, we would
be inviting them to make formal applications for permanent
posts in our group. But—horror!—the head of a rival group
in the BBC was advertising his vacancies already, and the
trainees in our group wanted to apply for them. What could
we do? There was a BBC staff agreement saying that every
employee must be free to apply for any advertised vacancy.
Did this mean we had to stand by and watch him cream off
all our best trainees, the young men and women we had
spent a year selecting and training to work on our own programs? Should we privately warn them that applications
would bring our displeasure? Should we put up a case to the
head of personnel to suspend the normal ruling? Should we
put up a case to the director of programs to impose simul-
taneity on all groups' advertisements? There were many possibilities, and six of us to discuss them, so it is not surprising
that the meeting lasted nearly three hours.

The important point about the problem was that it was
the corporation itself that created it. It had nothing to do
with producing good programs or controlling their costs or
developing new people or ideas. It was entirely concerned
with, and consequent upon, the corporation's internal organ-

ization, and yet it took half a day—10 percent of a week—of the time of six senior managers to resolve it.

The next morning I had one of my producers on the phone in a panic. The planning department wanted to take away his staff film editor and get him to put his work out to a free lance. For several reasons this was impossible, but the planners did not seem to understand why. I spent most of that day in a telephone battle, arguing with planning, appealing to the head of programs, going back to the producer for more ammunition, drafting powerful memos, consulting the film department, proposing alternatives. By the end of the day I had won. The planning department had seen reason, they had withdrawn the proposal, and my producer and his program were safe. But what had I actually achieved in positive terms? I had merely stopped a silly mistake from being made.

It is pointless (though it would be easy) to multiply these instances. Everyone who has ever worked in or with large corporations has his own parallel experiences. I wish I had spent a week noting how much of my time was spent doing my real job—the job determined by the needs of our market, the television audience—and how much in administrative machine maintenance, stopping the corporation from grinding to a halt. The ratio would have been impressive.

But it is not only time that evaporates in large corporations. Money evaporates as well. Just before I left, I went into a stationery shop to buy typing paper, carbons, paper clips, and so on. I actually paid money over the counter for them. Real money, the sort that gets you into theaters and out of restaurants, and buys groceries and furniture and presents for the children. Previously, all stationery was bought for me with corporation money, which bore no relation to human money. It was a purely notional currency that appeared on forms and memos, but never passed through pockets or wallets. Indeed, the budget for a single edition of a weekly program might be more than the producer's annual salary. Dealing with such large sums, it was only worth a very limited effort to save a thousand dollars of corporation money on a fifty-thousand-dollar program budget, even if there were any incentive to do so. By contrast, a thousand dollars of human money could take a year's hard and conscious saving to accumulate. Equally, you could save five dollars by shooting twelve seconds' less film, and five dollars was the difference between a glass of beer and a bottle of wine for supper. But it was impossible to make the connection: corporation money, like corporation time, was simply something that was there. It had to be used up somehow, and each of us was allocated separate quantities of it to achieve various objectives. There was a certain professional pride about keeping to your own budget, but a great deal of corporation money was not on your own budget: carpets, curtains, offices, and any number of other central facilities. These we wheedled and cajoled and argued and fought for without any compunction at all, and if we finished up with more research assistants or film units or studio time than we needed we would not have dreamed of handing any back: we could always use them in some way.

An illuminating manifestation of this attitude toward money appeared when I was discussing with a top executive a proposal which might earn a considerable profit. He was not very interested (it would have meant more work for him) and more or less terminated the discussion by saying, "You realize that even if it made a million dollars a year, that's still only one percent of our gross revenue?" So it was; but it was also a million dollars, which if offered to him privately, in human money instead of corporation money, would have been worth almost any effort or sacrifice. But for all the relationship he felt between it and the money in his wallet, he might as well have been playing Monopoly. But the classic case was the one hundred pounds that the BBC advanced to the comedy writers Frank Muir and Denis Norden for a program that was ultimately canceled. Some time later they received a request from the BBC to send it back, and they replied, "We regret we have no machinery for returning money." This apparently was a completely satisfactory answer, and they never heard about the one hundred pounds again. No individual human would accept such a reason for surrendering one hundred pounds of his own money—but obviously the rules for corporation money are totally different.

Even while I was a member of the BBC I wondered if this attitude to time and money was unique or unusual among corporations. After leaving, I worked with quite a number of big organizations, and realized that in fact the BBC was rather good. (I ought in fairness to point out that the present BBC, after an almost complete change of top management and a going-over from McKinsey's, bears little relationship to the corporation I knew: but even the old BBC would have shuddered at some of the examples of corporate behavior I have since collected.) My favorite instance happened to a friend who was also a free-lance writer. He had worked out a series of comedy commercials for a detergent firm, and the agency was so delighted they fixed up a day-long conference with him and the client at a London hotel. A dozen of them met in a room with pads and pencils and blotters at each place. Around the walls were waiters and waitresses manning three tables, one with urns full of coffee and milk, another groaning under bottles of every conceivable drink, the third piled high with plates of cold ham and chicken and tongue, salads, trifles and cakes, ready for the marathon session. The clients opened the proceedings by saying they thought comedy diminished the dignity of cleanliness. The agency men turned and stared at my friend. He agreed that it might well be so—he was a writer, not a market researcher. They thereupon agreed it was better not to risk it, and the meeting was over. They all trooped out into the London street, but my friend is convinced that he was the only one who was haunted for the rest of the day by the thought of the empty room, spread with a vast banquet which no one was going to eat. But then I suppose it was corporation food.

Outside the BBC I found that the corporations' incredible unreality about time and money also extended to people. Time and time again the best and most logical person for a job was passed over in favor of some unlikely and unsuitable candidate from outside, who proceeded to make a mess of it. Often the passed-over manager would leave and discover to his astonishment that he could quadruple his income outside, and devote to his new private enterprise ten times more energy and productivity than the corporation was ever able to release or harness. I found horrifying schemes for reporting on staff that tried to turn every manager into a cross between God and a consulting psychiatrist. I found people treated with an indulgent softness that in ordinary life no one would show to a plumber or car mechanic who had fallen down on the job a quarter as badly, or with an inhuman callousness that the same people would privately not inflict on a stray dog.

But once you start judging big organizations, not by other big organizations, but by the simple standards of an ordinary human community, there is a phenomenon that is even more extraordinary than all these. By organization standards, of course, it is quite common, not in the least extraordinary: it is the absence of a sense of belonging to the corporation. Of course, in all corporations there are some people who feel part of it, and in some corporations almost everyone feels part of it. They are the ones who say "we" when talking about what the corporation makes or sells or plans to do. But "they" seems to be the more common expression, and as mergers and takeovers create fewer larger units, the "they"-to-"we" ratio increases. And yet the individual members of the corporations nearly all like to belong to some organization, to feel part of it, to be proud when it succeeds or depressed when it is going through a bad stretch. The focus of their loyalty may be a football team or a golf club or a social club or a rose-growing association, but it is not the corporation which occupies by far the largest part of their waking life.

Of course, the corporations are aware that something is wrong: over the years this awareness shifts from one symptom to another, and each shift calls into being a new branch of management consulting and stimulates scores of postgraduate theses in management or social studies. If money-wasting is the focus, there is cost accountancy, management accountancy and all manner of stock and budgetary control procedures. If it is the use of time, the organization and methods and operational research men are standing by to help. If it is the misuse or alienation of people, there are shelves full of books on personnel recruitment and motivation, bonus schemes and personality tests, and management development programs. What they all have in common is that they do not go to the heart of the problem: they are like ointment for spots, fine if you have one or two spots, but if you have chicken pox you will not cure it by putting ointment on every spot; the disease has to be attacked at the root. The most recent corporate anxiety focus is "communication," and no doubt we shall soon be seeing a troop of communication consultants come galloping over the horizon, blowing their bugles and brandishing a score of lengthy comparative studies of vertical and lateral communication in General Motors, IBM and duPont. They will serve up the usual compound of common sense, jargon and nonsense in the name of Claude Lévi-Strauss or ·Marshall McLuhan or that professor from Harvard Business School or M.I.T. whose name I didn't quite catch, and the corporations will set up internal communication programs and send managers off to communication courses, and one more spot will be covered with ointment. But the disease will not be cured.

Perhaps the most significant objective finding about large corporations was published a year or two ago in *Economica,* the quarterly review published by the London School of Economics. It showed how the average profitability of companies increased up to two or three million dollars employed capital, and then descended steadily as the amount of capital employed rose higher and higher. And yet the tendency of all industrial countries is toward larger and larger industrial units. And of course it is this very largeness that is at the root of all the other problems: small private companies of twenty or thirty people, even companies of a few hundred, do not spend ages sorting out their own managerial muddles; they do not spend money as if it were a centrally provided facility; they do not tolerate continuing incompetence or behave with impersonal cruelty; and the people who work there usually feel they belong. When the Lotus sports car company was flooded out, the 600 employees heard about it on television and came in late that night to help mop up. That sort of loyalty at Ford or British Leyland would make headline news across the nation.

Does it have to be so? Do we have to accept that this is more and more the nature of the industrial world in which we shall spend the rest of the century? I am convinced we do not, and there are enough corporate exceptions to the rule to show that large does not have to mean impersonal, inefficient, and inhuman. But in that case, have the exceptional few found corporate success by accident, or is there some factor at work which can perhaps be isolated and used to help us improve the vast clumsy modern corporation not only as a place for humans to work in but also as a profit-making industrial unit? I believe there is; all these problems spring from a single root, and the root is deep in our own natures. The truth about how a great corporation should be organized is a personal truth which each of us can recognize in himself. But the scientific knowledge which enables us to relate our personal experience to scientifically authenticated fact is only now beginning to be published. It has already caused a revolution in science, and it is hard to see how it can avoid causing an even greater revolution in the corporation.

The name of the revolution is the New Biology. Its findings and theories are scattered over thousands of papers, books, theses, and learned articles published over the past twenty years and more, and most of them concern particular discoveries and observations, and experiments with individual species of animal. But in the past few years a handful of writers, bolder than the rest, have begun to arrange all these separate mosaic pieces into a new picture of the origins and nature of man. The best known are Konrad Lorenz, Desmond Morris and Robert Ardrey: and it was above all Ardrey's three books, *African Genesis, The Territorial Imperative* and *The Social Contract,* which started off the various trains of thought that have come together in this book. The New Biology is still very new, but before it is much older it will bring as profound a change in our thinking as Freud and his successors brought a century ago. Indeed, there is a sense in which the New Biology, although it compels the most profound revision of Freud's theories, is nevertheless the completion of his work. Hard though many of Freud's explanations were to accept, there was one element in them that struck a sympathetic chord in the minds of most of Freud's readers, and that was his assertion that the spring of human action was not the controlled logical working of the reason, but the uncontrollable surge of much deeper subconscious or unconscious emotional drives. There is nothing in the New Biology to conflict with that insight, though there is a great deal to modify our views on what those drives are, and where they come from.

The basis of the New Biology is evolution. Ever since Darwin we have understood the operation of evolution and natural selection on physical characteristics: we know that giraffes have long necks because somewhere back in time there was not enough food on the lower branches of trees, with the result that the longer-necked of each generation survived to breed, and the shorter-necked died without issue; we know that tigers are striped because the unstriped varieties stood out from the dappled shadows with the result that their breakfast saw them in time and escaped, while their better camouflaged brothers and sisters ate and survived. But the New Biology takes Darwin a whole stage further: it shows animal behavior, and human behavior, as the consequence of the same evolutionary pressures that produced claws and teeth, feathers and fur, or hooves and horns. Status-seeking emerges not as an unworthy failing of jealous executives, but as an immutable ingredient in man's make-up —an ingredient he shares with many other species including the jackdaw, the baboon and the domestic hen. The same is true of exploring, and aggressive behavior, and defense of territory, and protection of young: they are deep in our nature because our predecessors who lacked these qualities died, while our ancestors who had them survived.

It would be very tempting to lead off at this stage into a book on the fundamental nature of man. After all, I have now read some ten or a dozen fairly respectable books on the subject, which have started off any number of exciting ideas. And since I have not actually studied in detail any of the relevant sciences, the free flight of those ideas is not weighed down by any inconvenient facts or restricted by the disciplines of scholarship. But the temptation must be resisted; in the words of Donald McRae, professor of sociology at the London School of Economics, the trouble with Darwinism is that it explains too much. The Darwinian principle, coupled with an intoxicating absence of concrete evidence, can be used to prove almost any theory you choose. And so its importance to this book is not for the new ideas it provides, but for the unity it gives to a whole range of ideas, discoveries and observations recorded by many people over many years. Its particular importance to me is for the sense it makes of my own personal experience of the corporation, reinforced by the experiences of friends and colleagues discussed obsessively over many years. I feel as if I have spent the past ten years working at a jigsaw puzzle. The pieces have been assembled from my own experience and memory, from observation and consultation, from discussion and interview, from books and articles on history, politics, management, behavioral science and a number of related subjects. The New Biology has not provided any more pieces: what it has done is to reveal the picture on the front of the puzzle box.

The subject only took off when scientists realized that observations of animal behavior, and especially primate behavior, ultimately depended on observations made in the wild. And so for the past thirty years or more they have tramped over mountains and through jungles, across swamp and savannah, and lurked inconspicuously in silent discomfort to try and observe the natural behavior of their quarry. My own field work may have been less systematic but it has been a good deal more comfortable, since the species I have been studying—*Homo sapiens corporalis,* Corporation Man—flourishes in a much more accessible and agreeable habitat. I have also had the advantage that in contrast with other species, this one has been abundantly observed and recorded; accounts of its behavior have come in from every country in the world and stretch back over thousands of years.

There is one other unique factor which has operated in my favor. I have been able to do something which is impossible with any other species in the animal kingdom, namely to be accepted so completely by the objects of my study that my presence in no way inhibited or modified their behavior. Indeed, there were times when I could honestly say that I felt I was one of them myself.

I I

The Picture on the Box

I N one sense it is almost impossible to date my first observations of Corporation Man: it could be when I joined the BBC, when I was called up for military service, or even my first day at school. But in that sense, all of us have any amount of evidence as to how the species behaves in its natural state. There is, however, another way of looking at it: I have also observed the natural behavior of cats and dogs, wasps and spiders and flies and birds and bees, for all of my life, but I still have little more than a jumble of impressions of what they are doing and why. The reason is that I have never watched them with clear questions in my mind, with something precise that I was trying to establish. A scientist, on the other hand, although he may see no more than I do, will understand what they are doing in a way that I never shall; the actions which to me look haphazard and arbitrary are to him part of a pattern, a pattern formed by the imperatives of survival in a hostile world. He looks at them to verify theories, explain anomalies, and provoke new questions, so that the pattern may become even clearer. I cannot claim scientific methods or scientific standards, but as an enthusiastic amateur I have begun to see patterns in the behavior of men in large organizations just as zoologists observe patterns in flocks of starlings or colonies of ants or hives of bees. Until I encountered the New Biology it never occurred to me that there might be ancient survival imperatives at the root of them, but already several years ago a part of the pattern, a corner of the jigsaw, was beginning to fit together. And in that sense I can put a fairly accurate date to the time when my observations began.

It was the late summer of 1962. For the previous five years I had been working on *Tonight,* a television current affairs/ magazine program that was seen five nights a week, forty minutes a night, at the start of the peak evening viewing period. The starting of the program in 1957 by its founder-editor, Donald Baverstock, had been one of the success stories of the BBC in its competition with commercial television: twenty percent of the nation watched it every night, it had a high reputation for its treatment of current affairs, it regularly beat the commercial opposition, critics hailed it as irreverent, provocative, and original, and it was produced remarkably cheaply. I had worked very happily on the program right from the start, but in 1961 Donald Baverstock was promoted, and the next year his successor, Alasdair Milne, followed him into the higher reaches of management, and the editorship fell on me. It was then I realized that, as far as I was concerned, the party was over.

Some of the reasons for this lay in my own shortcomings and unfitness for the job, and there was nothing I could do about them: had they been the only ones, I might in time have overcome them. But in addition, I found myself up against what I came to think of as "the third factor." Previously, as a director, producer and writer, I had been aware of only two factors that limited what we could do on the program: on the one hand the equipment, resources, money, techniques and skills at our disposal, and on the other the interest, comprehension and tastes of the audience. Part of the fascination of the job lay in exploring and extending those frontiers. Now, as editor, I came up for the first time against the third limiting factor: the corporation itself.

Of course, I had been aware of the corporation before, of its various divisions and departments and levels of hierarchy, but I had just accepted them as permanent and unalterable features of the corporate landscape. Now I found it a frontier that had to be explored and attacked like the other two. At first I simply accepted these restrictions: if I wanted more studio rehearsal, I had to ask planning; if I wanted vision lines to Paris I had to ask engineering; if I wanted three film units one week and one the next, instead of two each week, I had to ask the film department; if I wanted to fill a vacancy for a production assistant, it had to be done through the personnel department; if I wanted to pay a researcher more money, the payroll department had to agree; and so on. There were at least twelve separate authorities who restricted my freedom, and if I wanted to challenge any of them I had to do it through the head of my department, who would then have to go up to controllers and directors until the lines of authority finally met in a single man. All too often it was the director general, who frequently had more important things to worry about than an extra twenty dollars a week for my research assistant. And in the intervals between meetings and memos and all the laborious paraphernalia of case-making, I had a forty-minute program to get on the air every night.

It did not occur to me in those days to read books on management, or to study organization theory; life was too short, and my time was oversubscribed by several hours a day. But it was abundantly clear that something was wildly and hopelessly wrong. It might have been the people, but I had to admit that most of them, when not refusing me resources I needed, were quite sensible and able. And so I was forced to the conclusion that it was something to do with the way they were organized.

In my early days as a television producer I used to find bad programs much more instructive than good ones. A good program you simply enjoyed and admired; a bad one made you work out why it was bad, what principles it violated, and this in turn made you work out what the principles were. So I now started to think in the same way about corporations and organization: clearly, the BBC was violating some of the principles of organizing television—very probably all of them; so what were those principles?

I had not the remotest idea what they were, or even where to look for them. It was clear, however, that, whatever they might be, their broad purpose must be to stimulate and facilitate the production of the highest quality programs at the lowest possible price while remaining within the terms of the BBC's charter. And so in the absence of any other guidance, the best course seemed to be to look around the television service and find out what actually worked in practice. And that was extremely interesting.

Television programs in the BBC had been built up around the individual producer and the department he worked in. The departments were drama, light entertainment, talks/current affairs, children's, and so on; within them, the producers were given budgets and resources for each program or series they produced. But already a new, unofficial organization was growing up inside the official one. Not surprisingly, some of the programs or series had been better than others. More were wanted, and the producer was allowed an assistant producer or two, to enable him to produce thirteen a year instead of six. Out of these, some would be wanted for even longer, in effect as permanent fixtures: the producer would then have quite a large production team on what was in effect a permanent basis. Moreover, instead of being given the precise resources and budget for each program, he would be given staff, studios, cameras, design effort, cutting rooms, viewing theater time, and budget for the whole year.

This system had grown up spontaneously in all the departments. *Tonight* was only one example: there was also *Panorama, Monitor, Sportsview, Maigret, This Is Your Life*—and these "production team" programs were by far the most successful, the shock troops of the BBC's effective counterattack on the commercial opposition. And when you examined them, you discovered why. It was because they united in a triumphant way the two forces which many people thought were doomed to irreconcilable conflict: administrative logic and creative logic.

The administrative logic was fairly obvious. Production teams responsible for output right through the year meant that studios, film crews, design effort, staff and money could be blocked out for twelve months ahead, instead of being endlessly juggled around for hundreds of separate programs, and projections could be made for even longer periods. It meant that the illness of a single producer did not throw everything back in the melting pot. It meant that an evening's viewing could be planned with some knowledge of what the programs would be like, instead of the sty full of pigs in pokes of the earlier days. It meant that orders and contracts could be placed for twelve months, with the consequent advantages of price to the BBC and security to suppliers, writers, and performers. And the relationship between the production team's budget and the audience research figures gave a quick and easy measure of cost-effectiveness.

More interesting, at least to me, was the creative logic. It was also more surprising. The accepted stereotype of the creative artist is as a solitary—the painter alone in his studio, the composer alone at his piano, the poet alone in his garret. When working on *Tonight* I came to believe that this was a lot of romantic nonsense: the act of creating a work of art has to be solitary, but the artist does not have to be a solitary. The busy Florentine studio-workshops that produced Leonardo and Michelangelo and Raphael, the German court choirs and orchestras where Bach and Haydn learned their art, the companies of English players that Marlowe and

Shakespeare wrote for—these groups formed the creative surroundings and attracted the patrons, the admirers, and the customers that the artist depended on.

It was on *Tonight* that I learned the creative logic of a production team, and although we produced no Raphael or Bach or Shakespeare I am privately quite sure that the same logic operated for them as for us. The basic requirement is a demand for something you can supply, which of course also operates for the solitary. But the team is much better equipped to supply it, for a number of reasons. We found, to start with, that although an idea can only originate in one person's mind, it can be greatly improved if six or seven people question it and add to it, elaborate it and refine it; and in the same way, after the program is over, six or seven people are much better than one at evaluating it, drawing conclusions, seeing new possibilities to exploit or errors to be reformed. A solitary producer is too prone to elation or depression, his own ego is too intimately bound up with every decision, to be able to achieve the objectivity of a production team.

Another advantage is the size and the variety of ideas that come from a team. It is not simply that six minds have six times as many ideas—they should also have six times the output, so that cancels out. It is partly that very many ideas are only half an idea—with the single producer they stay half, with a team someone is likely to produce the other half; but much more it is a question of executive ability and production capacity. A composer writes music for the sort of choir and orchestra that he can get to perform it, an author writes his play for the cast and theater he is likely to get: indeed, the closer the writer-actors-theater or composer-orchestra-choir relationship, the more fruitful the result is likely to be. As the performers become more skillful and his confidence in them grows, so he attempts more original, varied, and demanding works. In the same way a single producer's ideas would only be for programs he could carry out on his own, they were limited by the skill, experience, judgment, and inclinations of one man; but a production team could initiate ideas that used a far wider range—a good example was *That Was the Week,* which united musicians, singers, actors, political comment, studio audiences, comedy writers, news film, documentary film, studio cameras, benchwork, and other ingredients which demanded a range of techniques and expertise which no single producer could possibly command.

There was also something you might call collective wisdom. Of course, a single producer would add to his personal skill and experience with each program, but his programs were infrequent, and at the end he alone would possess the wisdom and, so to speak, it would die with him. This wisdom was a compound of knowledge of the audience and understanding of the medium, the residuum of many lessons painfully or excitingly learned about what the audience could and could not take in or enjoy, and what cameras and microphones and interviewers and writers could and could not achieve. A production team, with its greater frequency of output, could learn much more, much faster, and could share that experience with the whole team. This became a body of knowledge which remained even if some of the team departed, and for the higher management it was a much more significant and enduring guarantee of program quality than the talent of a single producer. And just as it was refreshed by new people who joined the team, so it was available to them as a guide and teaching aid: it made a production team the best place for any novice to learn the craft. And it did more than give the novice access to this body of accumulated folk wisdom: it also offered him a variety of different roles—writer, film director, researcher, studio director, interview producer—with a correspondingly better chance of finding a suitable niche than he would have if apprenticed to a single producer.

Still another advantage was flexibility. A solitary producer might be allocated a week's filming, a week's editing, and two days in the studio. If he later wanted to postpone the filming, that was too bad—the next week was allocated to someone else. Anyway, it would then be too late for the editor who had to move on to another program. He could not even trade two of his filming days for an extra day in the studio, for the same reason. But a production team with permanent facilities all through the year could do any amount of internal juggling so long as it came out right in the end. It also gave that bit of elasticity that made private experiment possible—the sort of experiment for which a single producer would have to put up a case for special budget and resources. A production team could just try it out with a spare hour or two in the studio or a half-day with the film unit, and if it did not work no one need ever know. This made it much easier to keep up with changing tastes and techniques, and to stop the program from solidifying or getting into a rut.

It did not occur to me at this stage that I had stumbled onto something with a relevance beyond television. All I knew then was that the production team worked in a way in which neither the solitary producer outside it nor the cumbersome structure above it could ever work. It had formed itself naturally, spontaneously, and almost in spite of the existing formal structure, and it was carrying BBC television. All the same, isolating the successful element did not solve the problem. How should production teams relate to the rest of the BBC, the institution entrusted by Parliament with the provision of the television service?

The answer came quite suddenly, and it came in the form of another question. Suppose *Tonight,* and all the other production team programs, were completely outside the BBC organization? Suppose they simply contracted with the BBC to produce a certain number of programs each year at a certain price? The prospect was Elysian, not just for the money I could save if it were my own, but for the simplicity it would bring to my life, the problems it would take out of the job, the freedom I would have to think about the program. Instead of the endless internal negotiations, the cajolery and threats and memos and proposals and meetings, I would use a very simple device called money. It would buy carpets and film and scenery and stationery, it would pay staff and performers and insurance and rent, and I could at any time apply it where it was needed and withdraw it where it was unnecessary.

There were several reasons—quite sound ones—why complete independence was not possible: for instance, the BBC had to answer to Parliament for its program content, and it also had a huge investment in studios and equipment as a result of starting up television in Britain and being the sole producer for many years. But there was no reason why the BBC should not simulate the system in organizational terms: it could give me a total annual budget, lay down its rules on political balance, financial procedures, and staff policy, and leave me to get on with it. I could hire the BBC's studios and other facilities or buy them outside as I chose. I need never ask for authorizations from the film department, or engineering, or contracts, or any of the other little power enclaves; I would simply report to the controller of programs or one of his team, and, if he was satisfied, that was that. If he was dissatisfied he could reduce the budget, curtail the program, or remove me. Too easy.

It was all so beautifully obvious that I wrote a brief paper to my superiors proposing the scheme, and although it rather spoils the story they in fact took it seriously and made a number of changes along the lines I suggested. Not enough, I felt, and not all for the better, but at least it showed they were aware of the problem and wanted to do something about it. In time I might have had another go at it, but the idea of working outside large corporations was becoming more and more attractive; and so I resigned, and started to make the discoveries listed in Chapter I. I also met Doug Hughes.

Doug is a production engineer with International Computers, and we met because part of my free-lance work involved making documentary films. He wanted a film made about the computer and the numerically controlled machine tool. At the outset I thought it sounded like a piece of straightforward technical exposition, but as soon as I met Doug I realized that it went right to the heart of how to organize an engineering business. He felt about the engineering industry much as I felt about the BBC, though at first that was the only connection I could see. However, as he led me further and further into the dark recesses of the average engineering factory, lightening my path with dazzling flashes of sarcasm fueled by his rich sense of the absurd, it all began to look unbelievably familiar.

To Doug, the average engineering factory was chaos. Metal came into it in a few basic shapes—casting and sheet, billet and strip and bar—and then went through thirty or forty processes before the finished machined part went to assembly: heat treatment, milling, drilling, grinding, reaming, then more of the same, with each process under a different manager's control. Away in one building were designers stipulating tolerances that could not be achieved, and in another were estimators playing happy games with fairy-tale figures that bore no relation to the nasty realities of the factory. If any part had to be scrapped, it was never anyone's fault—the milling foreman and drilling foreman each blamed the other and the factory manager's office turned into a law court. The system worked by a sort of selective panic called "expediting," which meant that urgent parts were rushed through at the expense of logic, order, economy, and efficiency. Machine operators alternated between waiting for parts and being submerged in a flood. Once when we drove past a strange engineering factory, Doug said to me, "Know how many parts they make?" Of course I didn't know. "Nor do I," he said, "but I can tell you one thing: fifty percent of them are overstocked and fifty percent are understocked." The BBC, in retrospect, started to look like a model of smooth management.

Doug had been in engineering factories all his life, but he hadn't been able to change anything until one day he was given the design of a card punch so complex that he knew it could not be manufactured by the normal methods. There was only one way; and with a remorseless logic which I now recognize, a production team took shape. A small group of men were put together in a separate shop with the necessary machines, and took the card punch through from raw metal to finished machine. The production volume, the degree of precision, and the delivery date were all met.

That could have been that. But Doug realized that in a situation almost totally wrong, he had stumbled on something right. And he began to see an engineering factory exactly as I had begun to see the BBC—as a collection of independent workshops with a boss in charge of each who was responsible not for a process but for a complete part or a complete product. He also saw that once these discrete groups were formed, with their known output of parts and hourly cost in men and machines, their production could be controlled by a computer in a way that was impossible for every single man and machine.

The film we made about all this was called *The Future Came Yesterday,* and among the first people to see it were two of Doug's colleagues. Both of them had separately come to conclusions very like Doug's, and had already begun to put them into practice in their factory in Belfast. It wasn't quick and it wasn't easy, chiefly because of the novelty of the ideas, but gradually their managers caught on. First of all they moved in on the pressing shop, and gave it the necessary drills and other equipment to turn out finished pressed parts, as if it were an independent little company. Once the other managers saw it in operation, they were over the hill: there was a hectic period of machine shifting and they were in business.

It was some time later that I made my first visit to Belfast, and by then I could see that they were getting close to every corporation man's ideal—gaining all the advantages of bigness without losing any of the advantages of smallness. Not only were the machines grouped so as to produce complete parts, they actually had white lines painted on the floor around each group. And a few yards from each group's machines, behind glass panels, were its offices: in there were the group boss, his administrative assistant and accounting staff, work study, inspection and production engineering; his stockroom was next door. For all practical purposes he had his own business, and he could keep his eye on it the whole time. Each day he would tell the computer what had been produced, and the computer would tell him what he still had to produce and by when. But the exact allocation of men and machines, the problems caused by sickness, machine faults, holidays, and so on—those were for the boss to sort out for himself.

Strangely enough, it was a strike which showed that the system was working. Always in the past, if any of the milling machine operators struck, they all struck. One day after the group system had begun, one of the groups struck, including the milling operators; but the milling operators in the other groups stayed at work. The groups had arrived.

So already in one corner of the jigsaw some of the pieces were fitting together for me. But things were connecting up in another corner, too. The BBC had stimulated in me a growing interest in how big corporations should be organized. By now several of my contemporaries were directors or senior managers in big organizations, and we found the topic even more fascinating because of the absence of any really satisfying and definitive book about it. There were some good books which touched on aspects—notably Alfred Sloan's classic *My Years with General Motors*—and there was no end of theory from the management writers, but very little that really connected our practical experience with general principles. It was at this stage that I read Machiavelli's *The Prince* and discovered that a sixteenth-century Florentine civil servant could see deeper into the heart of the modern corporation than any corporate executive or professor of management studies.

The unity between the modern corporation and the medieval or Renaissance state, the behavior of corporate barons and courtiers and princes, was the theme of my book, *Man-*

agement and Machiavelli. But even before I started to write it, it occurred to me that perhaps somewhere there was an even deeper unity that I could not see, a hidden root out of which the state and the corporation had both grown. Several people noticed that there was a part of the book, the part dealing with cell structures and creative groups, which owed very little to historical analogy and nothing at all to Machiavelli. I could only admit that this was so, but that I believed it was true and important so I was damned if I was going to leave it out. I do not think I even suspected at that stage that those two sections of the puzzle which had come together belonged to the same jigsaw. Now that the New Biologists have shown me the picture on the box, I know that they do: and the object of this book is to try and show that picture as I have seen it.

III

The Hunting Band

I N front of my house there is a short semicircular drive
which in a more gracious age allowed carriages to drive up
to the door, set down the occupants, and continue on into
the road again. In those days there were gates at each end;
but they proved a nuisance in the age of the motorcar, so
now there are two open gateways. A few months ago I looked
out the window and saw three strange young men walking
along the pavement. As they came level with the house they
had the unbelievable audacity to turn off the pavement and
in through the gateway, through my garden, past my front
door, and back into the road again. The insolence of it! Who
did they think. . . . As I watched them, the whole emotional
range of the Enraged Householder syndrome welled up
inside me, the same response that I myself used to provoke
when as a small boy I climbed over suburban fences to get
my ball back. But in this case it was different; I had just

finished reading Lorenz's *On Aggression,* and recognized that my instinctive anger was not a private and personal quirk, but an ancient aggressive response to a territorial threat. The knowledge could not subdue my feelings, but at least it restrained my actions and prevented me from trying to pretend to myself that the resentment was an entirely rational and logical consequence of an act which in fact was only the most harmless of adolescent larks.

This is the real fascination of the New Biology: not the data but the programs, not the new facts it unearths but the new way of looking at the world that it gives you—above all, the new way of looking at yourself and your fellow-men. Perhaps the best way to express this is by the phrase "acceptance of the irrational." The New Biology shows us how powerfully the irrational operates within us, and how much of our behavior is not the logical response of the intellect to the facts of the situation, but an emotional reflex set off by some primitive survival mechanism. I felt a surge of aggression toward those three young men because I belong to a species that for millions of years had to defend its territory to survive. Chance no doubt brought into the world many variants without any urge to defend their children or their cave; they could not continue their line, and they were selected out. I am here because there were some who fought tooth and nail against every intruder to protect their home and their young. It may be that in the orderly western suburbs of London in the 1970's the sharpness of that reaction is no longer necessary. That is not the point: my instincts and emotions are governed not by current social supply and demand, but by age-old genetic history. It is enough that an aggressive response to territorial aggression was a survival necessity once; and who is to say that it will not one day be a survival necessity again?

However, it was not an awareness of territorial aggression that made the pieces of the corporation puzzle come together. Territorial aggression is common to many species—insects and fish and birds and reptiles, as well as mammals. It was something more specialized, something which may be part of the reason why we developed so much more successfully than any of our primate cousins. It stems from the fact that we are not a solitary species. However far you trace our history and prehistory, you find groups: not just the family group, but something larger. Moreover, this is true of all species of ape and monkey except the gibbon and the orang-utan. True, the apes are only collateral branches of our evolutionary line; but if you go back seventy million years to a direct ancestral species, the lemur, you still find a larger grouping than the family as the basic unit. This is now so deep in us that we have to accept it as immutable: wherever we live, whatever projects we undertake, whatever dangers we encounter, we will form a group if it is remotely possible.

This simple primate grouping, however, is only half the story, and for the purposes of this book the least important half. It is something we all know instinctively: not just that the solitary hermit in his cave is a rare oddity, but that there is something very strange about the man who never mixes with his fellows at work, or the housewife who never talks to a friend or neighbor, or the family that cuts itself off from all the other families in the district. All this is obvious; it is the other half of the story, the half that makes us different from all the other primates, that has the profound implications for the modern corporation.

Most of the scientists seem to agree that this difference began well over a million years ago—more likely five million, and perhaps as long as fifteen million. Before then we, or rather our ancestors, were vegetarians like the rest of the family. But then, at some point in the Pliocene or Miocene era, we turned from vegetarians into carnivores. Perhaps we started by catching or trapping the small mammals—monkeys and rats and rabbits; but as the ages rolled by a new meat supply opened up—meat on the hoof: the great herds of large grazing animals where a single kill could feed a community.

There was, however, a drawback to those large varieties of antelope and waterbuck and oryx: they were too large and too swift for any man, or emergent ape, to catch and kill on his own. But they were not too large for a group of them working together. Already we were a social species; we traveled around together, and banded together for defense, even if each one collected his fruit and vegetables for himself. Now we adapted the existing cooperative way of life to a purpose different from that of any other primate: the systematic hunting and killing of game. Begotten by opportunity out of necessity, millions of years ago, the hunting band was born. And it has taken one branch of the primate family down from the trees and up to the moon.

It was this vision of the hunting band that came like the picture on the box of the jigsaw. There were still a great many pieces to find and fit together, but the search had become a very different operation. I think perhaps my realization was delayed by thinking of man's early history as a farming history; but it was only ten thousand years ago that we learned to plant crops, domesticate cows and pigs and sheep, and build ourselves a more comfortable and less precarious way of life. You only have to think about it to realize that ten thousand years of farming cannot possibly dissipate a genetic inheritance built up and handed down during five to fifteen million years of hunting. Indeed, if we go back a quarter of those ten thousand years we meet Plato and Sophocles and Aristophanes, whose intellects and emotions were so similar to ours today (and that is flattering ourselves) that it is impossible to think that the other three quarters can have had any noticeable genetic effect at all. The employees and the managers of the modern corporation, in their sprawling factories and towering office blocks, have been formed into what they are, not by three hundred generations down on the farm but by half a million generations in the hunting band.

Of course, Corporation Man is a great deal more than a hunter: he can speak and write, he can compose music and poetry, he can learn and reason, he can experiment and invent with an ingenuity and adaptability that are unique in the animal world. But all these are additions to, not subtractions from, the hunting primate. The hunting band is still there, and when we deal with the corporation, we are dealing with a very recent adaptation of it. Donald Baverstock with *Tonight,* Doug Hughes with the card punch, and all the thousands, maybe millions, of successful groups in industry, commerce, banking, government, and war—indeed every area of collective human enterprise—have not been forging a new weapon on the anvil of modern industrial civilization: they have picked up an ancient one and used it with only the smallest of modifications.

This book, then, is an examination of the primitive hunting band in the modern corporation. Survival no longer requires the hunting and killing of game, so this particular skill has been allowed to atrophy; it has been replaced by agriculture and mining and manufacturing, by the skills of devising, making, transporting and selling goods, by thousands of entirely new survival activities. But although the end product may have changed, it has changed very recently: the way we organized the hunting band, its method of operation, its communication system, its survival mechanisms, above all the instincts and emotions it calls forth—all these are still there, and we will begin to understand our human organizations in a new way if only we can see them; or rather, if only we can see them for what they are, since they have been staring us in the face all our lives.

Why have we not seen this before? Speaking for myself, I can only recall the answer I was once given by Francis Crick, the DNA Nobel prize winner, when I asked him what it was that kept one scientist from making a breakthrough which another scientist made. He said that it was very rarely an absence of the necessary facts: you always kicked yourself if you were the one who had missed it, because all the facts were in front of you all the time. There were various obstacles he mentioned—for instance, a piece of experimental evidence that was wrong—but the one I chiefly remember was this: an assumption you are not aware you are making.

I had unconsciously assumed until a year or two before that our organizations, if they were to be explained historically, must be explained in terms of *recorded* history. The trouble with that assumption was that it worked—a great many features of the corporation can indeed be illustrated in terms of medieval and Renaissance politics. But a demonstration of unity is not a demonstration of cause and effect. There is another reason too. Just as our farming and manufacturing history is brief compared with our hunting history, so too our hunting history, even if it stretches back for fifteen million years, is not all that long in evolutionary terms. There is certainly time in fifteen million years for a species to develop new instinctive responses, but it is very unlikely that they will have the compelling, overriding force of the older ones such as hunger, or fear of death, or reproduction, or defense of young. Konrad Lorenz talks of "the parliament of instincts" which governs animal behavior, and which debates and divides when, say, fear of a predator suggests one course and defense of young another. In that parliament the instinct to form hunting bands is a newly elected member whose voice will not be heard when the powerful older representatives hold the floor. It is still there, it is still an important instinct, but it is not an irresistible compulsion. So long as we have the family group and the purely social gathering, we can live happy lives without forming hunting bands, as indeed people can live happy lives without having children. Something may be missing, but it is not something indispensable, and consequently it is possible to fail to recognize the way in which the hunting band dominates every large organization. And the organization—government department, corporation, small company—does not have to form them, even though they are the best and most natural way to collective success. The tendency and the impulse are there, but they can be resisted—not everywhere, and not all the time, but in particular places and at particular times. Sometimes it seems that such resistance is the objective of the corporation.

And just as the hunting band is a comparatively recent development, so it has never been the sole form of organization for the whole community. The mothers had to stay behind in the camp to rear their slow-maturing young; the hunting band was only for the fit adult males. Lionel Tiger suggests in *Men in Groups* that the reason women cannot throw overarm in the way men can is that they never had to —they did not join in the hunt. Perhaps a strong and childless female could occasionally take part, but in principle the hunting band has always been and still is an all-male group, and the urge—perhaps I should say the instinct—to form such groups is almost irresistibly powerful in most men. No reason or objective is necessary, though once the group is formed reasons and objectives will be found easily enough: war has often been the most simple and, to many men, most satisfying objective, and their memories of comradeship in battle, in the trenches or the submarine or the tank crew, are still the high point of their lives. But battle is only one of the many possible objectives for a band when it has been formed. The drive is not particularly toward conflict with other hunting bands, nor even (which would be much more explicable) toward the extermination of the larger antelopes. The primary drive is simply toward the formation of the band: all objectives are secondary to that, and in a sense a consequence of it. It is the urge to form all-male hunting bands that has been the great instrument of survival down the millions of years that we have evolved as carnivorous primates; the object of the hunt has been a variable.

There is one other question we must answer before we know what we are looking for in the corporation. How many men are there in a hunting band? Obviously, there cannot be just one number which is the only possible one, and for a long time it did not occur to me that the question was worth asking. A group is a group is a group. If it works, then it's the right number. Obviously, it had to be more than one, but whether it was two or twenty or two hundred did not seem to signify. But, of course, the moment you start thinking numerically, you realize that you have in your own mind an upper and lower limit, and that they are not all that far apart. A group, a team, in the sense that I mean and operating as I have seen them operate, could not conceivably be two hundred. Nor could it be two, though it could be three; I would therefore put three as the lower limit. What about the upper limit? If it could not be two hundred, could it be twenty? Since there is no general evidence, I was forced back onto experience, observation, and reading. I had never worked in a group of twenty that had the unity of a hunting band, or seen one in operation; nor could I imagine how it could get down to serious business without subdividing into two or more groups. And from my reading, it was Parkinson's celebrated insight that came most forcibly to my mind—that no board, council, cabinet, or committee can ever function when membership rises above twenty. It will, of course, continue to meet, and membership may be a sought-after honor, but if it is that big a smaller group will have formed which does the real work and makes the real decisions. I had always believed that there was a truth in Parkinson's observation, and that he was talking about the right sort of numbers, but even twenty seemed too large. The feeling in my bones told me that six or seven was comfortable, and ten perfectly reasonable; twelve could not be ruled out, but fifteen sounded a little improbable. If it was twenty, I would need a great deal of convincing that it could operate as a single team: if a meeting of twenty ever worked, it worked because several people were subordinates of others present, or specialists advising on particular topics, and though there were twenty faces around the table, there were only ten voices that mattered. All the same, this was completely personal and subjective.

Then I thought about the army. I had spent two years of military service as recruit, cadet, and officer, and although I entered it with no enthusiasm for the military way of life, I emerged with considerable respect for the way it was run. So the army seemed to me a good place to look: the organization of an army is not a question of having fun with charts, it is a matter of life and death; its structure has been hammered out by the logic of survival over many centuries of bloody experience. With a strong organization you may bring a citizen army together at short notice and win a single victory over another scratch side, but if a regular army is to succeed over a long period of time there is a strong likelihood that it will find the best way. And it was quite clear that in the British army the basic unit of survival, the group that stood or fell together, was the infantry section. There were platoons, companies, battalions, and brigades, but all these were assemblies of smaller units; the section was a band of men, and the section was ten or eleven in number when at full strength. And this applies not only to the British army: the U.S. army squad is also ten men; the Roman army was based on units of ten, the squad who shared a tent; the army of Genghis Khan was based on units of ten; indeed almost every longstanding successful army, whatever larger formations it might adopt for battle, rested for its permanent organization on units of that sort of size. And it is not just the army. When we play games together, the same size keeps cropping up. Basketball has five men and ice hockey has six, but almost all other team games have teams of between eight and fifteen in number. Juries are twelve. Indeed, once you look around at human groups with the hunting band in mind, the number leaps out at you. Every practicing manager I have discussed the subject with agrees without question that ten is close to the maximum for a board or project team or work group, and if I had wanted any further corroboration of its application to industry, it was supplied by the paper on productivity bargaining that won the Institute of Management Consultants' Sandford Smith award for 1969. The author, Robert Spillman, says:

> Whatever the formal organisation, people develop an in-
> formal organisation, which may or may not coincide with
> the formal organisation, and within which certain of their

needs are satisfied. The basic unit of informal organisation is the work group; and this may consist of from three to eighteen persons carrying out a common task or engaged in linked operations. Each person in that group reacts or responds to the other persons in that group, and the result is that each group tends to act as a cell or unit with characteristics and needs of its own. Members of a social group will tend to subordinate their individual needs to the needs of the group as a whole; but in return the work group protects and shields its members.

By the time I had got this far, I was convinced. Since no one could go back to the Pliocene epoch and check up, I was sure that the only evidence we would ever have about the size of those hunting bands would have to be supplied by projecting back from Corporation Man or forward from the lemur, and as far as I was concerned they both pointed in the same direction. But I reckoned without the ingenuity of the paleozoologists. They approached the question like this: the hunting band would have to bring its kill back to the camp because of vultures and other scavengers, and it would normally have to return before nightfall for collective security against lions and leopards and to feed the women and children if stores were low. From this the scientists plotted the maximum hunting radius. Meanwhile, from other evidence, they discovered what the density of game population was in the part of Africa where man emerged. And they have worked out that within the human or emergent-ape radius there was about enough food to support a total population of forty, which would mean a male hunting band of something between nine and eleven.

This, then, is the premise upon which the book rests: that the tendency to form "hunting band" groups of about ten people, nearly always men, is a part of our nature; that these groups have been the instrument of our survival for up to fifteen million years; and that the modern corporation, or any large modern organization, still depends on these groups for its survival. I call it a premise because I cannot prove it; but there is a great deal of evidence to suggest that it is so, and most people who have worked in large organizations will know it in their hearts: they too will have an intuitive knowledge that if you want something done you form a project group, and that somewhere around ten is about the optimum to start working on it. Indeed, the project group is a quite common instrument of management: what the New Biology proves is that it is a great deal more than an instrument of management. The hunting band, the ten-group, is the foundation of every corporation, the base which supports the whole corporate edifice. No organization theory that does not rest on this base can ever make sense. Already I find myself impatient when I ask the size of a company or division and am given the answer in employed capital or turnover; it is the number of ten-groups—not the number of pounds or dollars—that expresses the size of the management task. I get impatient, too, with personnel management that concentrates on individuals; of course individuals matter, but it is the morale, effectiveness and output of groups—not of individuals—that is the proper measure of corporate health and strength. Every manager must know cases of men who collect glowing reports in one group and then leave it, perhaps for a solitary job, and dismally fail to live up to their reputation —or who have looked unpromising until they got into the right group and have turned into successes.

I have said that every corporation rests on ten-groups whether it realizes it or not: yet the tendency to form such groups is so powerful that they sometimes form within but in opposition to the corporation; there is plenty of evidence of this as well, and it will be discussed later in the book. But it emphasizes that one of the prime tasks of the corporation is to get the largest possible number of effective groups all pulling in the same direction, all hunting on the corporation's behalf. How can this be possible when a group has an absolute maximum of about fifteen, while a corporation employs tens or hundreds of thousands? And since ten people arbitrarily put together do not automatically form a band, when is a ten-group not a ten-group? How do ten-groups organize themselves internally? Which conditions make them flourish and which make them wither? These questions have to be asked if we are to understand corporate organization in the light of this powerful male urge to band together for survival, and the succeeding chapters will attempt to answer them. The answers are a fusion of knowledge and experience: the knowledge I have acquired from the New Biology and other relevant reading, and the experience I have gained firsthand in large organizations and secondhand from friends and colleagues. The knowledge is still new and some of it is still being challenged by scientists of repute, and the experience is necessarily narrow and limited; the answers must therefore be taken as tentative. And there is a third and totally unscientific ingredient which I might as well admit: my own feelings, emotions, instincts, and intuitions, insofar as I have been able to isolate and analyze them, as a group member, and group manager—the same emotional irrational reactions which I have seen provoked time and again, by the same sort of stimuli, in other group members. And is it so unscientific? If a member of a baboon troop could tell us how he reacted to different situations, what emotions were stirred up in his breast by the behavior of enemies, rivals, and friends—this would be evidence of a kind; if he could also report on many conversations with members of other troops and pass on to us what seemed to be the common elements of all their experience, we would take this into account as well. Why should not the self-observation of a past, and perhaps future, member of the subspecies Corporation Man be equally valuable?

I V

The Bond

A N Y O N E who has worked in a large organization knows that ten people set down around a table do not automatically form a ten-group; most of us have the scars to prove it. Obviously, there are certain conditions that have to be met—though of course the exact number of ten is not one of them: I use it only to designate that group between three and fifteen that is our modern manifestation of the hunting band. So what are the necessary conditions? Or to put it another way, what are the chief obstacles by which the corporation keeps these groups from forming?

The first and most important of the conditions can be seen very clearly in that interesting, delicate, and never entirely happy relationship between television production teams—the behind-the-screens men—and the performers who appear in front of the viewers. The essence of the problem is that the production team's measure of its own success is the success of the program, and the prestige and other rewards and satisfactions that accrue to them as a result of it. The performer, on the other hand, is not entirely dependent on the program's success, although it brushes off on him. As time goes by he gains a reputation of his own, and he can enhance it in a program that fails or diminish it in a program that succeeds. The producers want him to cover an automobile race at Daytona Beach, whereas he wants to interview the President of the United States or conduct a sixty-minute survey called "Whither NATO?" The producers think he has been overexposed; he thinks he hasn't been prominent enough on the screen. The producers want a fairly taut and tough interview; he finds his personal stock rises when he does the relaxed and lovable bit.

A very new performer does not feel this way—he is sufficiently rewarded by being on the program; it is also less of a difficulty when the performer is the star—when the production is built around him and there is a greater community of interest and interdependence. In between it becomes difficult. The production team find it harder and harder to discuss the program completely freely when reporters are present: they are aware that the reporter is thinking not simply "Will that work with the audience?" but also "Will that improve my image?"; and even if he is not thinking that, the production team will probably suspect that he is.

For the same reason, it does not really work to bring a group of performers together and discuss future ideas. If one of them produces a good idea and it is given to another to carry out, they all get the message very quickly and good ideas dry up. If they all execute their own ideas, none of the others will criticize with complete frankness because it seems like personal pique. The only really united meetings of performers take place when producers are not there, and result in joint demands for more money, more prominent credits, and fewer editorial restrictions.

Many newspaper and magazine editors make exactly the same discovery. They can have tremendously exciting meetings with their editorial staff, but if they bring in their regular named writers the meetings are a flop—and a flop in exactly the same way. And, of course, it is not only in newspapers and television that this principle applies; it is universal to human organizations, even if most of them display it with less temperament and drama. What is more, it applies more to the top level than to the lower echelons.

I once attended a meeting called by the chairman of an engineering corporation to which all the heads of the operating companies were summoned. It was a natural situation for a ten-group: there, around the table, were the eight or nine people who between them carried the top-line authority of the whole group. And yet nothing could have been further from ten-group behavior, though any poker player would have recognized the atmosphere at once. Cards were being played very close to the chest; remarks were studiously noncommittal, and clearly framed for their effect on the others— especially the chairman. The only subjects which relieved the taciturn caution of the meeting were the trivial ones, when suddenly everyone seemed to have a great deal to contribute about what business organizations the corporation ought to subscribe to at two hundred dollars a year, or what quality of car should be allocated to assistant factory managers. It would all have been very puzzling to me as an observer, if I had not at other meetings and as a participant behaved in exactly the same way myself.

My meetings were at a much less exalted level, back in the days when I, as head of a department, met with other department heads, but my motives were the same. I knew that my department's interests and my own ego were better served by keeping quiet about facts, figures, and intentions which might not meet with approval, or which might provoke the other departmental heads to outcry or rivalry or proof of their superior awareness or achievement. I would happily talk about unimportant subjects or general principles of policy, but my department's operations were my own business. Of course, my motives and my behavior were the same as those of the television performers, and they sprang from something that lies at the root of the ten-group, and of the survival of many other species beside ours.

The fact is that because, by our evolutionary nature, we could not survive on our own, the group, in the end, only survived as a group. We made our kill together, or we returned home empty-handed; we ate together, or we all went to bed hungry; we survived together, or we all died. The hunting band was dominated by the need to survive as a hunting band; it was composed exclusively of individuals who survived collectively or not at all. No one could hunt in that band who had a private meat supply to fall back on if the chase was too tiring, the ground too rough, or the risks too great. What held it together was the common objective, which meant survival for all if it was attained and extinction for all if it was not. No wonder production meetings do not work with performers who can succeed while the rest fail, or editorial meetings with writers who can improve their reputations with a brilliant article in a disastrous issue. No wonder the meeting of corporation executives was a failure when any individual executive could raise his personal standing by producing marvelous profits for his division while the corporation as a whole was declaring a loss. This meeting, like my departmental meeting, was in fact a threat to survival rather than an instrument of survival.

The first condition for a ten-group, therefore, is that there must be a common objective, a single criterion of success by which all succeed or all fail. If it is possible for one of the group to succeed while the others fail, he does not belong in the group and will impair its effectiveness if he remains in it. And so the ten-group must never be placed in a situation where someone outside the group distributes praise and blame, rewards and penalties, to the different individuals—a situation in which they see that their status and future success depend on whether they perform better than the other members in the eyes of an outside superior. The ten-group is rewarded, or it is not rewarded—other ten-groups may be rewarded instead. But if it is to be rewarded, it must know from the start that the reward goes to the whole group without distinction—it must not be a prize for which individual members of the ten-group compete against each other. They, and only they, know which individual really earned it. It does not signify whether the ten-group is composed of miners or salesmen or machine operators, or whether it is a management committee or a football team or a board of directors: if this condition is not met, the group is an assembly of individuals, not a ten-group.

It is in fact immediately noticeable in committee meetings how the atmosphere changes when a subject is raised which enlists the cooperative emotions of the members instead of the competitive ones. The meeting I described in Chapter I, when we discussed our trainees' applications for jobs in a rival's group, was an extremely united and cooperative one despite its fundamental futility. Indeed, that sort of meeting should hardly ever be convened to discuss divisive topics: they can usually be sorted out separately, and the underlying purpose of the meeting is almost always damaged by them. The chairman should go through the draft agenda to see that every topic concerns the whole group collectively, and that they spend the whole meeting discussing the difficulties, dangers, and opportunities that beset them all equally. Departmental litigation and treaty bargaining can be dealt with at other meetings for interested parties only—starting at 5:15 p.m.

A common objective does not, of course, entail working shoulder to shoulder; the hunting band was never a football team. Of course, they must meet regularly; the meeting when they all talk over the last hunt or plan out the next one is essential to the formation and maintenance of any ten-group —it is the source of all the group's strength and unity. But just how often they come together will depend very much on the nature of the work: for some kinds of task they may have to foregather two or three times a day, while for others a week or more may elapse before they all come together again.

Most of the time the members will very likely be working on their own—the solitary salesman on his rounds is the modern descendant of the solitary stalker creeping around upwind to drive the game into the trap—but they are members of the ten-group all the time. Sometimes a man will spend months on end away from the group, perhaps on the other side of the world; but as long as he is devoting all his efforts to the group's objectives, they will feel he is just as firmly embedded in it as their fellow members in the offices down the corridor. He, too, in his distant outpost, will be working not for his pay check or bonus or the greater success of the corporation, but for his ten-group back home, and his real reward is his knowledge (and their occasional acknowledgment) that his work is providing a vital element in their collective survival and success.

It is hard to describe the nature of the bond formed by membership in a ten-group, and perhaps impossible to comprehend it unless you have felt the force of it yourself. An interesting sidelight on the all-male nature of the group is the difficulty that many husbands have in explaining its compulsions to their wives. To the wife it is, very reasonably, just "work," something that has to be done to support the family and keep the home together. "But we don't *need* the extra money—the children need you at home much more than they need a holiday abroad." There are, of course, compulsions other than the ten-group, but the pull of the ten-group is the hardest to resist or convey. It recalls Kipling's ancient complaint of the Viking women to their warriors:

> "What is a woman that you forsake her
> And the hearth-fire and the home-acre,
> To go with the old grey Widow-maker?"

But it was not the call of the sea they found irresistible; and the complaint is as hard to answer for the modern executive as it was for the Viking warrior.

What makes it so hard is that the bond operates at a depth beyond language. Hunting animals cooperate without need of speech—their cooperative instincts produce what Carveth Read calls "perceptive and contagious sympathy." Any member of a successful sporting team knows how powerfully this still operates within us if we allow it to develop. To quote John Spencer, England's rugby football captain: "It's amazing what an understanding you build up. You know when a chap's going to stay outside you, and you know when he's going to come inside. You don't even have to shout." That sort of unspoken, animal understanding is clearest in sport but common to all ten-groups in a less physical way, and illustrates the primitive nature of the bond that holds the members together.

The strength of the bond is, of course, increased with time, but it is surprising how strong a bond can be formed in a short time if the conditions are right. The most extreme example is war, and I suppose the trenches in France during World War I are the outstanding example in living memory. If you read about the conditions men had to endure for those four years, it is almost impossible to understand why they did not desert in droves after the first few weeks. Different writers explain it in various ways—they were fighting for freedom and democracy, and for the forces of light against the forces of darkness, or else they knew they would be shot if they ran away, or it was a triumph of army discipline and training; but the men who were there, if they explain it at all, talk in terms of their friends. They could not let them down. The bond formed in the trenches was a true, primitive survival bond: each had been forced to depend on the others not to betray positions, to give covering fire, to warn of attack, to help the wounded, to cooperate day and night on a matter of collective life and death. It was not for themselves nor for their country that they endured so much for so long: it was for the ancient hunting band. As long as those bands remain, the fight goes on. To military historians, an army ceases to exist when those small basic bands are so depleted and dispersed that the bond is dissolved. When that stage is reached, the army becomes a rabble, and the factor which prevents degeneration into rabble is usually called morale: it rests on the ten-group, the section, the band who risk their lives for each other because an ancient survival instinct demands it.

Just how ancient that instinct may be is illustrated by the South African naturalist Eugene Marais in his book describing the two years he spent in a lonely mountain home next to a baboon colony. The book is called *My Friends the Baboons,* and contains a story about a leopard who appeared on a ledge above the troop. Two of the older male baboons saw him, detached themselves from the others, and crept along a branch overhanging the ledge. Then they dropped; the leopard killed one and wounded the other, but not before his jugular had been fatally severed by the teeth of the baboon who landed on his neck. The older baboons could easily have run away: instead they risked their lives for the survival of the troop. Greater love hath no baboon . . . did Christ too lay down his life for his ten-group?

If we are ever to understand what "morale" means in terms of any large organization, we have to understand the bond which unites the ten-group. A troop of baboons or the soldiers in the Flanders mud may seem a long way from the office block or the factory floor, and indeed Corporation Man is scarcely ever placed in a situation of such hazard. But corporate survival, the survival of the group within the corporation, the fear of irretrievably lost customers and markets, the fear of cancellations of big contracts, the fear of hostile takeover, of factory closure—these can turn on the heat and apply the pressure powerfully enough for most people. If the extra effort by one man can tip the scales for his group, that effort will be made even at great sacrifice. How many marriages have been sacrificed on the altar of the ten-group? How many warnings of coronaries have been fatally disregarded? But those who have belonged to a ten-group, especially one that has been heat-welded or pressure-welded in that way, know how great the rewards can be. When they have all had to depend utterly on each other, to trust each other's loyalty completely, and found that trust upheld even under great stress, the strength of the bond thus formed gives a tremendous sense of security through fellowship.

The experience is on an emotional and not an intellectual level, and those who share it are sharing the emotional bond of the primitive hunting band. All such groups feel a deep reluctance to let the group break up, and when they have to break up there is a profound sense of loss. Some people find it hard to understand how anyone could regret the end of the war, but anyone who has worked in a good research group or pit gang or production team knows the sense of loss when a heat-welded group is dissolved. The ex-servicemen's associations which meet year after year are evidence of how long this band can endure: many of them still struggle out to the meetings after ill health has forced them to abandon every other excursion.

Corporations do not have ex-servicemen's associations in the same way, but in the larger ones you often find annual dinners of a quite unofficial nature, instituted to preserve on at least one day of the year the comradeship of a successful group dissolved many years before. There was an interesting article in the Sunday *Times* in the mid-1960's in which an astute gossip columnist discussed what he called "networks." A network was a number of individuals who, while they had no formal or operational relationship with each other, had nevertheless such a close understanding and powerful informal relationship that the connection was a force to be reckoned with in the affairs of the country. He was particularly concerned with those networks in the political parties, journalism, banking, broadcasting, and other areas with direct bearing on public life; as far as I could tell from my own knowledge, he was quite correct. But the interesting fact was that all these networks could be traced back to an earlier ten-group, to a political reform group or newspaper or periodical or television program which had brought the members together, worked them extremely hard, brought them success and public notice, and then fizzled out as they dispersed to follow separate paths. Often the political group or journal or program continued after they had left it, but it was an extinct volcano: the glory was departed, and it never flared into life again. Yet for the rest of their lives each one knew that if he wanted an urgent meeting with one of the others he would not have to disclose the reason: the urgency and the bond were sufficient to clear a space in the most crowded diary at the shortest notice. In the same way, no one ever really understands the informal power structure and information flow of a corporation unless he can identify its networks, and trace back the directors and senior executives to the ten-group, perhaps twenty years previously, where they first came to prominence. Most of them would also privately admit that whatever subsequent honors and achievements they may have enjoyed, they have never since been as effective separately as they were collectively all those years before.

Once you have been part of a ten-group, there are several signs by which you can identify others when you drop in on them. The first one came to my notice very early in my BBC days, and it was particularly obvious because our part of the television service had overflowed into a number of tall, narrow Victorian houses that stretched down Lime Grove from the studios. There were always builders about the place, trying to adapt parlors and bedrooms and attics to the fluctuating needs of television programs: moving telephones, putting up shelves, knocking down walls, erecting partitions, taking filing cabinets up and down stairs, and composing an impromptu unfinished symphony of hammers, drills, saws, planes, and breaking glass. At first I could see no logic or pattern to their activity, but one day it dawned on me that the successful programs were always needing walls knocked down, separate rooms joined together, hatches and doorways built, and extra desks in existing offices, while the unsuccessful ones were having doors blocked, partitions put up, and desks moved out. In other words, the successful hunting bands were constantly trying to come together physically, to spend as much time as possible within sight and sound of each other, to share all the information and keep in constant collective touch with every move; while, similarly, there was a correlation between failure and the breakup of the hunting band into little producer-and-secretary caves where demoralized and fragmented couples lurked in lonely seclusion. Certainly it seems a common characteristic of ten-group members to keep popping into each other's offices, to go off to the club or canteen together, to seek contact and association far more frequently than corporation duties require. This goes with a great deal more laughter, and a great deal less formality; they are the first out of their jackets in the warm weather, they drop the polite corporation prefaces ("Would you mind if I . . ." "Could I just . . ." "You don't happen to remember if . . ." "I wonder if I could . . .") in their dealings with each other, their operational conversations are very brief, and after a period of time a number of words acquire special good or bad connotations that are not acknowledged by the dictionary.

One consequence of this is that the more confident and successful a ten-group becomes, the harder it is for a newcomer to join it. This could be because they have hammered out so many principles and shared assumptions that there is a lot to learn, but usually it is something far deeper. The initiation ceremony is a ritual which crops up all over the world, from the most primitive tribes to the college fraternities (it is discussed at some length by Lionel Tiger in *Men in Groups*), and it surely had a survival value for the hunting band. To admit a newcomer was to take a big risk: if he was to bear his full weight you would have to trust him with your life, and you do not put your life into another man's hands unless you have proved to yourself that they are strong and true. The risk is not as mortal in the corporation, but it is still big enough; and recruits to existing ten-groups find that it takes a long time to be accepted as a full member. There is no initiation rite, no moment of acceptance; but many who have joined could nevertheless put their finger on the action or project or special effort which finally proved to the others that they were fit to be admitted.

This resistance to newcomers looks from the outside like arrogance. Perhaps it is. But if so, it is one of the facets of high morale and, as such, essential to survival. Morale in corporations is regressive: at its highest, the identification badge of every member is the whole corporation—"I'm with General Motors," "I work for Texaco"; but it gradually works down, so that a British Leyland engineer building Jaguars is more likely to say "I'm with Jaguars" than "I'm with British Leyland." We attach our self-importance to the highest unit we can feel proud of, though that unit can be very small. But however low the morale of the corporation, so long as the ten-groups are intact it can be rebuilt. Even if the maximum claim of an employee is "We've got a damn good little design group, but what's the use if you're working for idiots?" There are still bricks there to start rebuilding with. Once those are gone, nothing is left. The Nazis were so conscious of this force that they regularly shifted the population of prisoners in concentration camps to keep these groups from forming or break them up when they had formed: if they left a prison population undisturbed for too long, groups formed and morale started to rise. There is a strange parallel today in the treatment of mental illness— doctors have found that in many cases a ten-group of patients can be helped collectively much more than by individual treatment.

The current preoccupation of personnel management in the corporations is the motivating and developing of individuals. This is in the best liberal tradition, stemming from the romantic movement which began two centuries ago and supported by Freud in his preoccupation with the individual psyche. But perhaps the time is coming when we can forget the Oedipus complex and think of the hunting band; when we can get back beyond the personal self-indulgence and romantic independence of Byron and Shelley to the older disciplines of the group whose members depend on each other for survival, as they have for fifteen million years. If that happens, the managers of corporations will come to see the formation, support, and development of effective ten-groups as their major task to ensure the morale and long-term future of their organizations. It may be a difficult switch, but there is a powerful force operating on their side: the ten-groups are trying to form themselves all the time.

V

The Instrumental Fallacy

F O R a long time I was puzzled by the comparative scarcity of ten-groups in industry and government and other large organizations. If they work so productively and give so much satisfaction, if there is a natural tendency to form these groups, and if all they need is a common objective, then why are they not the normal base of any corporation? And then it occurred to me to put it another way: why had it taken me as an employee and manager so long to catch on to it? What was my own blockage? And in worrying out the answer to that one I isolated a basic fallacy in myself that for most of my working life had dominated and distorted my view of organization and management, and had dominated it all the more effectively for being one of the assumptions I was not aware I was making. The best name for it I can think of is the instrumental attitude to management, and I suspect that it still underlies the thinking of most managers and causes more ulcers, unhappiness, disputes, inefficiency, and waste than any other single idea.

Someone who is a victim, or an example, of the instrumental attitude to management sees the people under him as the instruments with which he has to carry out his job, to execute his plans. Each has a separate role, perhaps a separate skill, and it is his job as manager to use it as a good carpenter uses his saw and chisel and plane and drill to turn the idea in his head into a final result. In the same way he sees himself as one of the instruments of his superior manager, being applied to the larger task as he applies his subordinates to the smaller one. He need not, of course, carry this sort of image or model in his head, but it nevertheless corresponds quite closely to his attitude. It certainly corresponds to mine for most of my managerial life, and shows up most clearly in the way I set about the most demanding, exhausting, nerve-wracking and ulcer-twitching job I have ever had to discharge: the job of directing a topical, last-minute live television program.

To recall those days in full detail would be an inexcusable exercise in nostalgic masochism and retrospective self-pity. To explain the task simply, I was given a running order by the editor and had two hours to turn it into a television program. The material would all come in during the last hour; it would include films, interviews, still photographs, charts, reports from remote studios; these had to be planned within the technical limitations and then carried out by cameramen, studio hands, designer, floor manager, lighting engineer, sound and vision mixer, and several other technical staff. The junction point between the editorial conception and the technical execution was me.

I had not the slightest doubt about what I had to do: get hold of the running order at the earliest possible moment, turn it into a camera script, and then brief each of the key figures on what I required of him. I told the sound man what the microphone booms had to cover, and what other film or disc sounds would be needed; I briefed the vision controller on film sources, camera positions, movements, and cuts; I told the designer where I needed chairs and tables; I explained to the floor manager about setting and striking caption easels and moving people on and off the set; I went through the plot with the lighting engineer. And then after a sort of dummy rehearsal (if there was time) we went on the air and I directed the program: I called out cues and cuts, gave stand-by warnings, passed timing information to interviewers, prayed the film would be there in time, tried to reshuffle the order if remote sound lines went down, and emerged at the end of it all more completely drained and mentally exhausted than ever before or since in my life. The others did what I asked them to, looked compassionately on my suffering, and went home relaxed and untroubled.

Of course, I can see now, fourteen years too late, what I should have done. The moment I got the running order I should have sat down not alone but with my five key technicians, and we should have worked it out together. Several times, in fact, the vision controller had suggested after the program a better or easier way I might have done it; once or twice the floor manager had suggested a camera move that was not strictly his business; once, the sound recordist came up with a suggested line of script which was better than the one we had transmitted. But, although I was appropriately commendatory, I never saw the point that was staring me in the face. The point was this: if we had all thought together about the whole program, letting the designer talk about shots and the floor manager about sound coverage and the vision controller about scenery, in a complete free-for-all, it would have done much more than take the tremendous pressure off me: it would have made a far better use of time and skills and facilities, and improved the program; they would have enjoyed it much more; there would have been six people instead of one to see a crisis looming and work out its implications for each sector; and we would all have learned much more about the whole business of television. Instead, because of my instrumental attitude, I managed to keep all those things from happening and nearly drive myself into a premature grave.

All this took place before Douglas Macgregor described Theory X and Theory Y management in *The Human Side of Enterprise*. But even so, Theory X management—"People don't want to work, they don't want responsibility, they have to be controlled and directed and coerced"—was anathema to me even then. I would have called myself a really advanced and enlightened Theory Y man ("People want to be involved and trusted") ; I sought to involve the technicians, told them what I could about the contents of the program, asked if my camera script set them any difficult problems, congratulated anyone who produced a specially nifty bit of work, and thanked them all at the end. What more could an encouraging, involving, Theory Y manager be expected to do?

There was one other factor which I might plead as an extenuating circumstance: the organization of the BBC itself was at least partly instrumental. The designer belonged to one department, the floor manager to another, the vision and sound and lighting engineers to a third, and none of them to the same department as me; this was the operational consequence of the power enclaves I described in Chapter I. As long as the picture and sound quality were good, it did not reflect on the technical staff if the program as a whole was terrible or marvelous. But I know in my heart that this is only an excuse, though quite a good one; I operated the system in that way, not because I was compelled to by the organization, but because I believed in it, just as the BBC believed in it. Had I at that stage really wanted to form a group on an informal, personal, and practical level I could have got a great deal closer to doing so without the system ever finding out. I did not do so because the instrumental fallacy was so deep inside me.

And, of course, it is not only the BBC; indeed, the BBC represented the rule rather than the exception. There was a computer firm with three different types of staff who called on customers: the salesmen to interest them in replacing or extending the configuration, the maintenance engineers to repair and service the equipment, and the software representative to talk about applications. All of them worked independently and came under different divisions with a consequence that any experienced corporation man could foresee without being told: the maintenance man privately told the customer that the equipment was at fault, the salesman mentioned (off the record) that it would have been all right if it had been properly maintained, and the software representative excused all failures in application by implying that the salesman had claimed a capacity of performance which was beyond the powers of the equipment and programs. If the three of them had been part of a single ten-group whose collective job was to keep the customer happy, they could have got to the root of the trouble among themselves and presented a united front to the customer and a true report to their company, instead of suggesting a state of civil war to the customer and each sending a selection of self-vindicating half-truths to their superiors. But the company's attitude was instrumental: they saw management as the business of making individuals responsible for functions, and not of making groups responsible for objectives (in this case keeping the customer happy) ; and consequently they provoked damaging instrumental behavior.

Where did the instrumental approach to management originate? Does it go back to the basic division of labor for manufacturing? Did it begin in the craft guilds of the Middle Ages, perpetuated or revived in the craft unions of the last century and this one, where a man's skilled function as mason or carpenter was more important to him than his membership of a group that built houses? Or was it devised by managers early in the industrial revolution, who thought the only way to get industrial productivity from farm laborers was to give them a single function to perform and make sure they did it? Perhaps in those days, with an uneducated and industrially unsophisticated labor force and starvation as the alternative to employment, it achieved its limited objective. The basic fears of pain, hunger, thirst, and death take precedence over all the other instincts until they are satisfied. But once they are quietened the others begin to clamor, and for many years now the fear of starvation has ceased to haunt the industrial worker, and he is no longer uneducated or industrially unsophisticated. Consequently, even though it achieved results then, the system is almost totally inappropriate now; yet the instrumental fallacy remains.

The reason the origin of the instrumental approach is puzzling and intriguing is not just that it so obviously does not work now, but that it cannot have worked even in early agricultural communities. If the crops were not sown at the right time, the community went hungry; there was no special store of grain for the plowman who cut such beautifully straight deep furrows and so succeeded where the others failed. No one refused to help with the haymaking because he belonged to the poultry department. Certainly, everyone can have had his own special skills—this is how groups work —but equally certainly they must have organized themselves for collective success. The plowman's reward, like everyone else's, was a good harvest, not a citation for furrow digging and an empty plate. Everyone knew the final objective and could contribute to the discussion on how to achieve it, even though he would have his own special role in the actual work.

And if it cannot have worked in an agricultural community, how much less can it have worked for the ancient hunting band? Perhaps it is only my deficient imagination, but I simply cannot picture a leader of such a band telling one member that his job was just to throw stones, and so he could shut up and stick to the job he was given; or saying to another that all he had to do was stalk, and he didn't have to worry about what the others were up to or what the actual plan was. I cannot see him assuming that it was his job and his alone to bring the kill back to camp, and that all the rest of the band were instruments provided for him to help in his private task. I cannot see it because a band organized with one leader and nine or ten functional automata would be selected out as soon as the leader was killed; none of them would have the experience or the will to take over the planning and directing of the band after years as a functional instrument. I cannot see it because the hunting band apparently formed long before the critical enlargement of the human brain or the development of speech, and a hunt is such a rapidly changing situation that to control it instrumentally instead of by common understanding of the objective is comparable in complexity to directing a live television program, and even less predictable. And privately I cannot believe it because it corresponds to nothing I have ever seen work in the ten-groups I have belonged to or dealt with. After all, it is known that when a pack of wolves has a large and strong elk or moose at bay, the leaders of the pack all put their noses together and somehow "decide" whether to risk trying for a kill or to call it a day. It is known that the leaders of baboon troops come together when a difficult choice has to be made, and after their "conference" they act in unison. How could a hunting band have acted otherwise? Can we imagine one of them knocking off halfway through the hunt to attend a trap-building course, or another refusing to kill the prey as it came toward him because it was not his department's responsibility, or another being feted back in the camp for a brilliant piece of running, even though they came back empty-handed, because he was running in the opposite direction from their quarry without realizing it?

This, then, is as important a condition for forming a ten-group as giving them a group objective: the whole group should be able to agree on the objective and decide for itself how it is to be achieved. The impulse to be involved in this way is actually a part of man's nature, a genuine instinct, even if it is not one of the more ancient and powerful ones; and to deny it is to deny a man a part of his nature.

Before going on to the implications of this assertion, it is perhaps worthwhile to establish what an objective is, or rather what it is not. Telling a man to stand in front of a machine and pull and release a handle ten times a minute is not setting him an objective, and telling ten men to do the same at ten machines is not setting them a group objective. But if you tell them to produce a certain result, a certain number of drilled parts or quantity of coal or cars loaded onto the ship, by the end of the day or week or month, then you are setting them an objective, and you leave it to them to work out how to achieve it. In H. Estes' words, it is "the difference between getting a janitor to keep the floors clean, as contrasted with sweeping routinely every half hour with a 20-inch broom, 10 strokes to the minute." The currently fashionable technique of Management by Objectives goes into this question in some detail; and although it is fashionable it is also, if properly understood, very close to the heart of our kind of human organization: more than any other management theory it brings Corporation Man into line with his ancient ancestors.

The idea that a group should decide on, or at least concur with, its own objective, and then work out for itself how to achieve it, will hardly come as a surprise to anyone who has worked on a management team, research group, or the board of a company. What is extraordinary is the readiness with which people who understand this principle intuitively in their own work deny it to their employees on the factory floor. But if it is a part of our nature, it applies just as forcefully there. Indeed, when people paint doom-laden pictures of the bleak future for the worker in a technological society, the industrial part never contains teams, only individuals pushing buttons. Perhaps this is a projection of what so much industrial work has been for many years. Some psychologists have seen this deadly dull, individual functional work as one of the major problems of industry, and have been studying ways of "enriching" jobs. Some have tried rotating these functional jobs, so that a worker does several in a day, but they have found (not surprisingly) that several boring jobs are still boring. But their problem has been the instrumental view of management: as long as a man is seen as an instrument to perform a function, no real solution to the problem of job boredom is possible. The only approach is to take the hunting-band principle down to the factory floor, and give the ten-groups problems to solve and objectives to achieve at the physical manufacturing level, in exactly the same way that management teams approach the problems of planning, organizing, and controlling the longer-term operations.

I always dislike utopian recommendations of that kind when I read them in management books. It makes me long to hear a practical man speak out for the realities of industrial life and blast the theorist back into the study where he belongs. But in fact this is not utopian or theoretical: it is the common practice in much of Japanese industry. To quote from *Modern Japanese Management:*

> One other feature of Mitsubishi Heavy Industries also typifies an important aspect of Japanese industry—the system of quality control, which centres essentially not on inspectors but on the workers themselves. In almost all Mitsubishi plants workers in each section meet together in their free time, possibly under the chairmanship of the foreman, and at the foreman's house, to discuss the way the job is done and how to do it better. Once this was done entirely without pay for the four to six hours a month that these discussions might take up—Now Mitsubishi pays a token two hours pay a month in recognition of these efforts.

If the Japanese have found a way of basing all their heavy industry on committed, participating ten-groups, this would go a long way to explaining their industrial achievement. But it is not only the Japanese. *Time* magazine (November 9th, 1970) reported how Polaroid now involves the workers in deciding which new machinery to buy, and how Donnelly Mirrors of Holland, Michigan, improved its results by turning shop-floor decisions over to employees (and also abolishing time clocks and putting all workers on a salary). And there are sufficient examples of this approach in Rensis Likert's *New Patterns in Management* to take the concept of self-organizing factory floor ten-groups out of the realm of theory and putting it firmly into the world of practical success. There is also a way in which the denial of ten-groups can not only fail to grasp opportunities but do actual damage. Since the impulse to form ten-groups is instinctive, it is likely that if it is repressed in one direction it will burst out in another. The enormous burgeoning of social clubs, sports clubs, recreational clubs, residents' groups, amenity societies, professional associations, and the like, represent, in a large part, the impulse to form ten-groups which is not satisfied at work. Their function is necessary and useful in its own right, but the drive to form a committee, start the thing off, get it moving, plan its activities and keep it running—that is the ten-group impulse releasing itself. It is only a hunch, but I'd be willing to bet that few members of strong and successful corporation ten-groups are prominent members of outside committees.

This activity, of course, is far from damaging: indeed, it is usually harmless and often beneficial. The damage comes when the ten-groups start to form within the organization but in opposition to it. This can easily begin if the ten-groups are there, but are denied any say in what their objectives should be or how they should organize themselves to achieve them. They make an attempt at having some say: for instance, the machine operators query the engineer's designs, and are told sharply to mind their own business and do what they are paid to do. Next day they receive a drawing with an obvious mistake in it: with dutiful glee they do exactly what they are paid to do and spend hours and hours machining an unusable part. This increases the mistrust and resentment and they are given even less of a hearing than before. So they meet and start airing grievances over their coffee break. Meanwhile, other groups are doing the same. Then a big grievance common to the whole factory is fixed on, a busy and energetic ten-group forms itself into a strike committee, and a familiar pattern begins to develop: the ten-groups which were not allowed to form and organize themselves to further the corporations ends are forced into the next best thing—they form and organize themselves to frustrate the corporation's ends.

There is one particularly ironic consequence of this which really "instrumental" management brings on itself and which makes the strike even more crippling than it need be; it is a result of the malignant cell. The term "cell" or "cellular organization" is a good one, since it implies that the ten-group, or larger unit, contains the necessary framework of a complete organization in microcosm, as the biological cell contains the framework of the full organism. The Belfast factory groups which we saw in Chapter II were healthy cells in that sense. But instrumental management, by putting all the lathes in one place and all the presses in another and all the draftsmen somewhere else, creates malignant cells instead of healthy ones. And so when the draftsmen resent their "instrumental" treatment, they find grievances which unite them. These can, of course, antagonize all the other cells and prevent the draftsmen from getting the support they might need. However, being a malignant cell they do not need it—they can destroy the organism on their own. If a healthy cell strikes, its own total production is lost but the other cells can often stay at work. If all the draftsmen strike—just as if all the drilling operators strike—there is precious little that the factory can go on producing.

Of course, the strikers will have a sensible-sounding pretext—more money or longer holidays or shorter hours—but the reason for these broad aims is that they serve as a focus for all the resentments of everyone in the group or the factory, for all the smaller and more detailed causes of frustration of natural ten-group activity. The pretext is secondary; it merely sanctifies a much more primitive emotional outburst. And the reason it can become so prolonged and bitter is that both the strikers and the corporation management find in each other one of the most powerful aids to forming, welding, and sustaining a powerful ten-group and encouraging it to expand: they find an aggression focus.

So far we have talked about the ten-group as a form of hunting organization some fifteen million years old. But there is a much older instinct that events can sometimes call up to reinforce it: the threat to survival. And in very many species of living creatures there is a standard response to certain kinds of threat: aggression. If a group, as opposed to an individual, is threatened, the response is group aggression which exerts a powerful binding force, and leaders for all recorded history have known and used this power of threat by finding an aggression focus to bind a large group: the aggression focus can be Catholics, Huguenots, Jews, Communists, blacks, whites, the management, the workers, or what you will—if people will believe they are a threat to survival, that is usually sufficient.

The classic case, in every sense of the phrase, of the inventing of an aggression focus is Cassius's speech to Brutus when he is enlisting him as one of the ten-group of conspirators to murder Caesar. He presents Caesar as the threat to everyone's liberty—the man who wants to become king and hold every other citizen in subjection, the object of fear and hatred—and does it with a sensitive skill that would have made him a masterly shop steward. But nearly all leaders of ten-groups, whether consciously or subconsciously, keep an aggression focus firmly in the group's mind. Usually the aggression focus is harnessed to an abstract principle: not "the newspaper that is competing for our readers" but "the newspaper that is debasing the standards of honest journalism"; not "the store that is trying to lure our customers away," but "the store that deceives the public with cheap and flashy goods that fall to bits in a week"; not "our rival car manufacturers" but "the manufacturers who pay for their glamour gimmicks with the money they save on safety." About four years ago I lunched with the chairman of a small company that was about to launch an electronic consumer product to compete with a product made by Phillips, and I decided to test the theory. I said to him, "I imagine you tell your staff how disgraceful it is that the public should have this low-quality high-price product foisted on them by an inefficient giant corporation, and how people have a right to high audio quality at a price that makes it available to a much larger number?" I had never actually seen a jaw sag before, though I had read about it. He did not see how I could possibly have known that those were almost exactly the words he used. But in fact it had been clear from what he had said earlier that Phillips was the enemy, and that price and sound quality were the weapons; the rest was a lucky guess based on the principle of the manufactured aggression focus.

It is obviously not very difficult to present the corporation to the labor force as a threat to survival. Logic, in a broad and general sense, may say that the corporation is the reverse —that it is the hope and cause of survival. But unemployment is the closest that most workers in industry can come to being in danger of not surviving, and the fear of unemployment can easily turn those who may terminate the employment into the aggression focus, with the attitude of "Let's get everything out of them while we can." Instead of being the focus of unity, the corporation becomes, as it were, a dangerous prey that can provide meat but also terminate life. It is not insignificant that the Japanese industrial climate in which ten-groups of workers can be so closely involved in the success of a giant corporation is also one in which it is almost unheard of to lay off employees or to sack managers.

The result, therefore, of the instrumental approach to

managing large concentrations of men is to force the growth of a natural organization of ten-groups in opposition. The corporation then has two management structures—the official one it draws up and circulates, and the one on the factory floor that controls the work. There were many cases during the war when, in the prisoner-of-war camps, officers carried no authority and corporals or sergeants emerged as the leaders everyone looked to. The principle was dramatized by J. M. Barrie in *The Admirable Crichton:* a wealthy industrialist is wrecked on a desert island with his family and staff, and the butler Crichton emerges as the natural leader of the community. When natural ten-group activity is blocked and defeated by the management as a means of achieving the corporation's objectives, it is inviting the Admirable Crichtons to rise up and frustrate them.

VI

The Leader

THE Macavity system of management is not widely discussed—chiefly because I have only just invented the term —nor is it advocated by any authority on personnel administration. It is, however, as common in most large organizations as the instrumental approach, and may perhaps be a consequence of it. I first encountered it in the BBC, though I have met it since in any number of corporations and government institutions. One year I was given a bonus in recognition of something or other, and I received (along with the formal notification) a heartwarming letter from my director explaining why he had singled me out for such an honor. In the course of the next few days several of my superiors expressed their pleasure at the award, and each of them let it slip out that it was in fact owing to his initiative and efforts that I had been enriched forty pounds (£24 13s. 8d. after tax). On each occasion I expressed the appropriate degree of gratitude. Then, some time later, I was left out of a general salary raise on the grounds that I had recently been given a special increase. The pretext was so flimsy and specious that I sought out my superior in a fever of righteous fury. He explained that it was not his doing at all. Nor was it his superior's, I discovered. Nor that of the personnel officer who notified me of the decision—he was merely the instrument of a greater (and apparently invisible) power. It was impossible to find anyone who had in fact given this ruling, or indeed whose hands had been soiled by it on its way down to me. Obviously, there must have been one Judas Iscariot among all the Pontius Pilates, but I never located him—a sharp contrast with the occasion of my bonus when it had transpired that there was a Father Christmas in every office. It was then that I found that couplet of T. S. Eliot's going around and around in my head:

> You may meet him in a by-street, you may see
> him in the square—
> But when a crime's discovered, then *Macavity's*
> *not there!*

But the Macavity system is only a symptom of a much deeper reluctance to talk about leadership, or accept it, or admit that it happens. The corporation has fabricated dozens of elegant euphemisms to avoid saying that someone is a leader: management, administration, executive responsibility, line authority, reporting to, immediate superior—all of these are used to hide the unpalatable or shameful fact that there is something called leadership which people, actual named human beings, have to exercise. Why are we so embarrassed about it? Perhaps it is because the army seemed so preoccupied with it, and the present generation is reacting against its prolonged and enforced service in the army. Perhaps it is because the word enshrines an old-fashioned fallacy that if a man had character and authority, all the other qualities like intelligence and scientific knowledge and market flair were unimportant. Or perhaps it is another aspect of romantic liberalism, whereby leadership is seen as an oppressive denial of human equality, with all its implications of curbing the will, restricting the freedom, and insulting the individuality of other human beings. Whatever the reason, the taboo seems to belong exclusively to the upper reaches of the corporation; lower down there is no such delicacy, and though the term may vary between governor and chief and squire and gaffer and boss, the concept of leadership is clearly understood and unambiguously expressed.

This inhibition is a pity, not only because of the tremendous importance of leadership in all human affairs, but also because of the wide divergence of beliefs about the nature of leadership that open discussion would reveal. The textbooks have many descriptions of management, marketing, profit, and similar corporate abstractions, but descriptions of a leader are hard to come by. It is hardly surprising: any list of qualities that meant anything at all would be bound to exclude someone who had succeeded in leadership and include many who had failed. This complexity came home to me when I was invited to speak at the biographies presentation at the Administrative Staff College at Henley. The students had to study and discuss six famous historical figures, and then each syndicate chairman had to make a speech about him at the presentation. The subjects chosen were Newton, Pepys, Rhodes, Cromwell, Lenin, and Marlborough. I looked at the list in dismay. What on earth could I contribute that would be remotely original or important on such widely known characters, or that had a hope of interesting sixty sharp-minded successful managers in their middle thirties who had been investigating them in detail for weeks? And then it occurred to me that it would be possible to look at them all as if they were candidates for the vacant post of chief executive in a company under my control. Along with giving a different perspective, it would be an interesting study of the nature of the leader. I do not know if the audience profited from the discourse, but I at least found it an intriguing exercise.

Newton was a washout from the start. There was no evidence that he had ever led any group of people in a successful enterprise; on the contrary, he was spiky, proud, obstinate, and prone to vicious feuds—the kind of researcher who is only really happy in his laboratory but who needs approbation and admiration lavished on him by the chairman to keep him with the corporation. All too many corporations would assume that the only way was to pay him more money, and the system would then force them to take him away from actual research and appoint him head of the research division, which would be a disaster for him, for the corporation, and for science. The wiser ones would leave him at his bench, pay him more than the chairman (and make sure he knew it was more than the chairman) and invite him to lunch regularly in the directors' dining room. He might be one of the greatest geniuses in history, but as a leader he would not even be a serious candidate.

It needed only a little more reflection to see that Pepys would not be a candidate either. Although he was a top civil servant—the secretary of the navy—he never seemed to have any urge to seize or shape events. Like so many successful corporation men, he was constantly trying to get himself noticed, hoping to get jobs when they became vacant, attaching himself to powerful men and glowing with spaniel-like pleasure when they gave him a metaphorical pat on the head. Certainly he was likable, and had an eye for essentials and a powerful grasp of administration and its problems, but he was in no sense a leader; he had the mind of a clerk and the soul of a courtier.

It was equally obvious that Rhodes, Cromwell, Lenin, and Marlborough would have to be on anybody's short list, and the moment you started to consider them in detail you came up against the difficulties of finding any common thread, of isolating any single quality of which you could say "This is the essence of leadership." Rhodes, for instance, had one characteristic which is the hallmark of a certain kind of leadership: it is sometimes called vision, but in his case it was the specific vision of his own destiny to unite the divided. It started with the uniting of a lot of South Africa's divided diamond companies into De Beers; then, having made his fortune, he turned to the wider task of uniting the separate African territories into a solid hunk of British Empire from Cairo to the Cape. But this kind of vision seems dangerously tied up with the ego of the visionary, and resistance (in this case Kruger's) calls forth intemperate actions in response. It also makes one question whether great size and unity really serve any useful purpose except that of enlarging the ego of the man who creates it. Many corporation mergers have prompted the same question. Hitler and Napoleon had a similar vision, and so did Rockefeller and Carnegie. Its great danger is when the desire to grow at any cost becomes compulsive, when expansion reaches the stage of addiction. My feeling about Rhodes was that he would be marvelous for restructuring a Balkanized industry based on small family businesses, and I would like an equity stake in his operations from the start; but I would not want him in my organization. The risks would be too great, and there would be every chance that the organization would end up as his instead of mine.

And then, for a contrast, look at Cromwell. Whereas you might think there was some quality in Rhodes that you could have picked out from the start—he was busying himself in the diamond fields in his twenties and had made De Beers and his fortune at thirty-five—I do not see how anyone could have spotted the young Cromwell. Without the civil war he would surely have lived and died an unknown country squire. He did not make any national mark until he was well over forty, and yet within a few years he had risen from a cavalry officer to the absolute head of a powerful nation, and was able to impose his own will on it with a breath-taking power and confidence. On the other hand, he was hopeless at delegating. A wonderful man to take over a vast, run-down business, sack the management, restructure the organization, and make it vigorous and profitable again, but not the man to run it once it was on its feet.

And what about Lenin? For a revolutionary leader, his behavior was quite inexplicable. He spent most of his life outside his country; when the fighting was going on in 1905 and 1917, he was not in the thick of it but lurking out of sight; he split the Marxist movement over points of principle. Yet he emerged as head of the government of Russia. It is easy to see the qualities of a leader in Stalin, or for that matter in Trotsky, but Lenin up to 1917 looks like a writer, the ideas man of the revolution. I saw him much more as a passionate management consultant who had written any number of papers on corporate restructuring and suddenly found himself as chairman being told to get on and do it.

Only one common factor seemed to unite these three disparate leaders: each one professed to act in the name of an idea greater than himself. Whether it was the British Empire, the Bible, or International Communism, it provided a unifying ideal for the faithful and a means of turning anyone who opposed or resisted the leader into a collective aggression focus. But as soon as I came to consider the final candidate, that last thread snapped. I had never seriously doubted that I was going to give the job to Marlborough. He was every manager's idea of a leader: he had been in the corporation (the British army) from the beginning, was tremendously skillful and made a success of every job he was given, shot up the management hierarchy on his merits (lieutenant colonel at twenty-five, lieutenant general at thirty-eight), stood up for his English managers when the new chairman from the Dutch company came over and started giving executive jobs to his friends, never lost a battle or failed in a seige, was respected by his officers and loved by his men; and yet for all his dynamic and thrustful leadership he worked diplomatically with overseas allies and (up to a point) tactfully with politicians at home. But so far from being impelled by a single ideal, he actually switched sides from James II to William of Orange at the critical moment for the control of the corporation, and tilted the balance. He had no grand vision of Britain in Europe; he simply saw a French competitor who had to be kept in check, and he outmaneuvered him time and again.

It would have been reasonable to take these four widely different yet indisputable leaders as proof that the gift of leadership, if there is such a thing, is subject to nothing except the purest accident. But a moment's reflection on the nature of the hunting band makes it clear that we must always have had leaders and that our species could never have survived without them; and if we reflect for something more than a moment, the logic of the hunting band can illuminate several aspects of leadership which might otherwise remain obscure.

It goes without saying that a leader is a prerequisite for a successful hunt. The prey moves so quickly and unpredictably, the situation changes so rapidly, that there cannot be a debate, a conference, a vote, or an adjournment; nor can there be two different courses pursued simultaneously, or each individual be left to his own devices. The decision must be made instantaneously and be binding on the whole band. In fact, all animals that hunt collectively have a pack leader, and current observation of our own species shows that every ten-group—every army section, football team, board of directors, committee, and cabinet—has adapted the ancient instinctive need for a pack leader, whether under the name of captain or corporal or foreman or chairman, to contemporary use.

So much is obvious. It is less obvious how the hunting band decided which actual individual member should become leader. But it can be stated with some certainty (and many corporations would do well to reflect on this) that it did not advertise the vacancy and interview the applicants. The leader was a member of the hunting band, and if he was killed another member of the band took over; to evolve a leader seems to be instinctive behavior, and corporation managers who worry about appointments of leaders for ten-groups are all too often wasting their time and sometimes playing with fire. A ten-group that has a group objective cannot help evolving a leader—it does not need to be told by some outside superior agency. The best such an agency can do is to confirm what the ten-group had already decided; if it appoints a different member from the ten-group's own choice, the result will be unhappiness for the leader appointed, the resentment of the "natural" leader who has been passed over, the contempt of the whole group for those who made the appointment, their alienation from the corporation, and the impairment of their effectiveness. All too often the result is an ineffective new foreman and an effective new shop steward. It is interesting that a survey of the American army in Vietnam quoted by Lionel Tiger found that a major source of tension within individual troops "arose from the fact that soldiers could have no hand in choosing their officers or in moving to another group if they could not respect their current leaders." The corollary of this is that if you want to form a ten-group you do not have to appoint the leader: you bring the people together, give them a stimulating and demanding group objective, and within a short time you and they will know who the leader is. This is not to say that you cannot appoint a leader, or that you cannot impose an outside leader on an existing group; only that you cannot hope to do better than the group would do on its own. Speaking for myself, if a leader has to be chosen I would rather pick him first and then let him form a group than try to pick a leader for a group that was already running successfully. Either way, the essential point is that it is natural for every ten-group to evolve and replace its own leader, and that any other method must be approached with great caution and in the knowledge that it is not the natural way.

But how did the primitive hunting band decide which member was going to be boss? The New Biology provides a very quick answer to that question: status-dominance. The urge to dominate the other members of the group—to be number one or, failing that, number two or three or four or five—is common to almost all social species, birds and fish as well as mammals. It has powerful survival value for the group: when there is internal competition for survival—famine, for instance—it is the weakest, the lowest in status, who go to the wall, and the strongest who survive to breed. In some species this is reinforced sexually: females will only mate with high-status males. It is not simply physical strength that determines status: strength of will, determination, courage and what you would call "character" in humans all contribute to this animal-dominance package. Status in the corporation is such an important and fascinating subject that a chapter will be devoted to it later in the book; for the moment it is sufficient to say that you cannot read about animal status and work in a corporation without being aware of its living force and relevance every hour of the managerial day.

But there is a snag in using status as a simple explanation of how we got and still get our leaders. It was evolved and refined over maybe a hundred million years or more for the survival of a social species. But not of a hunting species. Presumably the earliest hunting bands were automatically led by the number one status hominid, and the status qualities are by no means irrelevant to hunting. It is characteristic of high-status animals to lead the defense of a social group, and it is characteristic of low-status animals to follow where the higher ones lead; these factors would adapt quite satisfactorily to a hunting expedition. But—and here is the rub—they are not the ultimate determinant of survival. It is success in the hunt that has sorted out the winners from the losers in evolution's steeplechase; collective defense has remained important, but without food it becomes irrelevant. And so from the start of the hunting life a second quality appeared, a second selector came to sit at the table with the first to decide which teams should go on into the next round: the ability to lead the hunt to a successful kill and bring home the bacon, or the venison. There is, of course, no reason why both qualities should not exist in the same individual, but it is by no means inevitable that they will: sheer animal dominance is important, but not all-important, and if it goes with a complete inability to plan the surrounding or trapping of the prey, a total incompetence at choosing which of the herd to go for, and a tendency to stalk leopards under the illusion that they are impala, then the hunting band that follows it will hurtle to extinction all the more rapidly for being so firmly and decisively led. But if number two in the dominance order turned out to have a genius for knowing where the game was and how to kill it, then the hunting bands who learned to resist number one's leadership and follow number two would eat and survive and breed. After all, they were something like nine against one, so although number one could by definition beat up number two, he could not beat up the whole of the rest of the band together. Or individuals might detach themselves and join a better-led band. In "The Ineffective Soldiers," a study of the U.S. army, Eli Ginzburg writes:

A soldier knew that he might lose his life unnecessarily because of the lack of skill or judgment of his superior, and there was little, if anything, that he could do to prevent it. There was much talk about men who had shot or planned to shoot their officers—an indication of the tension that prevailed.

This was later confirmed by the Pentagon's admission that forty-three officers were believed to have been killed by their men in Vietnam during 1970 alone. I find that this (and many similar stories from other armies) suggests very powerfully that the hunting bands, the ten-groups which we now belong to, are the result of millions of years of tension and interaction between the social structure of the ape troop and the logic of the wolf pack, and both are still operative within us. School provides a good illustration: small boys sort out status in a very simple animal way—playground dominance is physical and basic. But the boys who dominate at school have no guarantee of continuing to do so all their lives; indeed, there is very little correlation. Many highly successful leaders were not leaders at school, but as they matured other qualities came to matter as much as or more than status on its own.

This does not mean that we have to reject the concept of the "natural" or "born" leader. Status is still a powerful force inside us all, and there is no reason why it should not coexist with effective leadership of the troop. But status-dominance does not ensure permanent leadership, as it does in most social species; the leader is always being judged on results by the rest of the pack, and if he starts failing to get results, his leadership is by no means guaranteed. All the same the "natural" leaders who are also effective can be dramatically so: Nelson, Napoleon, Hitler, Julius Caesar, Alexander, Henry Ford, and Rhodes are some of the most famous examples. The danger point comes when the maintenance and assertion of their own status seems to them to demand an action (like the conquest of Russia) which militates against collective survival. As long as the two impulses act in unison they are a powerful combination.

All the same, the irresistible born leader, the one who must at all costs dominate any group he belongs to, is comparatively rare. For practical purposes, the leader is the one who evolves from the group because he is the one they think gives them the best chance of survival and success. Status dominance is bound to be one of the factors that will influence them, but only one. If survival depends on strength and physical courage, the group will evolve one leader; if circumstances change and the emphasis shifts to knowledge and low cunning, it may evolve another. You may, on the football field, happily accept the leadership of a man who, at work, equally happily accepts your leadership: it is the needs of the task, not pure animal dominance, which tip the scales. And so Lenin, had he died in 1916, would be known to history as a fanatical Marxist agitator and pamphleteer. Cromwell, if he had died at forty, would be known as an obscure East Anglian member of Charles I's parliament. But a radical change of the political environment suddenly created a completely new survival task, and they were evolved by their groups as the most likely to lead the rest to success in the new situation. A radical change in the market has the same effect on corporations and industries: when the pop revolution struck the fashion and entertainment businesses in Britain in the sixties, it produced not only the Beatles and the Rolling Stones and Mary Quant and Carnaby Street, but also a crop of high-powered executives in their early twenties, and several millionaires under thirty.

Nevertheless, once status and hunting success have evolved their choice, another factor begins to operate. You can call it practice or experience, but its effect is to teach the evolved leader the job of leading. Leadership is a skill which, like all others, has to be learned by doing it, and sometimes doing it wrong. Once an individual has been evolved as leader in one situation, he has an extra qualification next time in that he has done the job of leading before; equally, those who have the experience of being led become less likely to contend for the role of leader next time. And it is more than just a skill or a technique: in time it becomes a role which out of custom and habit the non-leaders do not seek and the leaders expect and accept. Consequently, leadership can be created as much by the empty chair at the head of the table which the others do not want to fill, as by a struggle for the throne. All the same, someone with no experience of or taste for leadership could in some circumstances find himself the natural leader: for instance, in a group of much younger and equally un-dominant people where his knowledge and skills were the key to collective success.

The essential point is that leadership is not a quality at all. High status-dominance is an innate quality; skill and experience and the habit of leadership are acquired qualities; but leadership itself is a relative term. A man becomes a leader in relation to a specific group and a specific task: once he has evolved from his ten-group as its leader he can begin to learn the job, and he may go on doing it for the rest of his life, but the basis of his leadership is always that he is the evolved leader of his group. All too often the corporation gets itself into desperate trouble by not endorsing the evolved leader; it thinks it is choosing between one candidate and another, whereas in fact it is choosing between order and disorder. Nevertheless, the problem is sometimes a difficult one, as we shall see when we look at the way Corporation Man evolves his leaders.

VII

When Is the Leader
Not a Leader?

M O S T executives and senior managers will talk freely about the difficulty of selecting people to fill important jobs: how hard it is to know if you are right; how heavy the responsibility toward the man selected, the men rejected, and the corporation in which they all serve; and how grave the consequences of a bad choice. Further powerful proof of the depth of corporate concern is provided by the number of firms that earn a handsome income by specializing in management selection, and in the length of the reading list the library gives you if you ask for information. There is, however, another aspect, which managers talk about less freely—the enormous satisfaction and enjoyment which the selection process gives them. Think of it: anyone who ever has to be interviewed for a job knows the trepidation and awe with which he approaches the ceremony, almost as if it were a dress rehearsal for Judgment Day. He knows the special care he takes over his appearance, the questions he goes through in his mind, and above all the nearly mystical powers he attaches to the man sitting behind the desk. If you have joined the corporation as the result of such a ritual examination, it is impossible ever to think of yourself as the complete equal of the man who interviewed you; even if you subsequently become senior to him, always at the back of your mind is the memory of that first unequal encounter, and you find he splits into two men in your imagination— two quite different men, but both equally real. So it is not surprising that the converse is also true: if you are the man behind the desk, you taste something of the power that ancient kings exercised over their suppliant subjects. Of course, you are merely looking for the best man for the job, and it is just part of the day's work, and it is all completely objective and dispassionate; but there is no getting away from the fact that you have power over someone else. You are in a position to confer wealth, honor, and status on one of a number of other people, and they all know it; this power to confer status is absolute proof of your own status superiority, which each candidate implicitly confirms. If he does not, if he behaves as if his status were higher than yours, that is the end of him: there is no more certain way of avoiding selection. Deference and submissiveness are not often listed as job qualifications, but those who do not exhibit them during the interview rarely get beyond it.

The consequence is that under the cloak of a dispassionate appraisal by question and answer, irrational judgments are being made on the basis of qualities which are not mentioned in the job description. Sometimes the interviewer is trying to impress the interviewee; often he is trying to get his agreement to propositions, rather than discover his views; almost always he is seeking acceptance of his authority and confirmation of his status. Many personnel experts have been appalled by the problems of selecting the right candidate in such an absurd situation, and have tried to put the process on a scientific footing. They lay stress on establishing in advance the qualities the job demands and conducting the interview to examine how the candidate rates under each of a number of relevant headings. One of them described the normal corporation interview to me as "about as scientific as a couple of dogs sniffing each other's arses." Their writings on the subject, though lacking that vividness of expression, are a model of enlightened objectivity and systematic common sense, and the villain of the piece is the sniffer, the old-fashioned unscientific manager who "can tell without any of this mumbo jumbo" when he has found the man he wants. And yet the flaw in the "scientific" interview is at least as grave and probably graver.

When I first reached a managerial position in which I had to appoint people to vacancies, I was convinced that one of the greatest barriers to corporation justice was the selection of people for jobs on the grounds (probably never admitted) that the interviewer liked them. I was determined that I at least would always pick the best candidate irrespective of any irrelevant personal feelings. That resolution fell at the first fence. My very first vacancy produced a candidate who by any objective measurement was noticeably better than the others, but I just could not see myself working with him without a harsh grating sensation somewhere in the region of my colon. Nor could I see any of the rest of the team taking to him. There was nothing in the needs of the job or in his qualifications to exclude him, but all the same it simply was not possible for me to appoint him. At the time I thought that my resolution had weakened unforgivably, and I had better abandon any hopes of being a modern scientific manager. I now realize that wisdom had triumphed over intellect.

Qualifications and job descriptions would be all very well if we were appointing solitaries, but if the candidate is to join an existing ten-group then all the appropriate qualifications in the world will not counterbalance the gut feeling that he will not fit in, that he is not "our sort." You can try and describe "our sort" in objective terms, but in the end you are merely rationalizing the irrational. The only way to tell is by whatever corresponds to the canine sniffing procedure, and if you do not like the smell there is no point in going any further. Nor should you try. Of course, if "our sort" describes a type extraneous and irrelevant to the task of the group, if it is based on social or religious considerations when the task is electronic circuit design, then the group is giving itself an unnecessary handicap, and narrowing its area of choice. But mostly "our sort" is related to the sort of people who have succeeded at the task as members of the group, and although other sorts may be just as good they will not work in that group.

All the same, this irrational, instinctive feeling about people has no validity unless they are actually going to work in your own ten-group. If they are not, it is liable to lead to very grave errors. Few top managements are aware how well most groups know who ought to be given the job, and how strongly they feel about it. Frequently, it is not the candidates but the interviewer who is on trial: the candidates are the questions, and everyone below the job level knows the right answer—only the interviewer is in doubt. I have known a department meeting to break into spontaneous applause when the new department head's name was announced—and they were applauding the executive who had chosen correctly just as much as their former colleague who had now been so justly elevated and dignified.

I also remember a group board being exercised for months over the question of the successor for the departing managing director of a subsidiary. Should it be the technical director or the director of administration? The technical director had been with the company all his life and was one of the country's leading experts on their rather specialized manufacturing techniques, but he had a rather narrow outlook. The director of administration had joined only five or six years before, but he had run his own small family company before that; he was a much more sophisticated manager, well versed in management skills and with a much wider view of the company's problems and the larger financial context in which it operated. The management authorities would not hesitate for a moment—the director of administration must have the job; you do not appoint a man for what he has done in the past but for what he will do in the future. But it would have been a very bad appointment. The technical director was the evolved leader of the company, his brilliance at the business on which the company's survival depended was a legend: to pass him over would be not only a slight to him, but also a proof that the group board did not understand what the company was about, and a clear indication that success and preferment were no longer related to the ability to lead the hunting band to a successful kill. Management courses, not successful products, were to be the route to the top in the future. The group board, however, made the right choice. The technical director was given the job, the admitted skills of the director of administration were at his disposal, and once he was made to look at the company as a whole and not merely as a design-and-manufacturing entity, he started to develop the new survival skills that the new objective demanded. It reminded me of a shrewd observation by my squadron commander during my army service. I was objecting to his proposal to promote a corporal to sergeant, and he asked me why. I said that he just didn't look like a sergeant to me. His reply ought to be hung on the wall of every manager's office: "No corporal ever looks like a sergeant until he's got three stripes on his sleeve."

One of the chief reasons why a mistake was avoided in the case of the two directors was that a group of people, not a single omnipotent interviewer, discussed the appointment before it was finally made by the chairman. This is one of the best safeguards I have encountered. The BBC always has at least three, and usually four or five, people to sit together as an appointments board when posts of any importance have to be filled. I am sure that most of us who appeared before these boards were more inclined to believe that justice was done than we would have been in a one-against-one interview, and this impression was reinforced for me when I started to sit on appointments boards myself. I remember once having more or less written off a rather dull and un-communicative candidate who had a lowly job despite good paper qualifications, when someone asked him why he had applied for this post. Still uncommunicative, he said, "Ah, that's the sixty-four-thousand-dollar question." And then a senior colleague of mine, who had not yet asked him any-thing, chipped in. "No, it's not." he said, "*This* is the sixty-four-thousand-dollar question: why haven't you done better? Here you are with all these certificates and things, and you're not much more than a clerk. Why?" I was about to be profoundly embarrassed, but the young man just grinned with what seemed like relief. It was as if a barrier had suddenly been swept away, and he became relaxed and in-formative. "Do you know, that's what I keep asking myself," he replied, and continued in such a convincing and genuine way that we were interviewing a quite different candidate, who in fact got the job and was a sensational success. From that I learned more than the fact that it is unfair to a candidate to avoid asking him what you think is an awkward question: I also learned (since I would certainly have ap-pointed someone less suitable) that a small ten-group is a far better instrument for appointments than the solitary inter-viewer.

In an ideal world, or an ideal corporation, appointments and promotions would be no problem. Leaders would evolve from their groups and everyone would know: it would only be a question of officially confirming an accepted reality. But it must be admitted that in real life there are occasions when there is no evolved leader, or when the evolved leader is not up to the job. These occasions are much rarer than most corporations realize—I would guess that bad appointments through ignoring the evolved leader are at least ten times as common as bad appointments through promoting him—but they happen. Groups can fail, morale can drop, the task can grow or change beyond any member's capacity, a leader can quit and leave a successor who lacks the will or qualiifications to take over, a leader may evolve but fail when things get tough—there are many reasons why, even in the best corporation, a ten-group may find itself with a member in charge who is in no sense the leader except on the corporation's organization chart.

The first question, of course, is how do you tell that this has happened? When is the leader not a leader? In schoolboy fiction it is easy: a leader is anyone who is six foot six inches tall, well built, with fair wavy hair and steady blue eyes. This, however, quickly proves to be an unreliable criterion: the fact is that since leadership is relative, it is in the leader's relationship with his ten-group that you look for the signs of leadership, or their absence; and there are certain types of leader behavior which must have been essential to survival from the earliest days of the hunting band.

Fundamental to every real leader is the maintenance of his own authority. Without it, the band is doomed. There can be any amount of criticism and argument on most matters within the group, but there cannot be any argument about who is the leader. That is the surest recipe for failure, and any leader who cannot make a decision until he has "talked to the group"—gotten the approval of one or more members of the group whom he cannot compel, but only ask to comply—is not the leader. Of course, any leader will often want to talk to his group before giving an answer; but that is visibly different from having to defer to their will if it conflicts with his. It is therefore basic leadership to come down violently on any attempt to challenge the leader's authority. His decisions can always be challenged; but not his right to decide.

As well as his authority within his ten-group, the leader preserves with equal force his authority over his ten-group if it is threatened by someone outside. Any "leader" who willingly lets a superior within the corporation erode that authority is not a leader. This authority is eroded whenever members of the group have to seek authority from someone other than the leader to carry out the group's task; whenever the leader has to defer to an outside judgment on how tasks shall be allocated within his group; whenever the leader's orders to his group are countermanded from above; or whenever someone from above praises a group member for something the leader has criticized or criticizes him for something the leader has praised. If a superior wants to talk to one of the group on group matters, a leader will often start to twitch and insist on his right to be present, just as he insists on written communication to the group being made through him.

A consequence of this is that the leader will never excuse the group's failure by blaming, to his superiors in the corporation, a member of his group. The reverse side of authority is responsibility: if the leader has authority over the group, then he is responsible for what it achieves. He accepts that the group's failure is his failure. If the group is praised for success, he may single out one member as having done something meritorious, but he will not pretend (except within a convention of modesty) that the real credit belongs to anyone except the leader who trained him and set him to the task, and the same is true of blame for failure. But this personal acceptance of blame is for outward show. There is not and cannot be any such reticence within the group toward the member who let the others down. The leader is not particularly sensitive about people being easily hurt, unless it impairs their performance: anything that really threatens survival will call forth a powerful rebuke, probably in front of the rest of the group; the leader of the primitive hunting band did not have a private office, and anyway it is important for the whole group to see what will not be tolerated. These rockets are never pleasant to receive, but if they are justified they increase respect; the admiring glee with which people recount to each other how Charlie hit the roof when he found out what had been going on is a sure sign that there is a leader around. Equally, however loyal the leader may be to his group (and that sort of loyalty is a characteristic of leaders), he is prepared to discard any member who is a permanent liability. Age, length of service, and loyalty may condition where he is discarded to, but if any member is or becomes by his nature—as opposed to occasional and curable mistakes—a hazard to survival, then his continued presence in the hunting band cannot be tolerated; to put it in evolutionary terms, the bands which tried to carry passengers on the hunt were selected out, and we are descended from the ones which discarded them.

The third jealously protected area is authority over the means of achieving the objective. Of course, it can be discussed and questioned in advance, but once a leader has said how it shall be done he will passionately resist any instruction from on high to do it differently. A change in objective as a result of circumstances is another matter—it is one of the hazards of the chase and a leader's task is to adapt to changed circumstances; but if the objective is unchanged and a superior simply imposes a different plan from the one the leader has given his ten-group, this calls forth the same aggressive response as the other authority infringements.

You will also begin to suspect a leader who asks a superior to sort out for him a dispute within his ten-group. The "magistrate" function of leadership is as important to survival as the personal authority in which it is rooted. A quarreling and divided band will not survive, and a leader who does not instinctively stop the quarrels and settle the disputes on his own is not a leader. It is also suspicious if he modifies his plans "because so-and-so doesn't get on with so-and-so." This sort of consideration makes survival harder, and as far as the leader is concerned they get on or get out.

The real leader is also accepted by his ten-group as the final arbiter of status. Just as a band cannot hunt successfully if there are constant arguments about who does what and how they do it, so it cannot tolerate constant status squabbling. In a good ten-group every member knows his own status exactly, and knows that the leader confirms it. If a junior member tries to assert higher status than the group accords him, for instance by arguing not from a fact base ("Actually it started in 1964, not 1966") but from a status base ("I'm just telling you it won't work"), he is likely to be sat on by the leader very quickly. Any evidence that members of the group have a different view of the pecking order from the leader's is a sign that they will not be around for long, or that there is something wrong with the leadership.

It is, however, only the people above who need to look out for the signs that someone is occupying the position of leadership without exercising the function. Those immediately below are only too well aware of the fact; but they are also aware that the hardest and most thankless task is to tell the higher managers in the corporation that your immediate boss is no good. In the first place, they appointed him, so you are implicitly criticizing their judgment. In the second place, maintenance of corporate authority demands that they take his word against yours. In the third place, no one much wants to employ the sort of person who is liable to go behind his back to a superior and vilify him, even (or especially) if the person is telling the truth. In the fourth place, your motives are bound to be suspected. In the fifth place, the best policy for the boss on the defensive is to destroy the character and credibility of the informer. And yet survival demands that the band must have the best leader. So what happens?

Usually, (as you would expect in any hunting band), a collective challenge develops under the alternative leader. Perhaps the official leader will resist the challenge; it may be the crucial trial of strength from which he emerges for the first time as a real boss, and it may be a part of the process by which our species tests and forms its leaders. Or he may manage to hold on not from natural authority but from the authority the corporation gives him, in which case it is likely that the rebel chief and perhaps some of the others will walk out dramatically or detach themselves quietly, depending on their temperaments. But very often the natural leader takes over in fact, while the official leader remains at the head in appearance. From the outside, the official leader looks like the boss. It says on his door that he is, and in the chart and in the personnel files. But the real leader runs the group, and so long as the official leader accepts all his recommendations, he will be accorded the formulas of deference in public. The official leader becomes a deposed king, the one-time head of the family who is now the old man in the chimney corner.

If we accept that the ten-groups will always evolve their own leaders, that they know who their leaders ought to be and will throw off or slip away from under the wrong leaders if they are appointed, then the consequence should be that the only senior appointments that are necessary are those for specialist skills and solitary occupations; all the rest, all the line management and senior staff, will evolve organically from the recruits taken in straight from school or university. The leaders of ten-groups can at any stage bring people into their groups from outside, but these are not leadership appointments though they may evolve into leaders later; the corporation's leadership at every level will be developed organically, so to speak, and the corporation only has to know what it is looking for and confirm it when it finds it. But although this may be a theoretical deal, you encounter a grave difficulty when you try and put it into practice: as you rise higher the nature of the task changes radically, and the leaders evolved at the lowest level may be totally unable to cope as more and more importance attaches to under-standing technical arguments, assessing financial projections, foreseeing market changes, and formulating long-term plans. Of course, there will be many highly qualified staff working on all this; but the leader must be able to understand them, to know how to use them, to check that he is getting the information he asked for, and to sense that something has been left out or misunderstood. At the same time, he has to be an evolved and proved leader whose authority is accepted and respected—he cannot be a high-grade clerk, so to speak, who comes in at the top to run the whole corporation. But there is very little in the tasks at the lowest level to ensure that the leaders who emerge there will be capable of the types of skill that will be needed later.

Most corporations solve this problem by graduate recruitment and management training, but it has many snags. It can very easily lead to an us-and-them feeling—a separation (because there has never been any ten-group comradeship) between those who do the work and those who decide what work shall be done—and result in that alienation and absence of sense of belonging which leads to unrest and dispute. It also leads to rootless, interchangeable managers who have not grown up out of any craft or trade and who move from corporation to corporation and job to job in order to solve problems rather than lead people, and thereby encourages instrumental management.

One of the most interesting approaches to this problem was provided for me at the state's expense during my two years in the British army. Even my selection for management was interesting: I was summoned to a three-day War Office Selection Board, where we were divided up into ten-groups —mostly of eight, as far as I remember—and given a string of different assignments. For some we had no leader, for some we had an appointed leader; some tested the ability to organize people, others the ability to organize projects; some tested personal authority, others tested powers of communication. It was fascinating how a staff-work project, for instance, would evolve a leader quite different from the one evolved by a field-work project. I think (and hope) I would have thought it just as efficient and thorough a test if I had failed it. However, I was selected, and after several months in an officer training establishment I was eventually commissioned and sent out all wet behind the ears to a regiment in the Middle East.

I can still recall my absolute bafflement as to what on earth I was doing in a position of authority over men of such vastly superior technical knowledge, practical ability, military experience, and soldierly demeanor as the sergeants and corporals who had to salute me and call me "sir." They knew far better than I did what had to be done and how to do it, and I could at first see no role at all that I could fill. The first time in my own opinion I made any officer-like contribution was when Corporal Burrows came in very worried with a piece of paper in his hand. The problem was that we had asked all the troops to send an equipment deficiency return in triplicate to the squadron office, but one of the troops had sent four copies instead of three. Where should the fourth copy be filed? I held out my hand for the piece of paper, and Corporal Burrows relinquished it eagerly. I tore it into four pieces and put it into the wastepaper basket. He beamed with relief, saluted happily, and went out. I dimly saw how I might one day be of some use, though I cannot think that during my brief period as an officer the army was in any way a more efficient organization for any contribution of mine. However, I had to admit that the system worked rather well: the authority of the officers was respected—even mine, which I did not really believe in myself—and for all the rawness of the second lieutenants we did provide one useful function. Because our full-time responsibility was our troop of thirty men, with our troop sergeant and three section corporals, we were always able to represent them and their case to the management with just as much force as when we passed on management's instructions to them; and by spending so much of the day with them, a young officer gained over the years an insight into how you felt as an ordinary soldier—how you reacted and what pleased or irritated you— that would always be a part of any decisions he would make later on in higher ranks. It also meant that mutiny, or "strike" as it is called in civil life, unless the officers joined in, was a virtual impossibility with such a close working relationship in such a comparatively small group.

But why could leaders not be allowed to evolve? Why all the mumbo jumbo of saluting and uniforms and separate messes and "sir" and all the rest of it? I assumed at the time that this was just ancient tradition that no one had bothered to change; it was many, many years later that I met by chance a man who could explain it to me. He was (and indeed is) General Sir John Hackett, a scholar-soldier who went from the command of the British army in Germany to become principal of King's College at London University.

The army, he said, absolutely believes that leaders evolve. But it could never, by purely natural methods, evolve enough leaders with the technical knowledge, administrative grasp, powers of analysis and communication, and mental disciplines to fill all the positions in which those qualities were required. If they just let them join in the ranks and take their luck, some would evolve but others would yield precedence to less qualified but better leaders who would become corporals and sergeants over them. So they select, exclusively from people who have those qualities, junior officers who are not evolved leaders and some of whom quite possibly never will be. Then they dress them up as if they really were leaders, give them all the badges and status symbols, put them in separate living quarters, and make all the soldiers behave toward them as if they were leaders. They enhance this by giving them certain formal (if not very real) authority, and making them the main channel of communication by virtue of their access to more senior officers. Also, the senior officers treat them, and expect them to behave, as if they were the real leaders of their men. In a quite narrow sense of the word, it is a process of manufacturing synthetic leaders. Under such pressure it is very difficult for them not to act like officers, and in time nearly all of them, by habit and practice and the expectations of others, become real leaders. Like Max Beerbohm's Happy Hypocrite, they are given a mask which they wear for so long that in time the face underneath grows to the same shape: they by-pass the evolutionary process, but with time and experience they learn the skills and habit and role of leadership, and become acceptable as real leaders.

Whether this solution can work in the corporation is another matter; but it is interesting to see that something similar has been tried. Some corporations have turned their university intake into graduate foremen, giving them a year or two in a position very similar to that of an army lieutenant. But there is another approach, which was Napoleon's. At the end of a battle or a campaign, his question was *"Quels sont les braves?"*—who are our heroes? Those were the ones to be promoted: appraisal by results, the principle favored both by modern management theory and age-old natural selection. Napoleon, of course, encountered the same problem as the British army: there was no guarantee that *les braves* could read or write. So when they were named, they would be sent off to school until they had acquired the level of skill and knowledge necessary for their new rank.

There is no reason why the corporations should not apply both principles, and indeed the Napoleon principle, in a very limited way, is employed by many of them. But it is one thing to send a man on a three-week course, and quite another to spare him for a year or two of full-time training. As a consequence, Western society at the moment seems to be in danger of fulfilling H. G. Wells's vision described in *The Time Machine,* in which at some future date the human race has split into two species: the bright, gay, beautiful and delicate Eloi living in leisure and luxury aboveground, and in the dark caves below the pale hollow-eyed Morlocks endlessly bent over their machines that kept the system going. The enormous expansion of university education seems to be leading to a subspeciating of the working Morlocks from the graduate Eloi.

But does it have to be so? It all hinges on how we select for our universities, and I have an awful feeling that we have gone dangerously wrong. At one stage it was very easy: universities were for the reasonably wealthy, and were a finishing course for a small elite. The next stage was also fairly easy: the doors were opened a little wider to let in the intellectually distinguished, no matter where they came from. It is at the third stage that the questionable decision has been taken—to select the vastly enlarged numbers by just going further and further down the examination list; to say automatically that whereas we used to take numbers one and two in the class order, we will now take numbers three to eight as well.

Numbers one and two must always go on to further courses of the most vigorous, disciplined, and demanding scholarship. But Napoleon at least would have questioned the automatic acceptance of the rest. Why should they not all go to work for two years or more and see which of them emerge as *les braves?* They could take up their university places then, and be selected not just on their school record but on their performance afterwards as well; the ancient ten-group could have a chance to evolve its leaders by a test much older and wider than the university entrance examination, and then let them acquire the skills and knowledge that would be needed later. And it need not stop there: at any stage during the next ten years or more, the evolved leaders with abilities beyond their education could take up the university places at present devoted to educating numbers seven, eight, and nine beyond their abilities.

In 1969 I went to a lunch with a number of senior police officers at Scotland Yard. It was a time of student rioting, and I was surprised at the depth of hostility that the students aroused in my hosts. But the reason was clear: I doubt if a single one of them had been to a university, and all of them would have done anything for the chance. And they had to face abuse and violence from students who were frittering away, as they saw it, the precious opportunity from which they had been excluded. All of them were the evolved leaders, all had begun as ordinary coppers and been promoted on merit, and they had become the elite of one of the acknowledged star police forces of the world. And the higher they rose, the more keenly they felt the lack of the broader education that no specific job training could replace. They would also—if they had gone to the university then, in their thirties and forties—have been the sort of students that har-assed and despairing professors dream about. But they could not go, and many of the eighteen-year-old numbers seven, eight, and nine were apathetically and reluctantly occupying the places they would have filled so eagerly. Must it always remain impossible to temper the intricacies of academic selection with the simplicities of natural selection?

VIII

Leadership and Listening

L E T us take a breather for a moment and see what we have been doing. We have been looking at the way Corporation Man sets about his collective tasks, and trying to isolate from all the systems, structures, theories, and techniques those elements which are the enduring essentials of human collective behavior: the elements which go back beyond management theory, beyond political organization, beyond armies and cities and settled communities, back to the hunting life which over millions of years formed us into what we are today.

If this inquiry is leading anywhere at all, it is leading to the conclusion that there is, in the most proper sense of the word, a natural way to organize a corporation or government institution or any other human enterprise involving large numbers of people. Of course, other ways are possible, just as it is possible to make elephants sit up and beg, or lions jump through blazing hoops, or bears wear frilly skirts and dance. With time and long practice and will power, you can subject them by means of rewards and punishments to your unnatural disciplines; but untamed nature is always lurking just below the surface, ready to burst out the moment concentration wanders or determination weakens. And so, while it is possible to impose an unnatural organization on a corporation, the natural organization will keep trying to establish itself; it can be blocked and frustrated, but it cannot be destroyed. And why should we want to destroy it? It is far simpler as well as far more effective to encourage the natural order instead of fighting it, to use the age-old cooperative impulses of our species as the foundation of the organization, and to think of a corporate structure as a national park instead of a circus, and managers as game wardens rather than lion tamers.

So far we have agreed (or I have, anyway) that the basic unit is not the individual but a group, nearly always a male group, which varies from three to twelve or fifteen in number, and perhaps optimizes somewhere around ten; that this group is bound together by a common objective, with the bond of trust and loyalty thus formed capable of becoming an extremely powerful uniting force; that the ten-group needs to decide on (or at least take part in deciding on) its own objective, and to work out for itself how that objective shall be achieved; that it will evolve a leader out of its own members by a process of interaction between the needs of the task and the nature of the individuals; that the leader once evolved will resist challenges to his authority from inside and from outside the group; and that he will quell strife, punish dangerous behavior, discard passengers, and enforce the status-ranking.

I shall suggest a little later on that the ten-group is not the only organizational form which we have brought with us out of our dim prehistory to regulate and direct our collective behavior. But I feel that I cannot put off any longer some reference to one of the fundamental questions about human behavior: is this ten-group impulse perhaps not genetic, but cultural? Does it spring from nurture rather than nature? Do we inherit it not biologically from our parents but by learning it in earliest childhood? We know, for example, that a young otter, separated from its parents at birth and hand-reared by humans, will plunge into the first river it sees and catch fish. It has no training or practice or observation to guide it; its action is instinctive. But we also know that a young baboon similarly separated is liable on release to eat poison berries and die; it has to learn from its parents which food is safe and which is not. Do we, then, organize as otters chase fish or as baboons choose berries?

This is a hard enough problem at any time, and a frequent source of deep controversy among eminent scientists, but in this case there are three special difficulties. The first is that experiment is a practical impossibility—we cannot take large numbers of babies away from their parents at birth and expect to watch "normal" or "natural" group behavior developing. The second is that the fifteen million years of hunting were not static: they saw the evolution of our species from a carnivorous ape to the sophisticated hunting communities of a few thousand years ago, with weapons, language, culture, religion, and intelligence at least the equal of the primitive hunting tribes which have survived to the present day. All that time, selection pressures were operating in favor of some qualities and against others. Some, we may assume, were established very early, and these we would expect to be a part of our nature; others—painting, lighting fires, cooking food, horse-riding, the manufacture and use of the bow and arrow—probably arrived very late and have had to be passed down by teaching. In between there must be impulses and inclinations of varying strength, depending on how long ago and how drastically they were favored by selection. Is the concept of number, for example, built into us—or if not, is the brain structure to accommodate and use it built into us? Is is something every child has to learn afresh, or would any human community develop it "instinctively"? Quite simply, no one knows.

This brings me to the third difficulty, which is that I am totally unqualified to contribute to the scientific discussion. The debate already engages the best evolutionists, behaviorists, psychologists, and ethologists, all bringing evidence from their different disciplines. I therefore have to proceed by cutting the Gordian knot. I can merely look around me to see if there are any known human communities which lack this tendency to form male ten-groups, because they have never learned it, and look into my own nature and try and find out whether my own responses to the situations we are discussing seem like learned skills and acquired habits, or like inborn emotional impulses. In both cases the result is the same. There do not seem to be any present or past communities that have not formed this sort of group, and I can tell that my own responses go deeper than any acquired skill or habit, and have their roots in my biological nature along with (even if not as deep as) love and anger and fear. It is man's nature and not his habits we are dealing with; he needs a natural group organization as surely (even if not as urgently) as he needs food and drink and sleep.

And now, before we move on beyond the ten-group and its leader, there is one more question we need to answer: how did it come to its decisions? The process of making decisions is at the heart of higher management, and we have already seen how the denial of it can have disastrous effects lower down. Clearly, the hunting band had many decisions to make: which trail to follow, which animal to go for, how to set about the kill, when to call it a day and go home, whether to take special measures against predators, who should carry out which role, and many more. In its earliest days it had only the social instincts and apparatus of apes— the noises and signs and postures and actions which communicated in a rudimentary way certain simple warnings and information and intentions, and the responses to them;

by the end of the hunting era it had extreme painting skill and a well-developed language with complex grammar and syntax. But, however crude or subtle the instrument of communication, the band had to make decisions. A vegetarian life makes few demands on collective decision-making, though it must still happen from time to time when predators attack or new feeding grounds have to be found: but for the hunting band correct decision-making is a daily survival necessity.

The simplest form of decision-making is follow-the-leader. Let the leader make all the decisions, and the rest will do as he tells them. For all we know, this may have operated for many ages; but there is a better way, and it is beyond doubt that at some point in prehistory our ancestors evolved it. We have already established that hunting requires a number of separate skills: tracking, spotting, stalking, running, aiming, throwing, striking, and so on. While we can assume that all members of a hunting band were proficient at all of them, we can also assume that they were not equally proficient: one would excel in stealth, one in speed, one in accuracy, one in strength. Consequently, some sort of role specialization, by which each individual did most of what he did best, must have been favored by selection; the bands which used their pool of skills most effectively would have the best chance.

But hunting is more than the application of physical skills: it also requires knowledge and judgment, and these too are not likely to be evenly distributed. One member of the band may have the sharpest weather sense, another may be the best at understanding tracks, another may have a gift for sensing which member of the herd of game will be the slowest or stupidest, and so on. A hunting band that can bring all this pool of knowledge and judgment to bear when decisions have to be made is going to make the right decision more often than the band that just plays follow-the-leader and leaves every decision to the private judgment of a single individual. Of course, there can be no such debate in the heat of the chase: the leader's decisions there must be given instantly and obeyed unquestioningly. But at the start of the day's hunting, when there is no game in sight, or several herds in different directions, there is time to draw from the pool of collective wisdom.

This aspect of life in the hunting band, more than any other, takes my mind back to the late 1950's and the *Tonight* program. Of all the ten-groups I have worked in or known of, this came closest to the rhythm of hunting life; indeed, the similarity now seems almost uncanny. To start with, it was in the fullest sense a daily program. We arrived in the morning with very little idea of what would be in the evening's show. One or two items might already have been arranged, but the bulk of the schedule was left empty until the day. In the second place, we were a real ten-group—a central nucleus of about six, and four or five others. And in the third place, nearly all the group, and five of the central six, stayed together for over four years keeping the same routine of a new program every day. What is more, our daily routine followed the pattern of the hunt. We began every morning with a discussion on what to put in the program. The editor would then decide on a provisional program, and we would go off on reconnaissance expeditions, so to speak. We would ring people up to find if they could come on the program, or for advice about how to treat a topic; we would arrange filming: we would investigate the availability of film clips, still photographs, cabinet ministers, film stars, preservationists, and abolitionists; someone would be finding out how to get a three-ton truck into the London studio, another would be seeing if the Cardiff studio could accommodate an organ and a sixty-man choir. Sometimes a scent would go cold and we would have to meet again to think of an alternative. By lunchtime, we usually had sight of the prey: we knew what we were after, and it had become a question of getting it onto the screen by 6:50. During the afternoon the hunt would quicken, and the critical point would move from one member of the team to another: first it might be a question of getting an interviewee onto a train in Norwich by 3:05, then of getting some film to the laboratories before 4:00; next the pressure would move to the cutting rooms to get the film edited, then to the writer to finish his commentary in time; as the kill approached, the dubbing theater became the focus of anxiety, with commentary and effects to be added to film, while the live studio items became critical as interviewers arrived and photographs, musicians, charts, props, and scenery had to be assembled, plotted, lit, and rehearsed for cameras; finally the studio and its control gallery became the place where the day's hunt succeeded or failed, as the program was transmitted. Sometimes there was a splendid kill and we were all elated, sometimes our quarry got away and we were proportionately downcast. Either way, we would go off for a drink and post-mortem to draw what general conclusions we could and see that successes happened more frequently in the future, and that the causes of failure were isolated and eliminated.

The enormous stimulation and satisfaction of a daily routine, a new task each day and no precise foreknowledge of what it would be, prompt the reflection that perhaps one of the most unnatural of the boring elements in repetitive work is the knowledge of exactly what will have to be done tomorrow and next week and next month. The day-task comes most easily and naturally to us, and we are at our most productive and most satisfied when our group completes each evening the task it decides on in the morning. That, however, is by the way. I used the example of *Tonight* because, having now observed or taken part in many decision-making groups, I find it stands out as the model of how good decisions are made.

The first point to establish, and every committee should note it, is that only one person ever made the decisions—in our case the editor. The purpose of the rest of the group was to help him reach the best possible decision. This, I am sure, is a truth which holds for every group decision: in the end it is one man's decision, and the others' membership in the group means their acceptance that his decision when made is binding on them all. It is arguable that more delay and discord in great corporations and departments of state are caused by the delusion that committees can make decisions than by any other management myth. A committee's purpose is to help a man decide.

The second point is that the editor never decided anything on a majority vote. To give each person a vote would be to imply that each man's voice was equal, and it never was. As far as I can work it out there were always at least five variables, whose combination might vary on each topic. One was knowledge of the subject: since we dealt with almost any subject—politics, science, art, fashion, economics, films, industry, international affairs, music—the value of any individual's contribution would depend on his expertise in the subject. Another was production skill: how much experience and success the speaker had had in the production techniques that would be used. Then there was strength of feeling: was it just a casual idea, or something the speaker felt right down to the depths of his soul? Another highly important variable was judgment: did the speaker tend to be right in his assessments of what would work for the audience; was his judgment better on some topics than others; did he tend toward optimism or pessimism? The fifth variable—extremely important—was executive responsibility: was the speaker the one who was going to have to carry out the idea? If so, his feelings had special significance, and if he was really opposed to an idea that he alone could execute, then he virtually had a veto.

Obviously, there could be no way of reflecting all these variables by a distribution of votes, particularly since the weight of an individual's opinion would change even within a single discussion. And, of course, it never occurred to anyone to suggest it; we all knew it was the editor's decision and that it had to be. He was the evolved leader because we knew he was more likely than the rest of us to lead a successful expedition, and had the sharpest sense for keeping away from danger and destruction. A collective hunting expedition demands a fine and flexible grading of priorities—that route gives us the best cover but is more likely to hide leopards, this investment proposal offers the highest return but the country concerned is more likely to be plunged into civil war —and only the leader can keep them permanently in balance and adjustment. Also, any plan can be modified to put more weight on one member and less on another: a stiffer production target can give an easier job to sales, a shorter time in the dubbing theater gives the editor longer to cut the film, a brilliant piece of stalking can make fewer demands on running, and so on—and this too can only be balanced out from day to day by the leader.

But although the leader is the expert at the total objective and at the allocation of roles and priorities to achieve it, in any individual aspect of it there is always liable to be a member of the group with higher skill or better judgment or a more ingenious plan. If the leader does not incorporate these into his decisions, then the survival of the group is threatened. It is also threatened if a plan is decided on in the absence of someone with essential knowledge—the only man who knows the path through the swamp or the likely sales volume of the product at this price—or of the person who will be responsible for executing any significant part.

This is something that all of us understand instinctively. One of the prime causes of fury that crops up again and again in large organizations is leadership that does not listen. The decision to go ahead with a product without talking to the production manager, fixing the price without talking to the sales force, abandoning a development project without reference to the department doing the work on it, siting a new airport without discussion with local residents—these are happening all the time and arousing emotions which have nothing to do with reason, logic, or consideration of the facts. I can think of many cases when, in cool retrospect many years later, it is now clear that my fury was aroused by a decision which was substantially correct. I can think of other cases when I accepted an unpleasant decision philosophically because I had said my say, heard other people say theirs, and realized that the decision even if wrong had been reached in the light of all the available arguments and suggestions and information. It is the demand to be heard before the decision is made which has operated in favor of survival, and the willingness to listen first and decide afterwards which has sorted out the successful leaders from the unsuccessful.

There is another aspect to decision-making, which is nothing like so emotionally charged but still significant: the post-mortem, the reviewing of the decision in the light of its result—drawing conclusions, learning lessons, building up the store of shared folk wisdom within the ten-group, the talk around the fire at the end of the hunt; comparing today's events with past ones and looking for common threads, passing on pieces of observation, reviewing old beliefs in the light of new evidence, offering tentative judgments for refutation or confirmation, agreeing who had done well or badly, remembering any act of exceptional courage or skill. This sort of discussion tends to be intensive and compulsive in the early days of a group when there is much new experience and little precedent; and although it quietens down with time, it always goes on, and a radically new danger or opportunity can start it up again with the old intensity. In time this body of folk wisdom becomes a decision-making factor which restrains even the leader: it is difficult for him to go against the body of knowledge and custom in whose formulation he has taken so large a part. It is another of the reasons why the group and not the individual is the base on which the corporation rests, and why corporations should think of group promotion rather than individual promotion as the norm. To quote V. C. Wynne-Edwards, professor of ecology at Aberdeen University, "In general the characteristics and functions of a society belong to it collectively and cannot be completely represented or discharged by an individual member."

Most boards of directors and committees of executives understand these two principles of group decision-making—listening before deciding, and building up a store of folk wisdom by constant reviewing of causes and effects. What they less often seem to realize is the need for it, and the value of it, all the way down the organization. The subject matter may be different, but the process is the same. On the factory floor it will not be long-term expansion plans that people want consultation on; it will be design of parts, control of work flow, siting of machines, advance information of work load, as well as pay and conditions and holidays: and many factories are repositories of much ancient wisdom in these matters, as well as in ignoring instructions, concealing facts, and thwarting the objectives of management. In the same way the sales force, the office staff, the transport staff, and indeed every group in the corporation have little pools of knowledge and experience and judgment which all too often nobody draws on. The salesmen may know, privately, that a certain discount rate is unnecessarily high in their region; the machine operators may know, privately, that setting time could be saved if two jobs arrived in a different order; the accounts clerks may know that if certain bills to slow payers were sent out earlier the monthly statement could be ready much sooner: but this sort of knowledge, shared and discussed among the groups when they meet at lunch or over tea, never gets any further. Marks and Spencer, Britain's outstanding retail food and clothing chain which ranks high among Europe's most successful companies, insists that every director and senior executive visit at least one of the two hundred and fifty stores a week to keep themselves in permanent contact with this kind of group wisdom, but many corporations leave this most valuable source quite untapped.

Why? I suspect it is a legacy from the early days of industrialization when the manager was the only man expected to think, when work was simple and repetitive, products and production methods went unchanged year after year, and units were small enough for the boss to know exactly what was going on. But today in almost every corporation the reverse is the case. Units are larger, work is more complex; there is a constant flow of new products, new materials, new plant, new processes, new markets, new techniques, new procedures which demand the most intensive consultation on how to fit them into the existing practices, and constant review of how they are working out and what is going wrong and what can be learned for the future. It is here that the break appears, and the factory does not learn about the new data collection system until after the computer has been bought, and the second numerically controlled tool is ordered without the operators of the first one being asked what modifications would improve it. You can even end up with a brand new multimillion-pound container terminal lying idle at London docks because none of the dockers will man it.

If a break like this opens up in a corporation, separating the knowledge, experience, feelings, and reactions at the bottom from the judgment, plans, and decisions at the top, the situation is ripe for revolt. What has happened is that in collective terms there is a leader who will not listen and must therefore be overthrown. It was the error of Charles I and Louis XVI and Nicholas II, as it was the downfall of Henry Ford. Of course, the revolt may be put down, and the leader may maintain his throne by force, but if he does so he is still impairing his own chances of survival: not just because of the discontent and alienation and hostility in the ranks, which cannot help in achieving the objective and must give advantages to rivals, but because he is cutting himself off from this pool of knowledge, ideas, experience, memory, skills, and judgment—all the stores of folk wisdom built up over the years. These are just as much of a management resource as the skills and efforts of the employees. But when the break happens, when a leader or a leadership group does not come to decisions by listening but simply issues instructions and enforces compliance, it drastically reduces the size of the pool it has access to. Consequently, it can make a wrong decision because it lacks a certain store of knowledge or judgment, or fails to hit on an idea, which is actually available in the organization—but which it cannot get at because it has locked the door and thrown away the key. Survival depends on deciding right, and every available resource has to be brought to bear on the process of decision-making; and for the leader who has to make the decision, the ear is a more important instrument than the tongue.

IX

The Hunt and the Camp

WE have it on the best authority that no man can serve two masters, and it seems a fairly obvious truth until you reflect on the fact that many employees of large organizations are doing it all the time. I first had direct personal experience of this in the army. I was recruited into, trained by, and commissioned in the Royal Signals, and in the course of the ten or eleven months they spent turning me into something that would pass for a Signals officer I was made privy to a great deal of tribal lore. Much of it was to do with organization and equipment and techniques, and had no great moral authority, but some of it was as binding and as transcendental as holy writ. I remember a picture in the officers' mess—indeed, it was in almost every officers' mess—of a young lineman in Flanders who had just jointed a telephone cable that a shell had severed. The line was repaired, but he was lying on his back white and bloodstained and dead. The title of the picture was *Through!*. At first sight it recalled almost irresistibly Oscar Wilde's judgment that no man of true sensibility could read of the death of Little Nell without bursting out laughing, but in fact the picture had great emotional significance for older members of the Corps: it expressed one of the transcendental duties of every signaler —to get communications through at all costs. It was a duty that many of their friends had died trying to discharge, and there could be no doubt of the genuineness of their emotion. For them the painting was not a work of art but something closer to a sacred icon. If I did not come to share their emotion, I at least learned to respect it.

The same solemnity was attached to certain other observances and taboos which lay close to the heart of the signaler's job. Two will serve as examples. The first was rigid observance of radio procedure. It was in the nature of radio that the enemy could usually pick up your transmissions and work out your position, but they did not know who you were —for all they could tell you might be a battalion or an army. There was strict procedure to conceal that information, and a breach of it could lose a battle, so security procedure was dinned into us as a far more holy compulsion than the Ten Commandments or the Sermon on the Mount. The other solemn taboo attached to codes and ciphers: a slip that let the enemy crack one would profoundly imperil the survival of thousands of men, so the slip must never be permitted. All this was simple and straightforward in the training school; but what happened to the signals officer who was attached to the headquarters of an infantry brigade? If the brigadier told him to dump his radio in a ditch and retreat, did he obey? If he grabbed the microphone and bawled over the ether to a battalion commander, "Listen, you bloody fool, do you know who this is? It's Brigadier Howard," did you let him do it or switch him off when you saw what was coming? If you heard the brigade major ask a battalion what slidex code chart they thought they were using, did you let him wait for the reply or jam the frequency? Which master were you serving?

These are thorny problems, but only in theory. In practice they rarely caused any trouble. You could debate theoretical dilemmas endlessly, but in any given instance you always knew which of the two masters you had to obey. I was surprised to find how well this system of dual authority worked and for a time I thought it was peculiar to the army; but I encountered it again shortly after leaving. In the BBC, the cameramen belonged to a different division from that of the producers: a cameraman took orders from the producer of the program, but again there were certain taboos. The producer could not instruct him to breach safety regulations, risk damage to the equipment, or transmit pictures of a technical quality lower than the agreed minimum standard. The application of these rules might occasionally cause frustration and irritation, and they might be adjusted from time to time, but the system of dual authority was always accepted as perfectly natural.

Since those days, I have encountered the dual loyalty so often, and found it worn so easily, that I feel it has to be accepted as something we do naturally. It seems that the division is always the same: one master commands our day-to-day, operational activities, and the other our permanent, long-term obedience and allegiance. In the industrial corporation it is reflected all the way up: you respond to the disciplines of the department in which you are employed, but you also belong to the corporation. Your boss can give you all sorts of tasks, but he is limited by the overriding policies of the corporation. He can stop your going to Alaska, but he cannot stop your promotion into another division. He can load you with work, but he cannot prevent your taking an annual holiday. He can take away your company car, but he cannot reduce your pension. In hundreds of ways he accepts that he has operational freedom and untrammeled authority in certain areas, but in other areas his staff do not belong to him but to some different, higher, and more en-during authority.

This duality reaches its final corporate expression in the relationship between the chairman of the board and the chief executive officer. There is no obligation on any company to make these into separate functions, and indeed they are on occasion held by the same man—but chiefly when the company is actually being formed, or drastically reshaped. At such times the short and long terms are so intimately connected that they need to be united in the mind and will of a single man—the "old man," the founder of the firm. In just the same way the founders of the new African nations—Kenyatta, Nyerere, Kaunda—have to embody both the permanent state and the government of the day until a national identity is securely established. But once that has happened it soon becomes clear in the nation and the corporation that there are in fact two jobs at the top and not one. It happens with such regularity that it can be taken as the normal, orthodox way of running any large corporation—to have one man running the entire show is the exception.

The chief executive officer is the peak of the operational activities of the corporation. All the day-to-day and year-by-year research and development and production and sales are under his authority, and the year's profit-and-loss account is the index of his achievement. He stands at the summit of the corporation and looks down at all those who toil on the slopes and foothills and plains below. He marks strength and weakness, success and failure, scarcity and plenty, and decides what must be done to maximize the good and minimize the bad. And beside him, just a step higher up, stands the chairman—but he is looking in the opposite direction, not inward at the organization but outward at the world in which the corporation has to survive. He is preoccupied with long-term finance and relations with the capital market; with the community, and the corporation's reputation within it; with the governments it has to deal with and the laws that may be passed which will affect the corporation; with long-term shifts in technology and markets and materials which may affect the sort of corporation they will have to become in five or ten years' time.

When the chairman does turn around and look inward, he does not share the chief executive's obsession with results and return on capital and earnings per share. He cares about them, of course, but they are already being looked after. His preoccupation is with decisions that may change the whole nature of the corporation for the worse. Suppose the chief executive wants to sack thirty executives: in some corporations it would be accepted as a correct decision, but in others it would send a shock wave to the farthest outposts. In the latter case the chairman would have to balance the saving of salaries against the damage to morale. Suppose the chief executive wanted to start up a range of cheap products and enter a new market, or lower the excessively high technical standards of the corporation's engineering: the chairman might know that these decisions would do irreparable damage to the confidence of customers and the pride of employees even though the short-term profits would be impressive. Equally, a single unjust act, if it helps to avert imminent danger, may not worry the chief executive too much; the chairman sees that it may make all the most valuable staff start to reconsider what sort of organization they are offering a lifetime's allegiance to, and he may think the price too high. It is the chairman who is the more worried about recruitment and training and developing managers; as with his other preoccupations, these concern not so much what the corporation does or will do, but what it is and will be.

This distinction is not between two halves of a job that becomes too big for one man: on the contrary, the difference is so profound that it is practically impossible to discharge both duties properly at the same time. The present and the future do not run in harness: their demands and emphases move at a different pace and sometimes pull in opposite directions, and it is rarely satisfactory if the conflict takes place in a single man's mind. If one man tries to do both jobs, one of them is likely to go by default. Sometimes it is the chairman's job that goes, and the company is driven by a brilliant and thrusting opportunist who achieves outstanding short-term results, but is eventually overwhelmed by the unforeseen changes which he himself has precipitated; sometimes it is the chief executive's job that goes, and the company is wise, just and thoughtful, and returns two percent on its assets. There has to be a proper tension between the present and the future, and a tension requires the application of a force at each end.

It is not only in the corporation that this duality is expressed. Most states which have reached any size have evolved the same form of leadership. The king represents the permanent and the outward-looking aspects of the state, while his chief minister is answerable for its internal organization and short-term results. The king embodies law and justice, foreign affairs, long-term defense, and the capital side of the treasury; the chief minister and his government look after the preservation of order, the framing of individual laws, the revenue side of the treasury—tax collection and disbursements—and the balancing of national priorities from year to year. And it is not only in advanced civilizations that this has developed: many of the larger African kingdoms (Ruanda, Buganda, Ankole) evolved this same division. Indeed, one of the most profound troubles of countries like Britain and the United States is that they lack a proper expression of this duality. The British monarchy, by being little more than a formal and ceremonial office, and the American presidency, by being dependent on four-yearly elections, both leave the long-term, permanent authority— the chairmanship—to go by default. Neither the prime minister nor the president can easily sacrifice the short-term to the long-term, and consequently the long-term office becomes a vacuum which sucks into itself generals, civil servants, diplomats, bankers, judges, scientists, and industrial leaders who have to argue behind the scenes, and without any formal or democratic authority, for the future against the present. America has the additional advantage of state governments which, by filling the chief executive role in many internal affairs, leave the role of sovereignty vacant for the federal government and emphasize the permanent, monarchical aspects of the president's role because he has less direct responsibility for the measures debated and the laws passed by the state legislatures; but in national politics he is a victim of the same system that puts such conflicting demands on the British prime minister. Both have to weigh the long-term good of the country against the short-term need to be re-elected.

It is one thing to observe how this duality is inherent in all our organizational systems, but quite another to explain it. We have already seen that divided authority must operate against the survival of the hunting band; how can it also have operated in favor of the survival of our species? No one has offered an answer to this, chiefly because no one (to my knowledge) has asked the question. But once you ask it, there is an answer which I find so completely satisfactory, so thoroughly persuasive, that I do not think we have to look any further. So let me put it forward.

When we became collective hunters, the form of organization which that activity demanded, the ten-group, was an addition—not an alternative—to our older social organization. We are the product of some hundred million years of social living, as well as perhaps fifteen million years of collective hunting. As well as the ten-group, there was the camp. The hunt was the instrument of day-to-day survival, but the camp, the home base, was the instrument for preserving and continuing the species. The camp in the daytime was the place for the women, the children, and the old men. There was work to do—collecting fruit and roots and berries and water, bringing up the children, some rudimentary attention to hygiene and comfort—but it did not have the dangers or rewards of the hunting band. All the same, the species could die out just as easily by failure to keep the camp secure and free from disease and internal strife as it could by failure to kill the game. Consequently, the ancient primate society, which had long been used to living and wandering in small groups, must have preserved what it could of that form of organization while adapting to the compulsions of the hunting life. The hunt was a special, separate activity. When the hunters returned, they rejoined the older social organization. Communal defense against predators or other marauders of their own species, the prevention of lethal strife within the group, some means of making group decisions about which way to move on, some sort of social conventions and regulations—all these must have existed long before we turned carnivorous, and must have continued and developed over several hundred thousand generations to reach the refinement and complexity they show when we first encounter them in history.

Every modern corporation has its camp in addition to its hunting bands. It contains all those who are not actually devising, making, and selling the product that brings in the money. They may be physically only just across the corridor, but in all other ways they are in a different world. Many of them are women—secretaries and personal assistants, cleaners and coffee ladies—but in the modern corporation many are men as well. They are in departments with names like finance, personnel, planning, public relations, administration, registry, welfare, and so on; and, however devoted their efforts, however valuable their contribution, the members of the hunting bands look on them as the "women and children" of the corporation. Any hunter who is sweating his guts out to meet a production or copy deadline or a sales target thinks of them as, to some extent, a burden that he and his fellows have to carry, and I suspect there is even a submerged feeling that it is women's work they are doing.

Healthy, strong, active men ought to be sharing the exertions and perils of the hunt, not skulking in the warmth and safety of the camp all day. It is very difficult to say who in the corporation is in the camp and who is in the hunting band—but only if you are in the camp. You then think of the importance of your contribution—the tax savings you have devised, the pressure at which you work, and how you go home absolutely drained an hour after everyone else—and you almost kid yourself that you are really one of the hunters. But the hunting bands know with absolute clarity who are the hunters and who are the passengers. Some of the passengers may in fact prove their usefulness so clearly, in the way they make the hunters' work easier and more effective, that they will be accepted and even respected; but that respect has to be earned from the hunting bands, not in the camp. What the corporation's hunters find absolutely intolerable is the squaw-men in the camp starting to behave as if they were as important as, or more important than, the men who go out and kill the game. If this false importance is endorsed by the management, the contemptuous resentment is turned upward on them. Many industrial disputes are given an extra streak of bitterness when the men making the product that makes the money see their friends being laid off so as to support an army of smart young parasites in warm, carpeted offices.

There is also a biological limit to the size of the camp which a hunting band can support: there is only so much game to share out at the end of the day. But the safety and comfort of the camp are so tempting that the danger arises of more and more people trying to find themselves a job there rather than on the hunt, and putting an ever greater burden on the hunt to support them. It is sometimes called "top-heavy administration," and it is one of the greatest dangers to corporate survival: the corporation camp has a tendency to grow rapidly in good times, when game is plentiful, but when it gets sparse there are too many flabby stomachs to fill and a desperate shortage of trained and skilled hunters.

For all that, the camp has demands which are as powerful and legitimate as those of the hunters. A marvelous area for game may depend on a snake-infested camp with bad water and sparse cover. A better camp may mean harder work for the hunting band, but this has to be accepted. A higher price may mean a tougher job for the sales force, but the alternative of abolishing the patent department may be, in the long term, a much worse way of generating the extra cash. But the tension is always there, and it is the classic situation for the dramatist: the hunt and the camp—the chief executive officer and the chairman of the board—are both pulling in different directions, but the rope they are pulling is the bond that holds them together. The hunting band is part of the whole group which must survive as a group: if the rope snaps, both sides lose. One or the other may have to give ground, and the tension may vary from very low to very high, and a permanent point of rest may be an impossibility; but both sides have to hang onto the rope whatever happens.

This tension is felt right through the corporation, from the chief executive trying to get more development money at the expense of the training budget to the salesman fuming at the time he has to spend filling out sales reports instead of calling on prospects. I sometimes wonder if this tension is not the basis of all political division, at least in stable communities which are free from war or subjection or revolution. As I write this, at the end of 1970, it is certainly the fundamental political argument in both Britain and the United States. In Britain the conservatives have been returned to power on a national feeling that the camp has been favored at the expense of the hunters: too much national expenditure to subsidize health, homes, and schools, too much government restriction on, and interference with, the activities of industry, so let's sweep away this massive parasitic structure of controls, taxes, commissions, and civil servants and give people the freedom and incentive to produce and export and make us all richer—let's kick some of these boondogglers out of the camp so that the hunters can have a bigger share of the meat they bring back and go off tomorrow fitter and more eager than before. In the United States, the feeling seems to be exactly the reverse: "we've" been so preoccupied with giving the hunters everything they want that the camp is dirty and smelly, fighting and bullying are breaking out all the time, we can't drink the water because everyone is excreting into it, so let's divert at least some of the time and energy and manpower from bringing back more meat than we can eat to clearing the place up and stopping the fights and making the camp a better place to live in.

This tension between the hunt and the camp runs from the highest councils of the state down into every family, where the demands of the husband's job and the needs of the home and family can so easily come into conflict. But at some point in our distant prehistory we seem to have evolved a third force whose function usually serves to resolve the conflict, and it is a strange and intriguing evolutionary phenomenon.

Nature's requirement of every individual member of every species is that he or she should contribute to the survival and regeneration of the group. With certain exceptions (sterile castes of social insects, for example) this means the breeding and rearing of young; and when that is completed and the period of fertility is over, the individual is no longer required: he would be a passenger—a burden on the group—if he stayed around, and so he is given an honorable discharge by the natural selection board and dies off quickly and quietly. No group is imperiled by a disease or genetic defect which only strikes when reproduction is completed. This, however, is demonstrably not the case with man: we are one of those few species whose males and females survive long after they have finished bearing and rearing children. Why? What selection advantage could favor a hunting band with old people to look after, as against the young, active, unencumbered groups with a quick death at forty to prevent the old from being a burden on the young?

The answer offered by Professor Wynne-Edwards in *Animal Dispersion in Relation to Social Behaviour* is that the hunting bands who could draw on the knowledge, experience, memory, and judgment of their older members must have had a selection advantage over those who were not so fortunate. The elders were the custodians of a cultural tradition, a mixture of knowledge, experience, memory, and judgment, which was vital to the survival of the group when it needed to adapt to a new situation. The younger hunters might never have seen a really long drought before, but the elders remembered what happened forty years before. In the same way, many of Wall Street's brilliant young go-go fund managers who didn't need the oldies when the index was rising steadily were suddenly grateful for their experience and memory when they found themselves on a longer downhill slide than their own short lives had witnessed.

The presence of the elders in the camp acted as a countervailing force to the demands of the hunters, but as men who had themselves served for a long time in the hunting band they could understand and weigh the needs of the hunt as well as the needs of the camp. Their status and influence with the younger males would presumably be high, since they would have been the leaders of the pack when the present leaders joined it as novices, and their daily advice and warnings would reaffirm their value. Moreover, the fact that they had avoided death in the hunt for so many years was living evidence that they were experts at survival.

When we look at the ten-group in the corporation, therefore, we have to accept that it has never been a totally independent and autonomous unit. In the heat of the chase it can accept no interference, but when the hunt is over—when long-term decisions have to be made, when there are wider considerations than killing the game to be debated—they accept limitations on their freedom of action. Equally, my corporation experience tells me, they accept it only from those who have themselves been brave and skilled hunters, whose experience and achievement are respected, and whose leadership has brought success to many hunting expeditions in the past; they do not submit to the judgments of the women and children. But if the best leader is allowed to evolve both from the hunters and from the elders, then the dual authority of the camp and the hunt—the operational and the institutional, the short- and the long-term—is easily and naturally accepted. It is a duality that will become important as we leave the single group and look at the larger and larger organizations into which it combines.

X

The Corporation Tribe

O N C E you have accepted the application of the ten-group and the camp to the corporation, you can then use it as the sole building block and construct a theoretical organization from it in the form of a pyramid. When I first stumbled on the idea of the ten, I assumed this must be what happened; and the obvious way for it to happen is for the leaders of the ten ten-groups to come together and form the ten-group that controls and regulates a group of a hundred. Then the leaders of the hundreds would come together and form a group of a thousand, and so on. This explanation satisfied me for a long time, chiefly because it is very close to what does actually happen: we do indeed, as we shall see, combine ten-groups into larger units by exactly this method. Furthermore, it is very difficult to prove or disprove it by reference to corporations, because a ten-group can in practice be four people; the consequence is that as you get up to higher numbers, you can explain them in different ways. Twenty people can be five small ten-groups, and consequently five of those would, structurally, be a "small thousand" while adding up to a hundred. In this way any number could be explained as "natural" by the indulgent manipulation of decimal arithmetic. All the same, I felt a nagging unwillingness to accept this sort of structure. The deceptive neatness was part of the reason—that sort of simplistic extrapolation smells more of midnight oil than flesh and blood. But there was a much stronger reason, though as far as I was aware it had even less basis in evolutionary theory than the pyramid. It was simply that I had a feeling in my bones that there was another grouping of great importance, even if I could not understand why. It lay somewhere around four or five hundred—perhaps six. It was essentially a maximum size; smaller numbers, as far as I could see, were perfectly acceptable, but larger ones were not. It did not seem to fit in particularly well with the ten-based pyramid, unless it was stretched to give a thousand as the absolute maximum, but I had to admit that it was there.

It first came to my notice in the early sixties, when I started to get interested in management. Several people mentioned four or five hundred as being just about the maximum size for a one-man firm, the size up to which an energetic and managerially unsophisticated entrepreneur could build his business and keep it under his control. Sir David Brown, for instance, who inherited his gear company from his father in the thirties, says that the reason it was in trouble at that time was precisely because it had grown from its normal and profitable size of five hundred employees up to a thousand, which was too many. Profits started to slide, the old man's tight grip loosened, and the trouble had begun. The clearest symptom of this occurred when he sacked two men who were standing around doing nothing, and then found they were a contractor's employees. In the old days he had known every man by sight.

All this was very unscientific; nevertheless, when a number of practical men arrive independently at the same concept of an upper limit, and attach roughly the same figure to it, the evidence is not something to be dismissed just because it does not fit a theory. And when I came to think about it, five hundred turned out to be an extremely interesting number. Somewhere around four or five or six hundred is about the normal size for a village. It is also what most headmasters and principals think of as the "right" size for a school or college: a comfortable size, the size they would be very happy to run. And what about the army, where the logic of survival is at its strictest? A battalion in wartime was about six hundred; and the Romans—that most decimal of nations—had the tent of ten and the centurion for a hundred, yet the cohort was not the thousand that simple multiplication would suggest, but a variable between three and six hundred. Why?

Then I thought back to my school list. At the start of each year we were all given a printed list of all the boys in the school—a total of some four hundred and fifty. It became a competition among the junior forms to see how many you could identify, and you ticked each name on your list when you were able to put a face to it. I remember feeling some satisfaction when in the middle of my second year I completed the list. Next year the unknowns were junior to me and the game lost its savor; to have gone around in one's third year sedulously inquiring the names of the new boys would have been at best undignified, and at worst suspicious. Nevertheless, I had already proved to myself nearly thirty years before that it was possible to know all of a community of that size by sight. My feeling was that at a stretch I might have been able to recognize up to six hundred or so, but a thousand, for example, would have been beyond my powers.

There is a special significance about recognizing and being recognized, and it concerns identity. I am using the word in a very simple objective sense, the sense of how many people know who you are. This is profoundly important in a community, if only because it so radically affects what you can get away with. It might be worth slipping outside the school grounds or the factory gates if the chances are that whoever sees you won't recognize you, but if you know that the headmaster or the boss knows you, then the risk takes on a different complexion. Moreover, in a group of five hundred it is possible for the boss not merely to know you, but also to notice if you're not there. You could almost define your boss as the most senior man who will realize that you're not in today, and four or five hundred must be close to the human limit for that sort of knowledge. Or imagine trying to conduct a matrimonial intrigue in a village of six hundred people: you could reckon that the time-lapse between one person suspecting and the whole village talking would be a maximum of twelve hours.

So it did seem that this grouping of somewhere around five hundred might have a genuine significance as an "identity group" in which every individual recognized everyone else and—an important refinement—knew that everyone else recognized him. Since this seemed to be true for the whole human species, as far as I could find out, there could easily be a biological, genetic base for this phenomenon— some fact of brain composition, some limitation on our mental storage and retrieval system—that made it impossible for us to belong to an identity group of ten thousand, or perhaps even of one thousand. But that was as far as I could get.

I now know that I had at that stage seen slightly less than half of the truth, but the rest did not and could not dawn on me until I had grasped something fundamental to our understanding of any kind of organization, insect or animal or human: the principle of population genetics. I find it astonishing that this science, which absorbs so many distinguished scholars and bears so closely on the origins and nature of man, should have remained virtually unknown to the ordinary educated reader. But it is so important, and so fascinating, that I will try and summarize very briefly the relevant aspects.

The foundation of the science of population genetics was the realization that no species, however solitary its members might seem, could survive unless it was part of a wider population within its locality. The chief reason for this is the gene pool; no solitary creature, or pair of creatures, can procreate indefinitely, and resist all the hazards to survival, from their own genetic resources. No matter how multitudinous their progeny, if they all contain the same basic and limited genes, then a plague or climatic change or food variation or new predator will wipe out the whole lot. But if they interbreed within a wider population, the available pool of genes and the variety of possible genetic combinations and recombinations gives an enormously higher probability that some at least will emerge as a resistant strain, fill up the gaps, and replenish the population; moreover, the replenished population will now have a much higher resistance than before, just as the rats which survived warfarin poisoning have fathered a rat population which is now largely immune to it; and, of course, the same has happened with rabbits and myxomatosis.

To the layman, this is a fairly simple and straightforward idea, even if a new one; but nonetheless it compels a very different view of natural selection. It means that nature's law is the survival of the fittest *population,* not simply the fittest individual. Indeed, the individual who indulges his own instincts or inclinations at the expense of the needs of the group is a danger to survival, whereas selection will always favor the community in which the individual sacrifices his gratifications, or even his life, in the interests of the group. It is populations, not individuals, that have preserved and transmitted life from the pre-Cambrian oceans to the present day.

It is impossible not to reflect on the irony that after a

hundred years of bitter division, Darwinian biology should
so perfectly unite with Christian morality. But for the purposes of this inquiry there is one immediate conclusion that
we can draw: the hunting band and the camp, on their own,
could never have provided a large enough gene pool for
survival. They must always have been a part of a wider,
interbreeding population; there must always have been a
number of camps within an area, and those camps must have
been within a reasonable contact range. But how many
camps? Just a handful, or a vast population stretching over
hundreds of thousands of square miles?

I believe there is an answer to that question, but it
involves another short excursion into population genetics.
This time it starts from one of the fundamental problems
posed by group natural selection: what limits the total size
of a group? The simple answer is food; but when you look
closer, it is nothing like so simple. Our own species has discovered in modern times what happens if you expand till
you exhaust the food supply. The neatest example was provided by the flourishing nineteenth-century whaling industry, which kept expanding for as long as whales could be
found; the consequence was the disappearance of the whales,
and the collapse of the whaling industry. It is the universal
problem of overfishing, which applies not only to fish but
insects and plants and any life-supporting resource: there is
an optimum annual crop, beyond which you start to diminish, and ultimately destroy, the resource and consequently
the population the resource supports.

We shall never know how many billions of times this cycle
was repeated in the history of life on earth. But somehow,
over five hundred million years, the answer was found, and
some populations evolved a means of keeping their numbers
at the right level for optimum cropping of resources. Their
means of doing so are varied—limiting breeding territories,
eating newborn young, delaying mating age, and so on—but
the means are not in this case the relevant factor. What

matters is that before it can operate the control mechanisms, the population must reach a collective awareness that its numbers are approaching the danger point. And this is where it starts to get interesting.

Professor Wynne-Edwards has collected a mass of examples of how this is done: he suggests that the flocking of birds, the howling of gibbons, the croaking of frogs, the scent-marking of trees by dogs and wolves, the dawn chorus, and hundreds of other signaling devices are used by the populations as a way of keeping a check on their numbers, of asking "How many of us are there around this place today?" Some, of course, are merely counting absolute numbers; but there is strong evidence that higher animals are doing something further: they are recognizing individual members who belong. Observers have noticed that in the great herds of zebra there are smaller groups of about a thousand who keep together, however much they may move around within the herd. On one occasion when the herd panicked in a thunderstorm, the thousand "population" was completely split up; but it had completely reassembled within twenty-four hours. As a matter of interest, this number—around a thousand—seems to be the "population" size for a number of animals: the Alaska fur seal, the Uganda kob, the African elephant, and a number of others all seem to form discrete populations at this limit. Obviously these populations overlap slightly, which again has survival value since interbreeding across population boundaries creates a cross-flow between gene pools; but this is very much an exception—the rule is that a population keeps itself to itself.

It seems beyond question, therefore, that the hunting bands and their camps belonged within a wider group that was itself reasonably self-contained, and had some mechanism for controlling its numbers. It also seems virtually beyond question that this mechanism did more than measure and control absolute numbers: it identified whether all the individuals were bona fide members of the group, the genetic isolate, the tribe, or whatever you like to call it. After all, communities of monkeys are quite capable of recognizing and resisting an intruder of their own species, and various experiments have shown that it takes time for any newcomer to become established as a full member—a phenomenon not unknown in the corporation. This alone would suggest the need for mutual recognition within the population; but in our case there was a special extra reason.

I mentioned earlier how territory acted as a form of population control: with sea birds, for instance, only the pairs with nesting sites could raise young, so the population was stabilized by a "convention," and "conventional competition" for breeding sites replaced direct competition for food, since, as we have seen, direct competition for food involves everyone in taking all the fish they can get, with consequent collapse of both fish and bird populations. Numerous species of animals have evolved some such conventional competition as an alternative to resource-destructive competition—so many that Wynne-Edwards has defined a society as an organization capable of providing conventional competition. But in the case of our primitive and carnivorous ancestors, competition by fighting for territory could be just as destructive as overcropping the game. We were killers by trade, and to compete by killing each other would have been a sure route to genetic extinction. So the convention must also have precluded, or at least inhibited, fights to the death within the band or between bands in the population group. A brother's murder, as Claudius says, has the primal, eldest curse upon it, and if the population is to survive, then a neighbor's murder is only a little better. But who is my neighbor? There are other, rival hominid populations who in times of game shortage may descend in force and fury to take over the territory by that most unconventional and unanswerable of competitive devices, the sharp blow on the skull. Ten-groups who in this extremity turned on their neighbors within the same population, because they were unable to distinguish them from the enemy, would be at a selection disadvantage. Mutual recognition had a survival value of the most immediate kind.

If this is true, it begins to look very significant. But there is something else to look at before we come to any conclusions—three most interesting and unconnected research findings from three different continents. The first comes from genetics and France, where the marriage records were studied to establish whether there were such things as "breeding communities" still persisting. There were indeed, and the size of them provided a remarkable discovery: they numbered, on average, eleven hundred in the mountain communities, but in Paris they were only nine hundred. In fact Theodosius Dobzhansky, one of the most illustrious geneticists, has suggested that even today most human "genetic isolates"—the units within which breeding normally occurs, and across which it is unusual—are numbered in hundreds rather than thousands.

The second finding comes from anthropology and Chicago, and is even more relevant. Edward Hall studied the black neighborhoods, and found that within them there were very clear territories, sharply divided from each other, though without any visible boundary. They had the unity of villages, with many friendships inside the boundaries and very few across them; parents would reprimand neighbors' children, the gossip network was comprehensive and rich, and group attitudes on subjects where they were necessary were formed and then generally adopted by the whole community. The population of these informal, unofficial city villages was on the small side—up to two hundred or so—but their spontaneous development, their internal self-regulation, and their communication network have the precise characteristics of a tribal unit.

The third piece of evidence goes further back into our prehistory: it too comes from anthropology, from a study of the Australian aborigines. As one of the few surviving hunting groups, with their clear racial and geographic separation, they are likely to have preserved our prehistoric forms of organization with less change than any except perhaps the Bushmen of the Kalahari—though, of course, the possession of the bow makes them far more sophisticated hunters than our earlier ancestors. Their ten-groups tend to be on the small side, with five or six males and a total community of about twenty-five; the small number may be the result of having the bow to hunt with, or of Australia's unique freedom from predators, but in any case it falls comfortably within the three-to-twelve limit. However, it is the wider grouping that is the interesting one. It has been established that it divides into "dialectical tribes," that is to say, groups in which all individuals speak the same dialect, but are dialectically differentiated from all the other tribes in the area. These dialectical tribes are also "genetic isolates." What is interesting is their numerical consistency: all the tribes which were studied over the years tended toward a constant number of five hundred. If they fell below, the number was restored to five hundred before too long. If they expanded they could just about contain their numbers and preserve their unity up to a thousand, but then they would split into two, a new dialect would gradually develop, and a new tribe would be born.

There is one other most interesting example, though it is not the product of research but of experience. Mao Tse-tung's agricultural revolution was based on the concept of total mobility of labor within a commune of some seventy thousand people. Each man and woman would be told where to work each day, according to operational needs. The scheme proved impossible to organize. It was reconstituted with the village of a few hundred, and not the individual laborer, as the basic unit: each village was allocated its task for the day or the week. On that basis the plan worked and is still working.

The Chinese commune, the Australian outback, the Chicago slum, the Paris suburb; the school, the college, the village; the cohort, the battalion, the one-man firm; above all, my own inner sense of the size of community in which I could expect to know everybody, and the size which would be too much for me. I suggest that we have a natural population size of five hundred with a maximum of a thousand, which we have carried within us for millions of years. Once you start to think back to our African origins, there are other reasons that begin to jump out at you. For instance, the leaders of ten hunting bands, or more likely the leaders of the elders, would themselves form a ten-group as the council of the whole tribe and provide such rudimentary government and legal system as may have evolved over the ages. And there is a further point, which could have become important with the development of speech: five hundred is about the number you can comfortably reach with the unaided human voice in the open air, and a thousand is close to the absolute maximum even for a drill sergeant.

J. B. Calhoun defines any population as "the major unit in which the lives of individuals find reality." I believe we have to accept that for our species this unit is five hundred, with a thousand as the point at which it has to subdivide. Of course, we can associate ourselves in our minds with units of almost any size; we can think of ourselves as belonging to ICI or IBM, to Liverpool or Chicago, to Britain or the United States. But this, as we shall see later, is a sort of notional membership—we belong with our minds. I have lived in London nearly all my life and would certainly call myself a Londoner, but it would be nonsense to pretend that I feel for or even know about what goes on in any more than one ten thousandth of the homes that make up the city: not in the way that a villager knows and cares about what goes on in every house in the village. If you go away from your village, people ask each other where you have gone; I cannot pretend that if I leave London I provide five million people with a topic for conversation. A unit of five hundred or so is something you actually feel a part of: not with the compelling bond of the ten-group, but nevertheless with a membership that cannot be shrugged off by a change of mind. You know that if you leave, everyone will notice the gap you have made. A soldier can belong to this corps or that corps, this army or that army, and if it is successful he will be proud of his membership; if not, he will feel he is a member of a great regiment or battalion in a lousy formation. But his regiment or battalion membership is of a different order: it is not notional but real; it is a part of his permanent identity which he cannot disclaim in the same way. Less powerful than his section, his ten-group, it is nevertheless real and personal and human; he knows them all, and they all know him. It is the major unit in which he encounters reality. He belongs not only by accepting, but by being accepted.

The importance of the five hundred-unit (let us call it the tribe) to the structure of the corporation is enormous. It is impossible to assemble ten-groups into tens or hundreds of thousands without excessive multiplication of management layers, but with tribes it becomes not only possible but comparatively easy. All the same, I think we have to be conservative about the size of a corporation tribe: if a thousand is the maximum, it is the maximum for a tribe whose association is lifelong, whose membership changes not with hiring and firing but only with birth and death. Moreover, the corporation tribe disperses every evening; even its ten-groups do not go back to a communal camp. This can, of course, be counterbalanced by how much the different ten-groups see of each other during the day—a battalion on active service, for instance, will have far greater opportunities for mutual recognition than an insurance company in a skyscraper block —but the combination of lifelong membership and frequent opportunities for recognition is rare enough (though it certainly occurs) for us to think of the corporate tribe as around five hundred, and to accept that, whatever other groupings we may attach ourselves to intellectually or emotionally, five hundred is the largest group any of us is ever really a part of. We shall begin to understand what that means in terms of the life of the corporation as we start to look at the tribe in operation.

XI

The Tribal Chieftain

T H E corporation tribe is neither as powerful nor as pervasive a working unit as the ten-group. The impulse to form ten-groups is so strong that, if necessary, it will happen despite the corporation; the tribe, by contrast, is far more optional. Many successful small concerns stay at ten-group size: professional partnerships, R&D groups, consultancies, studios—these can manage very well without ever expanding or combining into a tribe. I have a feeling, privately, that they are in fact often part of a larger informal tribe: that their clients and suppliers and colleagues, or rivals in the same area of business, do form a larger unofficial community in which they have an objective identity, and that if they are in business for long enough this network will build up into the hundreds. I also feel, with greater certainty, that what may seem to be a completely separate and independent ten-group within the corporation usually belongs in the same way—however much it may proclaim its autonomy—to some larger unit. But these are not operational tribes in the full corporate sense, and nonetheless they work well and happily.

All the same, there are two powerful reasons why tribal structure is of prime importance to the corporation. The first is that it is large enough to be a satisfying community for those who belong to it. It recalls de Tocqueville's perceptive and charming observation about the township: "The township serves as a center for the desire of public esteem, the want of exciting interests, and the taste for authority and popularity, in the midst of the ordinary relations of life: and the passions which commonly embroil society change their character when they find a vent so near the domestic hearth and family circle." With the words appropriately altered, the corporate tribe provides exactly this. It is a rich network of scandal and gossip, friendship and feud, romance and rivalry, and if our language was furnished with a word that meant the exact opposite of loneliness, that would be what the tribe offered to all its members. It is large enough to be satisfying, but not so large that you cannot feel yourself a part of it; unlike the ten-group, if you belong to the tribe you normally accept that you are part of the corporation: from the corporation's point of view, it is the prime focus of loyalty for most of the employees during most of their working lives.

The second reason is that it is tribal structure alone that makes the management of really large organizations possible. Managing a hundred thousand people, or even ten thousand ten-groups, is almost a contradiction in terms; but managing two hundred tribes is quite possible. They must, however, be allowed to become, or remain, genuine tribes, and it is at this point that so many corporations go wrong: they fail to utilize the nature of the tribe as a positive instrument for corporate success and profit, and in all sorts of ways they manage to destroy those elements they most need while leaving the others intact. It is not so much that there are rules which they break; rather, it is a lack of understanding of what a tribe is and what it is not.

Because I worked in a new and rapidly expanding industry, I have seen over the years the growth of a number of new tribes, and watching individual tribes grow can give a valuable insight into the nature of any tribe, however long established. Indeed, one of the first questions to ask about any corporate tribe you encounter is how and why it began, and who started it. Who started it is particularly important. A tribe can, of course, be started by an act of management, but that is not the way most successful tribes come into being. By far the most common and most successful method of tribal formation begins around the nucleus of a single dominant ten-group. There is hardly a product group, department, or factory that cannot be traced back to an explosion at some point in the past, when a new ten-group came together, seized an opportunity, developed it, and expanded to tribal size. It is not hard to think of the ancient hunting band finding a new territory with a new plentiful food supply, and expanding their numbers, forming new hunting bands, attracting stragglers or other less successful bands, and building up a new tribe around them. It would be harder to find any evidence to support the idea, but then it is observation of the present, not speculation about the past, that furnishes the idea of the dominant ten-group as the nucleus of the tribe.

But whether the tribe originated in this sort of "extended family" or was founded as a confederation of ten-groups, it still takes its orders and style and direction and standards from the ten-group that leads it: the tribal chief and his council of elders. And it is, of course, the tribal chief who is the keyman—not only of the tribe, but of the corporation. Since a large organization is in fact administering tribes, the good tribal chief is at once the guarantee of his tribes' efficiency and success, and the channel of communication between the corporate leadership and the multitude of tribesmen.

Great corporations can make great mistakes. A single error of judgment—like the Rolls-Royce costing of the RB 211—can destroy the corporation. A single stroke of good judgment—like Rank's alliance with Xerox—can save an empire. If you are running a giant corporation, you have plenty to do without worrying about who is minding the shop. Yet the corporation may be crumbling away beneath you, and your customers may find it out before you do. It will not be dramatic, with millions of dollars suddenly changing sides on the balance sheet; it will be myriads of tiny, almost imperceptible failures. The car key that jams in the lock after three days, the shop assistant who does not know what she has in stock, the service engineer who says he will call and doesn't, the sullen, unhelpful girl on the switchboard, the traveling salesman who is obviously just going through the motions of selling, without any conviction—all these and hundreds like them will happen from time to time in any corporation, but if allowed to multiply they can build up almost insensibly until they are a talking point among customers and the start of a long slow slide down the hill. They are beyond the direct control of any top corporate executive, but with a good tribal structure the offender will be personally known to the tribal chief, who will be personally known to the top executive: a very different matter from six levels of corporate hierarchy.

And yet any hierarchical system will reach a point where someone on the chart has roughly five hundred people working under him: that is not the problem. The problem is to turn him from an official in middle management into a chieftain, and although it is by no means easy, the hardest part of it is to grasp what the difference is and to see the need for change. The rest is still hard work, but not beyond the powers of any experienced manager.

The difference is rooted in the freedom and authority of

the chieftain. He is not just one more link in the chain, with authority and responsibility slightly wider than his subordinate and narrower than his superior: he is much more like the boss of his own independent firm. Nevertheless, he has to be very much a part of the corporation; he has to be simultaneously separated and integrated. There are no rules for the resolution of this paradox, but there is a principle: the area of the chieftain's independent authority should be defined so clearly that both he and the corporation know the boundary line with great precision, and within that boundary no one should interfere with his operations; and wherever the boundary is drawn, he should be left with enough authority to be accepted by those under him as the personification of the corporation and the only channel through which they encounter its authority. It is this last point that lies at the root: whatever authority he may or may not have over money or policy, his leadership of his people must be unquestioned. A tribal chieftain can have very limited management authority indeed and still be a chieftain, but unless his subordinates realize that for all practical purposes his word is their law, the tribal structure does not exist.

That is very abstract and oracular, but the difficulty of being more precise is well illustrated by the practices of two corporations, both employing about thirty thousand people. They have in common the reputation built up over many years of being among the best managed corporations in the Western world. I have chosen them because of the extreme contrast in their approach; the difference will demonstrate why precise rules are so hard to formulate, and the residual similarity will illustrate the underlying principle. The companies are 3M of America and Marks and Spencer of Britain.

I became interested in 3M because of a saucepan scourer. I had known of them for some time as one of the world's largest producers of recording tapes, so it came as a surprise to find that such a large organization was interested in such a small object as a saucepan scourer; conversely, if a firm so large and successful was bothering to launch a new saucepan scourer, it must surely be very good (which it was). On investigating further I discovered that this was not just a whimsical experiment: they actually had more products than employees, and they had, as I said, around thirty thousand employees. This tremendous diversity was only possible because of dedication to the principle of forming ten-groups and allowing them to expand into tribes whenever they could link a new product with a growth market. Often it was simple adaptation of an existing product: Scotch tape adapted for surgeons, Scotch tape as curling tape for the cosmetic market, Scotch tape for masking in paint shops, Scotch tape for protection in packaging departments—if it looked promising enough, a ten-group would form and go out hunting. Equally, if a researcher came up with something new, his tribal chief encouraged him to form a ten-group and try to find a market. If he succeeded, he could expand until he became a tribal chief himself, the head of a division; there are some thirty divisions, mostly up to a thousand each, and one or two considerably larger. He would be given the maximum freedom to make his own decisions about the product—its package, price, market, and production volume—to hire the staff he needed, and in fact to become virtually an independent entrepreneur within the corporation.

The Marks and Spencer tribes are the stores, nearly two hundred and fifty of them, of which the largest employ several hundred staff: the store manager is the tribal chief. By contrast with a 3M chieftain he might appear to be powerless. All the goods are selected for him by the tribe of merchandisers at the head office; they determine style, color, sizes, and price, and, for seasonal goods, starting and stopping times. All his layout and display and relative space for goods are laid down by another headquarters tribe called store operations. The number of staff and their wages are laid down, as are procedures for dealing with customers' complaints and queries. He could hardly be more different from the 3M tribal chieftain developing new products and new markets on a very loose rein from the head office.

And yet everyone in Marks and Spencer knows that the difference between a good and a bad store manager is crucial. In each area, a good store manager has scope to improve his results by enterprise and good judgment. He can pay a really good assistant more than the fixed rate. He can move rainwear to a more prominent place in a wet spell, or woolens in a cold snap. He can have more pink dresses and fewer blue ones sent because of a local preference he has noticed. He can extend the space for footwear if he sees the new range of shoes moving faster than was forecast. But more than all this, he is boss of his people; he is responsible for the efficiency and helpfulness of his staff and the focus of their loyalty. He is the arbiter of their disputes and the solver of their problems. This may not match the responsibility of a private owner running his own show, but it is critical, and it keeps him watching, thinking, learning, and experimenting all the time.

What he has in common with his fellow chieftain in 3M is absolute clarity about his tribal boundaries, about what actions lie within his discretion and what are outside it. Moreover, it is not a private piece of knowledge which he shares secretly with his immediate superior: in each case it is known to everyone. How wide or narrow the boundaries are will affect the size of the job and the power and importance of the tribe; the presence or absence of clear boundaries determines whether the tribe is being allowed to function as a tribe at all. In the case of Marks and Spencer, if divisional supervisors or merchandisers or store operations staff could walk into the store and start giving orders to the salesgirls about changing the knitwear display, or telling them to go and comb their hair, or ordering them to sweep the floors again, or sending them to the stockroom to get more shirts, then the tribal authority of the chieftain and the operational efficiency of the store would be destroyed. It is the manager's job. He does it well or he does it badly, but no one else does it for him.

There is a consequence of this which is equally important if the latent energy of the tribe is to be released and harnessed to the success of the corporation: there must be an objective criterion by which success and failure are measured. "Objective" is the most important word. It is not enough that someone upstairs should be pleased; tomorrow he may be angry at the same result. The measurement must be drawn from the marketplace, if possible by making the tribe a self-contained profit center, and always by setting a target in advance. It is remarkable how often industry's tribal chieftains, if allowed to set their own target, come up with a tougher one than anyone would set for them—but then it is remarkable for the same reason how interior decorators always take a fortnight over a job they say they can do in a week. A 3M tribal chief asks for his year's investment allocation in proportion to the profits he hopes to make: he expects to be judged in the marketplace. A Marks and Spencer store manager knows equally clearly what the turnover of his store should be, and there are his previous year's records and the results of the other stores to compare it with. In neither corporation is there secrecy about these results—every tribal chieftain knows how all the others have done and how his achievements compare with theirs.

Not every tribe, obviously, can become a profit center. All the same it is surprising how often a market measurement can be found. It is often possible to compare the cost of a year's work by the legal or financial department with the cost of similar quality work from an outside firm of solicitors or accountants. It is also possible to put work out to such firms from time to time as a check. The same is even more true of the in-house supplier of parts: the front-line tribes should be free to purchase from outside if they get better service that way, and a part of General Motors' success in controlling such a vast empire so profitably for so long has been a resolute opposition to corporate protectionism: GM component manufacturers have to sell to GM vehicle-producing divisions on a level footing with everyone else; if they cannot compete successfully, they are selected out.

The creation of a tribe, therefore, demands complete and detailed agreement with the tribal chieftain on three subjects: the resources available to him, the results required of him, and the limitations on his freedom of action. He must also be the ultimate source of authority among his tribespeople. Their holidays, wages, uniforms, and conditions of service may be determined by a higher power; that does not matter. What matters is that orders should be given only by him, or by someone acting on his authority; that requests should go to him; that disputes should be resolved by him; and that for all practical and operational purposes his yea is yea and his nay is nay: he is the father of the tribe.

There is one other factor which can be of great assistance: the actual authority over physical territory. A store manager, a factory manager, a headmaster, a destroyer commander—all acquire an increase of stimulus and satisfaction by being able to walk around a place and feel it is theirs. It may not actually belong to them, but then Buckingham Palace does not belong to the queen or the White House to the president. It is sufficient that as long as they hold the office it is under their command. Physical territory enables the manager to ask anyone what he is doing there, with the clear implication that he recognizes the man as a stranger and has the right to remove him from the premises. I have never seen territorial authority recommended in any book on management; but I have never seen a department head in a vast office block walking down the corridors with the pride and authority of a factory manager going around his factory.

It would have been much easier, I suspect, to recognize

the tribal structure of industry in the early years of the industrial revolution. The mines and mills were mostly tribal in size, many had been established for a generation or more, and the difficulty of travel gave them a closer cohesion. Above all, they were comparatively static; it is the rate of change that has blurred or obliterated tribal boundaries in the modern corporation. A group of five hundred can become two or three thousand much faster than the human capacity for organic enlargement, and it is all too tempting to try and manage them within the original structure. Sometimes tribal logic takes over, and within a complex of several thousand people a number of separate tribes develop. A determined, efficient, and truculent manager has his own ways of making sure that nobody messes with him. He has the inestimable advantage of knowing everything that is going on in his tribe, and why, and this is a powerful weapon with which to fight his superiors. Another is the respect he has from his tribesmen. Above all, he is getting the results that keep his superiors in their jobs, and the threat of walking out is the most powerful weapon of all so long as he does not wield it too lightly or too often. Consequently, you find informal and unofficial tribes which are acknowledged in fact, but not in theory. I have met such a tribal chieftain who was installing machinery costing upward of 200,000 dollars before the application for capital appropriation had been given approval. He knew it was necessary, he knew it would more than pay for itself, he knew the money was there, and he knew there were five jobs waiting for him in other corporations if his bosses wanted to make anything of it. But equally there are groups of thousands, or even hundreds, where no tribal structure remains. Orders are given by one authority and rescinded by another; nobody knows who he is working for; bad work is unreproved and good work unrewarded; managers are constantly saying, "I don't know, you'd better ask x or y or z"; and only a few scattered ten-groups preserve their little pools of efficiency and self-respect.

But even when there is a sound tribal structure, it is often in a transitional state. The ten-groups expand, and several of them form subtribes within the tribe. It is often hard to recognize the point at which the division has to be made, the umbilical cord has to be cut, the new leader has to lead his tribe over the mountains toward the promised land. It is sometimes hard even to recognize that this has to be done as a deliberate act of management organization: it is easier to leave an uneasy agglomeration where the overall chief no longer has real personal knowledge of his whole tribal operation and the headmen of the subtribes do not have the independence and authority to do their job as they want to. It creates the friction of the young man who is grown up and earning his own living but still staying at home with his parents. Respect and affection do not diminish the friction—on the contrary, they prolong it. A time comes when the break has to be made, the young man has to leave home, the intermediate manager has to be established as the head of his own department, and a new tribe sets off.

And yet, in a situation where markets, technology, processes, and materials are changing so fast, the tribes are the most powerful force for stability, for making sense out of the change, for assimilating and turning to use and profit the valuable innovations, and discarding or modifying the others. But tribes, unlike new machinery, do not arrive overnight. They may be formed in a hurry, but it takes time to build up a body of tribal wisdom, to agree on tribal frontiers, to sort out group relationships, to establish standards and principles, and to confirm the status and authority of the chieftain. But when this has been done, when a tribe has had a number of years to establish itself, it can be a corporate asset as important as (or more important than) cash or plant. It is a cliché to say "Our people are our greatest asset," especially when we all know that some of them are our greatest liability; but a successful tribe that has been going for a long time establishes traditions, standards, a reputation, a depth of relevant knowledge and experience and memory, and a capacity for adapting to and cashing in on change, which are indeed an asset. But they are not held by any single person, like, say, the ability to speak Japanese; they are a fixed asset vested in the whole tribe, an asset which can continue to provide profits but cannot be exchanged for cash. Of course, there can be bad tribes—they can be badly led, they can lose touch with the market, they can become ingrown and blinkered and inflexible—but very often the capacity for regeneration is there if it can be stimulated and the barriers removed. And this repair and regeneration of the tribes ranks with the formation of them as one of the prime tasks of corporate management, just as the destruction or dispersal of a successful tribe in a merger or takeover or corporate reorganization, because of the logic of administration or accountancy, can represent a loss to the corporation which it is beyond the wit of any administrator or accountant to make good. But if we are to understand what it means to build tribes and maintain them in good health, we shall have to look more closely at the inner workings of the corporation tribe, and the stresses that can threaten its survival.

XII

Tribal Unity:
Rebellion and Civil War

I T is much easier to describe the tribe as a single organism than to open it up and see what happens inside. To the outside corporate world it is, or should be, an independent entity. Something goes in one end, something else comes out the other. If it is a manufacturing tribe, it is raw metal and castings and wire and subassemblies and coolants and lubricants and paint and electric power that go in, and finished products that come out. If it is a store, cases of consumer products go in, and bags full of cash come out. If it is an infantry battalion, fuel and food and ammunition go in, and newly acquired territory comes out. If it is a school, raw, untreated, unprocessed children go in and refined, processed, certificated children come out (at least that is the current theory). With service organizations, government departments, and so on, the input and output are less visible and measurable, but even here a good tribe will have a clear role and those who control it will know if it is functioning well or badly; and if it is going well they will be happy to leave it alone.

If a tribe is not functioning well, sometimes the reason is outside tribal control—a shift in the market or a new technology or a change of government policy may take away their livelihood almost overnight. Sometimes the reason lies in the inadequacy of individuals or ten-groups—failure to make decisions in time, or inability to plan the work and control the people who are supposed to do it. Sometimes the reason is to be found in the corporation—too much interference, too little guidance, decisions delayed or made without full information. But when all these occasional variables have been removed, there remain certain permanent factors which make the tribal chieftain's task harder or easier, and influence the collective behavior of the tribe; not factors like whether the work is hot or noisy or smelly, but much more fundamental, tribal considerations. Very little useful discussion of the internal workings of a tribe can take place without reference to them.

The first consideration is the balance of tribal population between male and female. An all-male tribe is much more liable to bouts of collective aggression, and a reasonable proportion of women working with the men dilutes the concentration of aggressive energy and makes the chieftain's task easier. If the tribal population is almost wholly female, the dangers of explosion are very small indeed. A strike is the ultimate expression of the collapse of the corporation's tribal system (though it may also express a flourishing tribal system within the union), and it is historically the all-male tribes in mines and docks and car factories which have provided the longest and bitterest strikes, whereas strikes of all-female tribes are extremely rare.

The strength of collective aggression rises with numbers, so absolute size is the second important factor. A small tribe of a hundred or two is far less of a problem than a tribe that is rising up toward a thousand and beyond. But there is a third factor which can enormously diminish or intensify the importance of numbers: namely their concentration or dispersal. If they are in small groups and widely separated, with little or no chance of forming larger groups, then the problem is much less than if they are concentrated in one place. Every schoolmaster knows that a group of forty or fifty boys in a single group on the playground is something that has to be investigated at once, whereas ten or a dozen can be left alone. Every factory manager knows that a knot of forty or fifty men together on the factory floor during coffee break needs the same urgent investigation. A work situation which encourages that sort of spontaneous congregation is far more inflammable than when it takes a lot of prearrangement.

The easiest tribes to control, therefore, are small, widely dispersed, and chiefly composed of women: stores, schools, banks, offices, hospitals. These factors are, of course, no guarantee of enterprise, efficiency, or success; the work can still be extremely badly done. What they mean is that the simple fact of organizing people is not one of the major problems, and therefore the internal structure is not critical. Many different groupings and subgroupings can work perfectly well, depending on the nature of the job.

At the other end of the scale is the large, all-male tribe concentrated into a small area, with plenty of opportunities for mingling in large numbers. This has to be recognized as an inherently explosive situation, and in this situation more than any other the corporation is in danger of losing control. The first necessity is a proper structure of ten-groups, with none of them getting too large: if they can be divided up so that the groups correspond to an operational function, so much the better, but if not then the evolved leaders of the natural social groupings—the informal ten-groups—need to be given proper recognition and representation. There are many decisions which are not operational—holidays, shift-working, conditions of work—which can easily cause grievances and build up a head of steam. If each ten-group has an acknowledged identity and an official spokesman or representative, the steam can find an outlet. It can also help the sense of belonging, of being part of the tribe, if each ten-group has its own territory: even a group of machines arranged in an open square instead of along an endless line can help to build this sense of group identity, just as it is easier in cities to create a sense of community in the houses around a square than in the ones along a road.

With a tribe of this composition, the further groupings of ten-groups become extremely important. In theory, the leaders of ten ten-groups ought to form a ten-group of their own to sort out the work of a hundred. In practice, this rarely seems to happen: the next grouping seems to work out at thirty or forty, three or four groups, with someone in charge who is not (though probably was previously) a full-time leader of a ten-group. He is the foreman, the subaltern, the supervisor; and just as this size of thirty or forty corresponds to the size of the camp to which the hunting band returned, so he corresponds to the head of the elders who does not go on the hunt himself but who is the final arbitrating authority between the needs of the camp and the needs of the hunt. He is the most underrated figure in the corporation. Just as the tribal chieftain is the keyman in the wider corporation—the link between the highest level of planning and the real events on the factory floor—so the foreman is the link between the chieftain and the hour-by-hour progress of the tribe's efforts. He is the pivot. All information and instructions reach the ten-groups through him, all the problems and resentments and long-term worries of the ten-groups are interpreted, evaluated, and then expressed by him to the chieftain. So long as he and his dozen or so colleagues in the tribe are respected and trusted by the ten-group (they do not have to be liked) and are fully in the confidence of the chieftain and his council, the tribe is properly bound together. If not, that is the point where the break comes and where the union starts to build its alternative organization, its own revolutionary tribe.

If the foreman or supervisor is the naturally evolved leader from the three or four ten-group leaders, then half the battle is won: an outsider superimposed on the groups has a tremendous task to get his authority accepted and is all too likely to be treated as a joke or an irrelevance. It is much easier to forge the link in the other direction, to take someone who is respected on the shop floor and weld him into the tribal leadership structure. What is more, there is an instrument for doing this, though it is all too often neglected. The man who saw it most clearly, though at a far more exalted level, was Alfred Sloan. He recognized that at the very top of General Motors there was exactly the same danger as this: a fatal separation between the hunting bands and the camp, the corporate management and the divisional operations, the future and the present, the theory and the practice. And so he established a regular meeting between the divisional heads—Chevrolet, Buick, Cadillac, and so on —and the government of General Motors, his own four-man executive committee. No decisions were ever made at this meeting; that was not its purpose. Part of its purpose was to enable those who were planning the future to have a sense of the current mood of the divisions—were they chafing at restrictions and bursting to go, or feeling overstrained and hoping for a letup? Part of it was to test out new ideas on the practical men. Part of it was to find out how past decisions were working out in practice. Part of it was to lift the eyes of the divisions from the floors of their factories up to the horizon, and see where the whole enterprise ought to be heading. Part of it was to keep each side aware of the other's problems and aims. This meeting between warriors and statesmen is needed at every level in the corporation, but at none more urgently than the lowest when the foremen sit around with the tribal chieftain and his elders. It is also the easiest meeting to neglect, since it is not related to this day's operations. And even when it is held, it can too easily degenerate into a string of detailed trivia ("Item 34, the cold tap in no. 2 washroom . . .") or simply become the boss's briefing session where he issues his orders. At least half the purpose of the meeting is for the boss to shut up and listen, and half the agenda should normally be decided by the foremen: the boss should raise on his own initiative only those questions that require a decision from him.

There is very often another obstacle: many tribes have to divide into subtribes for operational purposes, and groups of foremen may report to a departmental manager; a tribe may well contain four or five such managers, and they will necessarily form the chief's operational group for most practical day-to-day purposes. But these departmental managers can also form a barrier between the chief and the foremen, since he will not now need to meet the foremen operationally; they will get their orders at one remove. This in fact makes it necessary to hold the meetings with them more frequently than if he were in direct operational contact, but in practice (and especially if the intermediate managers do not understand the difference between the hunt and the camp) it tends to stop it from happening at all.

This meeting, of course, if properly conducted, serves another purpose. Not only does it enable grievances, ideas, and problems to rise up to the top—it enables people to rise as well. Most tribes are run by a ten-group, which often seems to work out as the chieftain with two or three elders (finance, planning, personnel) and the three or four operational group managers, perhaps with a works manager in a chief executive relationship to the chieftain's chairmanship. This occasional wider meeting where they collectively meet the whole group of foremen together is perhaps the only opportunity to form a tribal judgment (as opposed to a number of separate private judgments) of who are the coming men and what is the real status-ranking of the foremen. One of the prime causes of disaffection, sedition, and revolution is blocking the upward route of the best men, the men with ambition, status-dominance, and a popular following. The fortunes of a factory or a kingdom can hinge on whether such men are allowed to become gamekeepers or forced to be poachers. At each level this meeting is the arena where they first show their mettle.

These three factors—numbers, concentration, and male–female balance—determine the danger of a horizontal division within the tribe, a fatal separation between the top and the bottom, between the managers and the men. There are, however, three other factors which, when they become critical, can create not a horizontal but a vertical division, not subversion and revolution but baronial warfare; conflict between rival groups within the tribe.

The first of these is change in the volume of tribal activity and prosperity: as long as the volume remains constant, the existing boundaries between ten-groups or other subdivisions of the tribe remain unchallenged, but if the volume of work either contracts or expands with any rapidity, the boundaries come under pressure. With expansion a small group is likely to grow bigger and start to assert itself, new men become important and older ones resent their assertiveness, and friction begins. ("Why the hell do we have to clear our plans with them? We're bringing in twice the business they are. Let them clear their plans with us.") With contraction, the groups see their importance and even their jobs disappearing, and each tries to keep hold of the work that will continue, or grab some from somewhere else. Of the two, expansion is by far the more liable to cause strife since in a contracting situation few people will press a quarrel to the point where they become a nuisance, because nuisances are so easily disposed of: but when business is expanding the nuisances are also the most necessary to the future prosperity of the whole tribe, and they know it.

The second of these factors is change in the type of work. Even when the volume remains fairly constant, there is sometimes frequent change in the sort of tasks the tribe has to undertake. If the factory simply turns out ball-point pens year after year, responsibilities become clearly defined and universally accepted: if it is constantly having to adapt to new products and processes and materials and machines, the weight of responsibility is likely to shift around, with much the same result as the increasing volume of work which so often accompanies it. And the third factor concerns the antiquity of the tribe: if they have all been together a long time, they can adapt much better to these shifts and innovations than a group which has been newly formed or rapidly expanded to twice its original size or even larger. The easier of the two extremes here, therefore, is the old established tribe which is still doing much the same sort of work in a fairly constant volume. In such a situation there is unlikely to be any serious clash over function and jurisdiction and boundaries of responsibility. At the other extreme is the newly formed or suddenly expanded tribe with an expanding volume of work of a constantly changing character; and this brings a major problem.

The problem is rooted very deep in our animal nature. I have already referred to the territorial instinct, the inborn compulsion to acquire and defend your own exclusive territory, which is common to many species including man; but I have found in the corporation something that I can only explain in territorial terms even though it is not strictly territorial. It is a kind of territorial defense of role or job, and although it certainly operates within individuals it is at its most powerful in groups: "my department's responsibility," my salesmen's area," "my union's job." A hunting band, after all, would defend its camp, but it would also resist intrusion into its hunting area even by other bands from the same tribe. On the other hand, an intrusion without hunting intent into a part of the area where there was no game would be unimportant: the significant factor would not be territory as such, but a threat to compete for the same source of food. The result is something I can only call a quasi-territorial response, a defense of your means of livelihood calling upon territorial instincts but not precisely or exclusively territorial in its application.

Once a ten-group or tribe or any other grouping within the corporation is given a clearly defined task and an area of responsibility, it has the title deeds to a piece of quasi-territory; but a changing situation will constantly call the boundary line into question, and if it creates uncertainty or overlap it will provoke the most formidable animal reactions from Corporation Man. There are monkeys who have a way of standing in troops, each on their own side of the territorial boundary, and howling at each other in fierce and deafening concert; departmental managers and craft union officials often behave in a very similar way.

One of the most passionate quasi-territorial battles of recent years was fought out in Whitehall shortly after the election of the Labour government in 1964. The Treasury, the most powerful of all the ministries, had historically controlled all government expenditure, long-term as well as short-term. The Labour government believed this was too much conflicting responsibility for a single ministry, and set up the Department of Economic Affairs to take over the longer-term part. To the politicians it may have seemed a simple and sensible piece of administrative reorganization; to the Treasury it was a monstrous and intolerable assault on their ancient quasi-territorial rights. They fought with the desperate passion of men defending their homeland, and in the end they won. The DEA never managed to pry out of the Treasury the control of longer-term investment they needed, and were left with the dregs of economic power—regional planning, the control of prices and incomes—while the Treasury went on drinking the wine.

And yet despite the emotional intensity of the quasi-territorial responses, there is no guarantee that the existing boundaries are the best ones to serve the corporation's ends. A manufacturing company which was in grave trouble with its customers because of bad workmanship decided that the trouble lay in quasi-territory: the manager responsible for meeting delivery deadlines was also responsible for inspection, and with frantic customers and salesmen on the phone demanding instant dispatch of the product, it was always inspection that was scamped. So they removed inspection from his authority and set up a quite separate inspectorate reporting straight to the director of production, with the not surprising result that complaints and returned products dropped dramatically. And, of course, border conflict can be to the corporate advantage; the competition between Birds Eye frozen peas and Batchelor's canned peas is more rather than less intense because they are both part of Unilever.

And yet if Birds Eye and Batchelor's were to start competing by privately knocking the other product, retailers might decide to move over to some third supplier outside the corporation: so do you encourage border conflict or discourage it? This is one of the most common of management dilemmas; publishing houses constantly encounter it between their various magazines and newspapers; government departments meet it all the time. They realize that it can be a positive source of alertness, efficiency, and enterprise: from the corporation's point of view it provides the ideal form of "conventional competition" when it works, since whichever group wins or loses, the corporation itself goes from strength to strength and constantly improves its stock by expanding through the victorious groups and economizing in the unsuccessful. A large part of the success of General Motors was due to their seeing the logic of internal rivalry earlier than most people. But when it does not work it can be damaging and divisive, as rival departments try to encompass each other's downfall. So what should you do?

Obviously there is no simple rule, but most people seem to have hammered out certain principles. The first is to abandon the fiction that we are all a big united family, sharing our delight in each other's success and our disappointment at each other's reverses. The tribal chief must expect rivalry between the ten-groups and subtribes, and expect it to manifest itself in competition between the leaders; equally, tribal chiefs must be expected to compete against each other. It is in the strictest sense natural behavior: competition between individuals and groups for each other's territory is common to many species and ensures that the weak and irresolute and unfit are kept down while the strong and determined and courageous survive and expand. Since group competitiveness has got us this far, there is little hope of outlawing it successfully in the corporation, and a great deal to be gained by channeling it in the right direction.

The second principle was best enunciated by Robert Frost (or more accurately by his neighbor) in the poem *Mending Wall*: "Good fences make good neighbors." His insight has recently been confirmed by a psychological experiment designed to find how people get on each other's nerves when forced to live in each other's pockets for long periods. Several pairs of sailors shared small cabins for several weeks, and it was found that friction and quarrels were lowest where they agreed early and clearly which space and seats and cupboards and table area belonged to which. Lack of certainty and definition was the prime irritant. Corporation Man needs exactly the same clarity and certainty, and an important part of the tribal chief's job is to see that these fences are firmly established and in the right place to further the success of the whole tribe. It is one of the most important of organizational tasks, and failure comes most often through drawing fences around functions which are part of a single entity. It can too easily result in production competing with engineering by proving that making up the design takes twice as long as the designer said, and sales competing with them both by proving no one wants to buy it. Fences around complete products or projects or sections of the market stimulate the right sort of competition.

There is a third principle which follows from this: just as everyone has to be absolutely clear where the boundaries are and where overlap and quasi-territorial infringement are forbidden, so it must be equally clear where competitiveness is permitted and encouraged, and this too must be constructed to further the tribe's interests. Robert Frost's neighbor was right, but Frost was right too when he said, "Something there is that doesn't love a wall, that wants it down." Any group needs room to expand, to test its strength, to break into new hunting grounds. It must not be completely hemmed in—there must be a gap in the wall, a place for locking antlers with the others in conventional competition. It would have been perfectly possible for Alfred Sloan, when establishing his five main car divisions to correspond with five different market levels (Chevrolet, Oldsmobile, Buick, Pontiac, Cadillac), to lay down that the top price in one division should stop short of the bottom price of the next; instead, he encouraged overlap at each end, so that as a customer approached the top of the range in one GM division, the next division up was competing for his custom at the same price.

Nevertheless, with the best designed fences in the world there are still going to be disputed frontiers where the warfare does nobody any good and a line has to be drawn. The best guidance here comes from observing Professor Carpenter's rhesus monkeys. He took three hundred and fifty of them from various parts of India and released them on an island in the West Indies. There was plenty of food, plenty of room, and no predators, yet within a year they had split up into groups and each group had established a clear territorial area—an exclusive space where no other group was permitted to trespass. My experience of the corporation suggests that the same thing happens there too: groups work out their own frontiers with each other, and too much or too rapid intervention by the chieftain can make him spend most of his time in arbitration. When *Tonight* was disputing with *Panorama* and had no real case, I knew it in my bones and I am sure it came out in my voice. Equally, when I felt so strongly that I was prepared to take the matter up to the director general if necessary, this too was clear from my demeanor and they retreated with the appropriate threatening or derisive gestures. Observers have noticed how a monkey who has trespassed onto a neighbor's territory behaves with the furtive guilt of a schoolboy raiding an orchard, and hurtles out in the same way if he is spotted. Corporation Man, or Corporation Manager, has just the same sense of guilt and nearly always knows when he is on his own territory and when he is trespassing, just as he knows when his neighbor is burning with a passionate grievance and when he is just trying it on. A judgment from the chief of the tribe only works if it confirms what both of them know in their hearts anyway, and very often the dispute is better settled by offering to give a ruling only if they cannot agree by negotiation within a limited time.

There is one other weapon at the disposal of the chief: the meeting between the warriors and the elders. It can be very difficult for him to be constantly in single combat with a territorially aggressive leader, particularly when the boundary dispute becomes, as it too easily can, a challenge to the chieftain's authority. It is true that the warriors–elders meeting is concerned with issues that unite the tribe rather than those which divide it; but in fact the unity of the tribe is threatened if one of the headmen is constantly marauding his neighbors, and the united condemnation of all the others, particularly if they have been welded into an effective ten-group, is too powerful for even the most egocentric expansionist to defy. The wise chieftain will, however, privately assure himself that such united condemnation will indeed be forthcoming before he raises the issue.

XIII

Status and Hierarchy

REBELLION and baronial war are the two most obvious consequences of weak tribal leadership or inadequate tribal structure. There is, however, a third; it is less spectacular but much more pervasive, and is a far more personal source of anxiety and friction than the other two. It concerns status.

Of all the driving motives inside Corporation Man, his concern for personal status within the corporate hierarchy is the least understood. There seems to be a generally accepted view that the desire for status is comical and unworthy, and that status-seeking is the mark of the worst sort of organization man. Everyone subscribes to the pretense that status considerations do not operate. "I just need a larger office because I have to have meetings of twenty people." "It's not the size of the car, it's the silence of the engine I need because of the dictating I do while I'm driving." "A carpet gives much better sound insulation than linoleum." But in fact, so far from being shameful or unnatural, the drive for status is one of the principal tools of evolution and natural selection not only in man but in a wide range of other species, and in particular those species which go around in groups; indeed, it is a question whether there is any animal society that does not have a status-hierarchy. Baboons, jackdaws, monkeys, hyenas, antelopes, rats, hens, swordtail fish—the list goes on and on, and man has his place in it as clearly as any of the other animals. The function of status is to select for survival the best individuals in the group—the best both individually and for the group. When food is short, the status-dominant will eat and the weak will starve. When females are hard to come by, it is the status-dominant who will mate and breed. Equally, when disorder breaks out in the group it is the status-dominant who move in and quell the strife, and when the group is attacked the status-dominant head the defense. A driving force which has been one of the instruments of our survival for so many millions of years is not going to disappear because it clashes with corporate organization theory.

All the same, there is a profound difference between status in animal communities and status in the corporation. It is very rare for animal status-rankings to change, except with the normal processes of maturity, aging, and death. Contemporaries usually sort out their pecking order early in life and keep it thereafter. Life in the jungle is not a status struggle —rather, it is the reverse. Animals know their own status and the status of all the others in the group; the leader evolves and maintains his leadership, the others all know their respective places, and although occasional challenges and squabbles develop the normal consequence is stability, security, and—in both senses of the word—order. It is the large numbers, the anonymity, the changing forms of organization and the frequent new groupings and relationships which make corporation life so much more anxious and insecure than life in the jungle.

The unit of the corporation which comes closest to the fixed and secure status-ranking of the jungle is, without any question, the ten-group. I cannot recall ever encountering a ten-group in which status maneuvering or dispute was ever a significant factor. Occasionally, the arrival of a new recruit might cause temporary disturbance, but he would quite soon find his ranking or depart. It is this complete certainty and security about status that makes it so satisfying to work in a ten-group—and there is the added advantage that you also have a clear status within a wider circle by virtue of your known membership of that ten-group. "I'm in no. 3 platoon, B company" gives you immediate identity within a regiment of six hundred men: you have your own established status within your section and platoon, and the platoon has a distinctive identity within the regiment. This internal status-balance of the ten-group has been used with extraordinary astuteness by IBM in their factory at Greenock in Scotland. It employs nearly two thousand people, and there is a leader to every ten workers; and each leader determines the relative payment of the men under him by grading them from A to E. According to reports, the result has been extreme harmony and a very low level of dispute and discontent over pay. This must be a very tentative judgment, since I know of no objective evaluation of the system, but the idea of pay differentials being fixed by each ten-group leader has a great deal of natural common sense behind it.

The ten-group is the only unit in which status is almost invariably secure. All the same it is by no means impossible (though it is less common) for this same security to extend to the subtribe and even the tribe. Carveth Read in *The Origin of Man* quotes one of the most basic statements of status-security from the memoirs of an American pioneer: "All along the frontier between Canada and the United States everyone knew who he could lick and who could lick him." In a long-established and self-contained corporation tribe, the tribesmen have much the same security. They know that everyone else knows; consequently, they do not have to keep asserting anything. This may well be yet another reason why five hundred or so is the normal limit for an effective corporate tribe: it is difficult to achieve this sort of status-security with a much larger number. Of course, within the tribe the ten-groups will have their own status-rankings, and in a changing situation these can alter and cause exactly the same friction and division as disputes over quasi-territory: if, for instance, the manager of one department finds that his job is graded lower than that of a manager of another department which he believes to be no higher than his own, the stage is set for a battle in which group status and personal status are inextricably intertwined.

It is as numbers grow larger and tribal boundaries become less clearly marked that status becomes more and more of a problem in the corporation. It should, of course, be a straightforward matter, in direct proportion to each individual's unique personal contribution to the survival and success of the group. In a ten-group this is what it does indeed reflect, and in a completely self-contained company of four or five hundred the group status would reflect reality in the same way: everyone would know which of the different groups—the manufacturing groups, the assembly groups, shipping, sales, design, accounts, and so on—carried most responsibility for the success of the firm and would be the hardest to replace, and status would be determined by operational imperatives and the logic of survival. There is no point in the accounts group trying to get more money than the sales group when everyone knows the salesboys are keeping the firm alive by busting their guts, whereas you could pick up a new set of accounts clerks tomorrow. There is no point in shipping trying to get the summer holiday date moved if it is the one that manufacturing and assembly have asked for, for the same reason. And everyone knows there is no point: they know what the answer would be, so the question is never put.

This sort of stability, however, depends on everybody knowing how much weight he and everybody else are carrying in the task of collective survival. In the primitive hunting band it must have been perfectly clear, and the relative dominance of the different hunting bands within the tribal area must have been equally firmly settled, even if it was revised from time to time in border clashes or by fiercer and more lethal conflict. But in the higher reaches of a great corporation, particularly when there are no clear tribal divisions, who knows how the weight of his burden and the success with which he bears it compare with the others'? It may be clear enough within his own department, but there are many departments, and their functions are so interlocked and interdependent that it is impossible to judge them separately. And yet Corporation Man desperately needs to know his own status, to know the status of everyone around him, and to have his status known by them. In addition, his evolutionary nature has given him an urge to gain the highest status available to him. What is he to do?

It is, of course, a problem we have already encountered. We know that a society is defined by its ability to provide conventional competition for conventional prizes. Direct competition is impossible: it involves killing everyone else in the search for food until you are killed yourself. On the Canadian frontier in the 1840's, the convention was a fight until one competitor licked the other. In our small status-secure company the convention is unique contribution to profitability and long-term survival. In the giant corporation it is only a question of discovering what are the conventional rewards, and what are the conventional ways of competing for them; these become immediately obvious when you look at the people around you, above you and below you, and see what distinguishing marks the higher have in common with each other, how these differ from the lower, and how they got them. Then you go ahead and compete.

This procedure would be perfectly satisfactory, given one condition: namely, that the corporation had constructed its conventions of competition and reward so as to improve its performance and increase its chances of survival. But the source of all the friction and anxiety is the corporation's pretense that it is not respectable to be concerned with personal status; that people come here to do a job, they get paid for it, and they can keep the status-struggle for home and the Joneses. No single private individual I have ever met in any corporation believes this, but the corporate attitude enshrines the creed. The consequence is that Corporation Man, unless he is in a small and status-secure tribe, is constantly trying to find out how the corporation rates him, how it rates those around him, and how the corporation's expressed ratings compare with his own.

The first place he looks is his pay check. Since salary is one of the simplest ways in which the corporation conventionally grades its staff, it is a quick and reliable guide. It is, however, often extremely hard to find out other people's salaries. Nevertheless, when it does emerge that a colleague you rank below yourself is being paid more, the discovery strikes at the very heart of your security, identity, and self-respect. I have known some terrible corporate battles over money, but none of them have been motivated by the money as an absolute. If you are concerned over money as an absolute, you can—assuming you are underpaid—always leave and go to another company. You only fight if you want to stay, but have received an affront to your status. Always the cause of anger has been money relative to the money someone else was getting. This, however, cannot be openly stated, so the battle is fought in disguise, and the argument rages around the difficulty of the work, the time it consumes, the level of responsibility borne, and comparable salaries in other corporations (where they help the case). The BBC had a grade for every job, and we went through unbelievable contortions to get a job regraded simply because it did not reflect the higher status of its actual incumbent. All too often the regrading was effected as he left it, but the fiction of the job's importance had to be preserved and as a result a low-status successor found himself with a grade and salary beyond his deserts.

Salary is in fact a very poor instrument, if used on its own, for the corporation to employ as its internal status index. One reason is that money is the prime instrument of corporate survival, and if employees are encouraged to compete by seeing how much of it they can take home, the competition is damaging; the kingdom is using the gold in its treasury for medals and challenge cups instead of defense and expansion. And there is another reason: a sudden need for rare skills may put up the market value of comparative newcomers—systems analysts and programmers, for instance —whose personal status is nothing like as high as the salary they can command. This can cause deep grievance among men of higher status if they have been brought up within a convention where salary was a direct expression of status.

But salary, of course, is not the only conventional prize in the status race. There is another of equal or even greater significance, which is perhaps even more damaging than salary when it becomes a source of status conflict. It is function, the actual job you are given; and the battlefield is the corporate or divisional or company organization chart. The organization chart causes more agonized exasperation than any other piece of paper, and for a very good reason: it is drawn up in good faith by men who are trying to arrange the most effective means of deploying the corporation staff for success in the survival battle, but everyone on the chart is looking at it as evidence of how the corporation judges their status, and they see the lines and boxes as conventional prizes for which they are invited to compete. Again the naked status argument has to be clothed: this time it wears the guise of operational theory. "If I have to go through the controller it will cause the most appalling delays." "If he reports direct to you instead of through me, we're going to get the most ghastly crossed lines." "Won't it simplify the lines of communication if all those twelve come under me— wouldn't that make your span of command more manageable?" Or more menacingly, "If I have to clear everything with him then the job can't be done, and that's that." The poor well-meaning fellow who drew up the chart does not know what has hit him: he had no idea the corporation contained so many passionate experts on the theory of organizational structure. But every compromise he makes to soothe ruffled feathers is a compromise of operational efficiency; and after he has been through the performance once and got it over, he privately vows never to do it again. The existing organizational structure will have to serve unchanged for the rest of his career.

Salary and function are unquestionably the two most significant status indices in most corporations, but they both suffer from the same drawback: they are difficult to display. You cannot really have "$15,500 p.a." embroidered on your tie, and even if your card and office door say "Chief Assistant to the Assistant Supervisor of Engineering, Southeastern Region," its precise import in status terms does not instantly leap to the mind. And yet status badges are extremely important in many animal species, since they obviate the need for aggressive status behavior; with a badge of some sort, status is instantly visible. Among vervet monkeys the status of adult males in the troop is demonstrated by the color of the scrotum—deepest indigo for number one, shading down to the palest pastel blue for the monkey at the bottom of the heap. It means that a quick glance shows each member whether to push in front or stand back. Number one gets all the food and females and deference he wants, then number two gets his turn, and finally the last one gets the leftovers, if any—the females are not interested in him and all the males shove him out of the way. This observation was confirmed when an experimenter removed the lowest status individual and painted his scrotum an even deeper indigo than number one's and returned him to the troop. No human act could ever come closer to the magic of Cinderella's fairy godmother: suddenly all the males deferred to him, all the females clustered around him, and he had all the best food and as much of it as he wanted. The poor little chap suddenly found himself living out the wildest fantasy of every downtrodden underdog from Bottom the weaver to Charlie Chaplin. I have never found out what happened when the paint wore off.

The corporation very rarely believes it deals in status badges and displays, but in fact it is a treasure house of them. The only one most corporations acknowledge is the tie, and perhaps blazer or tiepin or cuff links, simply denoting corporation membership. This in fact is usually a low-status badge, worn by those who are proud to belong to the corporation at all; higher-status Corporation Men have more to say about themselves than that, and sometimes form higher-status groups—even with ties and cuff links—within the corporation. They have occasional dinners and meetings and sporting events, but the main attraction for members is the status by association, and the means of displaying it.

The real status badges, however, are less formal and contrived. I remember the day I became head of a department, and exchanged the measly green windshield sticker which allowed me to use the general parking lot for the proud red badge of the senior executives' lot. I remember going to lunch for the first time in the senior executives' dining room, and the slightly exaggerated geniality of the welcome from colleagues I had known for many years and who would hardly have noticed my arrival in the bar of the club downstairs. I remember the official from accommodation department who brought me a slide viewer with pictures of the new selection of office furnishings I was now entitled to. I also remember two moments of deep shame. One was when I found my red leather chairs did not go with the carpet, and asked for blue ones instead, and the other was when I asked for a waitress to bring coffee to my office: on both occasions a junior official had to convey to me, in an agony of embarrassment, that blue chairs and waitresses were badges of a status higher than mine. Since one of the rules of status is that you can only allocate relative status to your subordinates, never to your superiors, I had violated a convention instead of competing within it, and so we both lost face.

All the same, this introduction to a system of allocating status badges, which I had never been consciously aware of before, started me thinking and inquiring among other corporations. Quite quickly I discovered that they all have a complex honor system with at least a dozen different orders and any number of grades within each order; not every corporation has all of them, but few are without some. There is the secretary, ranging from access to the pool, through a secretary in your office, then a secretary in a separate office, to two secretaries and finally an assistant with her own secretary. There are flowers, from zero when your secretary has to bring her own, through rubber plant and then flowering plant, up to fresh cut flowers every day. Office area is another, from cupboard size to ballroom size, and office furnishing from light oak and linoleum through endless gradations to fitted Indian carpet, Sheraton or Chippendale furniture, and genuine Impressionist paintings. (In the Civil Service, wall-to-wall carpeting is reserved for a certain level of seniority, and if a junior takes over the office someone comes and turns the carpet back two inches from the wall before he moves in.) Then there is stationery, rising from thin printed to thicker embossed and culminating in something very like cardboard, embossed with your own name. Drinks are another order, from the pub across the road through the executives' club, then the office cocktail cabinet, up to a bar with a waiter in a corner of your office suite. The Order of the Bath, in the corporation, starts with sharing the general concrete-floored lavatory, progresses through various grades of more refined toilet facilities, until you have a key to the executives' washroom and finally a complete suite with bath and shower in your own office. Tea and coffee start at the vending machine in the corridor and go through trolley service to room service while the receptacles progress from thick canteen cups to fine bone china and silver coffeepot brought in on a silver tray by a butler. Where you eat is another universal badge, with grades rising from a special table in the factory canteen through a range of more elegant and exclusive dining rooms, until a butler serves lunch in the dining area of your office suite. The make of company car provides a long series of different grades from a secondhand Chevvy to this year's Cadillac, and the place you put it goes from the street, through the company lot, to a reserved space in the company lot, then to the directors' garage, until finally you do not have to care since the chauffeur always drives your Cadillac to the door and is always waiting there when you come out.

The precise conventions will, of course, vary from corporation to corporation: just as the sovereign is the fount of all honor in Britain, so the chairman or president or chief executive is the fount of it in the corporation. If he believes it is wrong to have drinks on the premises, he does not have to ban them from offices: they will disappear, except as a badge of nonconformity or rebellion. If he thinks directors and executives and managers should eat with the rest of the staff, the order of private dining rooms will vanish from the honors list. If he uses a Rover instead of a Rolls, there will be a corresponding reduction in car luxury right down the list, and the economy will be many times greater than the few thousand he saves on his own car. All this, however, affects only the type of status system which operates in his corporation: he cannot avoid having a system even if he were foolish enough to want to.

The beauty of all these corporate status badges (and there must be many others) is that they have developed without the intention and often against the will of management. But management's wishes are irrelevant beside man's ancient evolutionary compulsions, and they demonstrate more clearly than any theoretical argument the power of the status instinct and need for display. It is equally noticeable when there are no visible marks of status how conversation is used to demonstrate it—careful mention of high-status groups or people with whom the speaker is or has been associated, criticism or condemnation of people whose status is lower but who seem to be trying to move up, threats or promises of action in order to show that the speaker is important and influential enough to take that action, use of Christian names when referring to high-status figures; where there is no other indicator, these signs pop up all the time until relative status is properly established. Ironically, the waving of status flags is usually itself an admission of lower status—you do not try and register your status with your inferiors, you simply snub them if they try and behave as if they were your equals. But whether by badges or conversation or salary or function or all four together, Corporation Man needs to have his status established and accepted.

Why then is the corporate honors system so often shrouded in secrecy, embarrassment, and pretense, and allowed to become a focus for tension and resentment instead of a source of pride? Almost certainly the trouble springs from a failure to make the crucial distinction between the hunting band and the camp, the day-to-day operation and the corporation as a permanent institution. Corporations which establish the difference, and make it clear that there are two routes and not one to recognition and reward, save themselves endless difficulty. Success on the hunt brings its own rewards in fame and bonuses and operational authority, but these are essentially for specific performance in a specific task. Next year may be different. Corporate status, however, is something more permanent; it is not tied to a specific job. It is the status-order of the camp, and although it can change with time the adjustments are normally gradual and infrequent. This permanent nature of status is, of course, recognized by a number of institutions. The armed services have it clearly established and displayed through rank, with special merit in the hunting band separately distinguished by medals and decorations: you do not make a corporal into a colonel for gallantry, though you may give him the Silver Star. Japanese corporations tend to be very clear and logical about it: Toyo Rayon, for instance, has thirty ranks which are related not to function or job but to seniority and qualifications. Promotion is automatic after a certain time, but whiz kids can be promoted earlier, just as they can be given jobs, on an acting basis, with authority above their ranks. Unilever, too, has an extensive grading system on the same permanent basis, an expression of camp-status rather than hunting success. It is extremely important that this status-ranking should reflect the general view of relative status, and that it should be made known to all those who are included in it—not just for their private information of their own allotted status but so that they can know that everyone who matters knows their status too, just as they know everyone else's. It is also important that there should be plenty of different grades both to reflect fine distinctions and to give everyone a good sense of steady progress. And, of course, it is vital that unusually rapid progress up the ladder should reflect, and be seen to reflect, outstanding service and loyalty to the corporation over many years, a recognition of permanent qualities and not single achievements. It is this ranking that should be marked by the various grades of honors in the corporate honors system.

Once a permanent status-ranking is published (annually if necessary), a great deal of the steam is taken out of the salary struggle. Each grade will presumably carry a salary or salary range, and this will be the salary guaranteed to everyone in the grade even of the most minimal efficiency; it will also be the salary for pension purposes. Any higher sum can in fact be paid in a given year for special merit or responsibility or scarcity value, but it will have no effect on the status of the recipient, though of course continued success will move him faster up the ladder than his contemporaries.

Established status-ranking also takes much of the heat out of the organization-chart battle. On a reconnaissance into enemy territory a brigadier will happily take operational orders from a corporal who knows the ground; when they get back, the brigadier is still a brigadier and the corporal is still a corporal. Operational needs often entail a junior giving the orders, or being given authority equal to that of men who are senior to him, if he is the only one with all the necessary skills or information; and many corporate projects would be much easier if the services' sort of short-term flexibility could be achieved. As long as camp status and hunting-band function are tangled up together on the same chart, this flexibility looks like an assault on status and is impossible. Once that threat is removed, it starts to become a possibility.

There is one other instrument which few corporations use as explicitly or as frequently as they could, and that is the citation for gallantry. Just as status in the camp has to be displayed some way or other, so does success in the hunting band. An important job and a high "acting" salary both enable the successful young hunters to know they are recognized, but they are not easy to display. All too often the display is carried out in conversation by saying how pathetic and hopeless everyone else is, thereby illustrating Sir Thomas Browne's observation, "He who discommendeth others obliquely commendeth himself." A proper citation system whereby achievements of exceptional merit are described in the corporation newspaper or magazine (with photograph) or put up in weekly notices on bulletin boards, can satisfy the desire for fame and recognition without disturbing the status system or stimulating aggressive, assertive behavior. If the brave hunter knows that everyone has heard about his triumphs, he does not have to keep telling about them; he has been awarded his conventional prize without having to claim it.

XIV

The Folk Culture
of the Corporation Tribe

IN the autumn of 1968 I paid a visit to the school I had
left twenty years previously. It was an interesting experience,
since it was not, in any physical sense, the school I had left;
it had moved to completely new buildings in a different part
of London. Nor was it the same school in terms of people;
only two or three of the sixty-odd teaching staff were still
there. And yet it was easily recognizable as the same school—
the same balance of subjects, the same attitudes to learning
and games and the arts, the same academic reputation, the
same tolerance of eccentricity, the same relationship between
boys and masters; the conformists were the same sort of
conformists and the rebels the same sort of rebels. Anyone
from outside, for instance in a university, would have described the school in almost exactly the same terms that his
counterpart in my day would have used.

Quite clearly, there was something about the school that

outlasted people and buildings; something that kept it different from other schools, and different in the same way, despite a pupil turnover of twenty percent a year and a staff turnover of about five percent, and despite changes of physical environment. I asked the headmaster how conscious he was of this enduring quality, and his reply was extremely enlightening. He had come to the school some six years before and quite soon had decided that changes were necessary. The chief instrument by which a headmaster can change a school is the appointment of faculty, and he took the opportunity of some vacancies to introduce a new kind of schoolmaster, of the sort he felt was necessary. These were excellent men with good records, but the experiment simply did not work. They did not get on with the boys or in the common room, they were frustrated and unhappy, and quite soon they left. The headmaster realized that, although it was not impossible to change the direction in which the school was going, it was impossible to change it very much or very rapidly. It was almost like an organic transplant—anything not very similar in cellular structure would be spontaneously rejected; any new organ had to be within the acceptance limits of the host.

I quote this particular case because the change of location emphasized it for me, but in fact it is true of every corporate tribe that stays reasonably intact over a period of time. This enduring quality is sometimes referred to by shorthand phrases like "tradition" or "continuity" or "group identity" or "cultural transmission," but these are often used to avoid the effort of analyzing the separate elements that compose it. However, if we are to understand the corporate tribe, that analysis cannot be postponed. So far we have dealt with the biological, evolutionary factors that ten-groups and tribes all have in common: maximum size, leadership, structure, aggression, territory, status, and so on. But it is also important to understand what makes tribes different from each other. Many categories of difference are widely discussed in other books—type of product, annual turnover, profitability, capital intensiveness, manufacturing methods—and, of course, they are extremely significant indicators. But this cultural tradition and continuity is at least as significant to the success of an enterprise, and because it cannot be quantified it does not follow that it cannot be clarified.

I shall be talking about these elements of cultural tradition as they appear in the context of a single tribe—a factory or small firm or school or other institution around the tribal size of five hundred. After all, it is within the single tribe that we all have direct experience of a cultural tradition; if we can see how it develops and operates there, it is easy enough to trace it in larger units. And because it has its origin in the time when the tribe was the largest permanent operational unit we knew, it is still in the community of tribal size that it operates in the most visible and natural way.

But although we will be examining these elements of cultural tradition at the tribal level, they are in fact the same ones that give unique identity to a larger company, to a giant corporation, or even to a nation. When we say, "What is Ford like to work for?" "What is IBM like to deal with?" "That's typical of duPont," we are assuming a continuing identity going right through the corporation and back over many years. Insofar as we can generalize about nations—"Just like the Italians," "Typically German"—it is this same cultural tradition, not a specifically Italian or German combination of genes, that we are referring to. It is something you build up over many years, and can destroy overnight. It is what you have to change if you take over and incorporate another tribe. It can be a bastion of defense or an obstacle to advance. It is almost impossible to teach, and almost impossible not to learn. At the lowest level, it is what keeps a firm in business; at the highest level, it is what has preserved and developed all the civilization we have.

This culturally transmitted tribal identity is, of course, a single unity, and the separate elements are all interconnected and interrelated. Nevertheless, they take separate forms within the tribe, and can easily be looked at separately. The first and most obvious is the tribe's external identity: the position it occupies among other tribes, the reputation it has built up, the behavior it stimulates or inhibits among those who encounter it. When you start up for the first time, the options are wide open. Suppose you open a chain of restaurants: if you are to succeed, you must carve out a special niche for yourself, you must exploit what marketing men call a market gap. You can offer continental food, or a relaxing leisurely atmosphere, or good value at low prices, or unique specialty dishes, or very quick service, in all sorts of permutations and combinations. In fact, you will probably be expanding on the basis of a formula that has worked for a single restaurant. But once you have got your chain going successfully, it is a chain that binds you. Your customers come for the sort of food and price and atmosphere you have encouraged them to expect, and you cannot significantly alter any of them without losing their business. Suppliers have a picture of your nature and needs in their minds, and come to you with new products and services selected to fit into that picture. The staff who stay with you do so because they are happy with the pay, conditions, treatment, and management climate you have created, and these in turn condition the new staff who apply. That, too, becomes harder to change without losing the most loyal and experienced staff. Your rivals, too, come to give implicit confirmation to your niche; they accept the strength of your market hold on the central part of your business and compete only at the perimeter—the upper or lower income end of your market, casual snacks rather than main meals, the youngest or oldest range of your customers, and so on. All the options that were open at the beginning are very nearly closed: the niche you cut for yourself becomes the mold which forms your identity and shapes your future.

This, of course, was precisely the headmaster's problem. The external identity of the school determined the sort of parents who sent their children to it and the reasons why they chose it over other similar schools; it was the idea which united the old boys and guided the policy of the governors; it was the reason why the new masters had applied for their jobs and the older ones had stayed on instead of going to other schools. A sudden change of that identity would have been a massive breach of confidence and have provoked tremendous resistance from every group which combined to form the total community.

It would have been different, of course, if the school was failing. A part of every tribe's external identity is its status among other tribes, and like personal status it is very close to the business of survival. If possible it must be enhanced, but at least it must be preserved; as long as that happens, most people are happy with the identity that secures it. If it starts to slip, they try for as long as possible to pretend that it is not happening, or that it is a temporary reverse, or that nothing can be done about it. But in time the self-deception becomes harder and harder, and rebellious ten-groups clamor for the removal of the group that has presided over the decline; if they fail, the slide may go on to extinction, but if they win then all sorts of changes and innovations become possible which were unthinkable in the days of success.

The second element in the culture of a tribe is very close to the first: it is the internal status system. The principle of an internal status system is, of course, universal to all tribes; the individuality of tribes lies in the differing status they accord to different people and groups and functions and achievements and personal qualities. In one firm it will be the scientist, in another the salesman: in a healthy firm the status-ranking will follow the priority order of importance to the firm's success and survival. The convulsion comes when the conditions of survival change faster than the normal organic change of the individuals on the status ladder. Many manufacturing firms by the start of the 1950's had survived for generations by efficient, dependable, low-cost production, and their tribal status-hierarchy rose out of the production line. When the sudden change from production-orientation to market-orientation struck the manufacturing world during the 1950's, it rapidly separated the conventional high-status skills from the actual skills needed for survival. Men who had spent respected and successful professional careers and climbed to the top of the ladder entirely by their skill and knowledge and experience in organizing production suddenly had to realize that these skills were only of secondary importance. They had to vote not to buy the superb new German machine tool, but to invest the money in a bunch of fancy boys who talked about brand images and consumer motivation and depth research. No wonder so many of them failed: it was not a simple matter of open-mindedness and seeing facts—it struck at the heart of their status and self-respect.

Almost exactly the same thing happened in the BBC when television started. The prestige of BBC radio during the war and immediately after it had been enormous: it was the prime instrument of national unity, and men became famous all over the country simply by reading news bulletins. Moreover, by broadcasting truthful and objective news on their overseas services even when it was bad news for the Allies, they gained a reputation overseas which still makes them the most respected broadcasting organization in the world. And then television started, and inexorably the audiences moved over to it. Of course a great many radio producers and broadcasters moved over with them, but some— and above all the most senior—remained behind. I was constantly astonished by their bitterness and hostility toward television, their stream of anti-television jokes, their refusal to see any merit in television or any limitations in radio; but of course what they were suffering from was a mortal blow to their status through no failure of their own but simply because of a sudden shift in technology, and a consequent shift of survival-status to a range of skills which it was too late for them to acquire. I discovered later that this was by no means an exclusively British phenomenon; one of America's leading radio commentators became physically ill under the stress of television: he suffered from acute skin sensitivity and had to wear gloves the whole time, until he had successfully learned the new skills and established himself in the new medium.

The tribe whose long-established status-structure is tied to the wrong skill is a problem for any corporation (unless it is the leader's tribe itself, in which case the problem is transferred to the shareholders), but the BBC stumbled on the answer. I honestly believe that if there had been room for television studios in the radio headquarters at Broadcasting House, British television would now be dominated by the commercial networks. Television would have grown up in the shadow of radio, and as a rather vulgar appendage of it; it would have been dominated by the radio hierarchy, and radio would have remained the best route to the top for the ambitious and successful. Consequently, the start of commercial television competition in 1955 would have been too much for it, and since radio was still free from competition it would have been to the improvement of radio rather than to fighting commercial television that many of the top people would have bent their energies. But that was not how it worked out. The nearest space for studios lay across several miles of London, in the old Alexandra Palace, and when bigger premises were needed, those too were several miles away in Lime Grove. It was physically impossible for anybody looking after a radio department to exercise authority over television programs as well. As a result, a completely new tribe was born, with its own territory, its own technical facilities, and its own audience (or market). It was peopled by the innovators, the adventurous, the people impatient with the hierarchy and the restrictions of Broadcasting House, and there was also an element of impatience with radio's middle-class assumptions. Consequently, when the new, young, aggressive commercial television started up in 1955, it found itself competing not with old Auntie from Portland Place but with her new, young, aggressive nephew —and the nephew had several years' start. It was only when commercial television began that the elders in Broadcasting House realized that if it wiped out BBC television, then their great dread—commercial radio—would be irresistible. But BBC television more than held its own. The device of starting a new tribe for the new skill instead of trying to incorporate it into the old one had saved the citadel—even if only by a geographical accident.

A third element of the corporate tribe's cultural tradition is the means by which leadership operates. Every tribe has to have a system by which it determines what shall be done, who shall do it, and how it shall be done, and some way of making sure that it has been done properly. This system is bound up with territory and quasi-territory, since most of the time the leadership operates through the jurisdiction of those who have established their authority within certain boundaries. No one ever draws this territorial map of the tribe, but it is a powerful reality. Anyone can reorganize lines and boxes on a chart, but the internal territory is far less easily changed. People quickly find that if George says yes, it's yes, and you don't have to ask the manager, or that if you can get Mr. Wilkins on your side then the project will go through. This is known as "informal organization" and is discussed by Rosemary Stewart in *The Reality of Management*; it grows up slowly and changes gradually, and time and again it saves the formal organization from grinding to a halt. It has a remarkable talent for coming unscathed through endless top-level corporate restructuring. I remember reading a children's story about Teddy and Andy-Pandy: they were planting seeds in the garden, and then fixing the packet in the earth with a stick, as a label to mark which seeds were in which place. But the next day Teddy thought of a better arrangement, so he changed the nasturtium label with the love-in-the-mist label. The next day he improved it again by switching the candytuft label with the marigold label. Several times he changed the labels around, and then waited for the flowers to come up. He was furious when they all came up in the place where they had been planted, instead of where he had put the labels. "Stupid things—can't they read?" he asked. I was in the middle of a corporate reorganization at the time, and I realized that it was a pure Teddy and Andy-Pandy operation: labels were being moved around with impressive decision, but the flowers were going to come up where the seeds had been planted long before; the informal organization, the real instrument of organizational achievement, was totally unaffected.

The tradition of leadership style goes beyond quasi-territory and the informal organization tree: it affects the way decisions are made. Some tribes believe in fixed, formal meetings, others in casual dropping-in. Some believe in telling the chap what you want and leaving him to get on with it; some like to clear the lines in advance. In the former you are liable to get slapped down for seeking guidance—"For God's sake use a bit of initiative and don't keep pestering me!"; in the latter, a bit of initiative will bring a reprimand from the other direction—"What on earth do you mean by issuing these safety regulations without my authorization?." Neither style is either right or wrong in itself; it is a part of the leadership tradition and has to be learned by every newcomer.

The fourth element is one of the most interesting and significant of all. It is the central faith. Whereas the other elements take time to grow up, the central faith is there from the start. It is the belief at the root of the business, and I call it faith because it rests on a number of unproved assumptions. "People want quality," "If you can make a better mousetrap the world will beat a trail to your door," "It's not the product that matters, it's how hard you sell it," "If you want to stay in business, you've got to deliver on time"—all these expressions of commercial and industrial dogma spring from the central faith of the tribe. The faith usually starts from the leader of the central ten-group around whom the tribe grew up, and it can be the unifying idea of anything from a small partnership to a giant corporation. Most businesses start from an act of faith, a risk which comes off, an inspired guess about a market gap. Thereafter, the faith which made the man or group take the risk becomes the central belief of the tribe. Equally, a near disaster in the early days can create an image of the devil which is quite as distinct as the image of God: "Never again will we . . ." IBM has a devil—the employment of too large a proportion of the local community in their plant, dating back to a traumatic early experience—and many companies are still encountering different aspects of the Evil One. The devil in Marks and Spencer—or one of his faces at least—is profit-seeking: the central faith on which Simon Marks built his firm was that science and large-volume sales could give ordinary people much better quality goods (especially clothes) than they were being offered, and that they would be willing to pay a little extra for something a lot better. The faith was amply justified, but in the early days Marks and Sieff had to combat the image of sharp traders on the make: they did so by extreme honesty and straight dealing and an ethos of service to the community which still animate the whole firm, and the slightest suggestion of sacrificing quality for gain still horrifies them.

A good way to find the central faith of a tribe is to get its members to see who can formulate the biggest blasphemy. In Marks and Spencer it would be: "So what if it falls to bits when they get it home—we've made our profit, haven't we?" In the BBC: "I admit it wasn't really true, but the Home Secretary was very keen we should say it." In Rolls-Royce: "It's a lousy bit of engineering but it will sell like hot cakes." Parke-Bernet: "It doesn't look like a Tiepolo to me, but if you say it is, I'll have to take your word for it." Almost any corporate tribesman can formulate his own for you, provided he still retains a modicum of philosophical detachment; indeed, it is a mark of a good corporation that its central faith should be clear enough for a good blasphemy to be easily found. And the separate tribes in the corporation, like monastic orders, have their own special emphases within the central faith: a special *Tonight* blasphemy would have been "Who cares if it's a P.R. handout—the morons will lap it up," since a part of the program's success (and one of the founding concepts) was based on a high respect for the audience's intelligence, and their desire to find out what was really going on, especially the facts that vested interests wanted to conceal. Anyone who talked of the audience as morons would have been absolutely unemployable, however impressive his skills.

With such a variety of central faiths, you might expect more religious warfare between, for instance, the strivers for quality and the seekers of profit, and, of course, between highly competitive corporations these are emphasized—religious difference becomes an aggression focus of the sort described in Chapter 5. But the philosophical difference is in itself very small; after all, the quality people have to make a profit, and the profit-hungry must reach a certain quality. Marks and Spencer has a brilliant profit record, even if it disparages this as an objective, just as most successful profit-oriented firms turn out good products. The worshipers of Venus do not deny the divinity of Apollo. Indeed, the classical gods, in a sense, represent most of the types of central faith and all have their own worshipers among modern corporations. Mars, the god of war and tough competition and price-cutting, clearly inspires the aggressive corporations like Tesco. Mercury, the traveler and messenger of the gods, has always seemed to me the symbol of Coca-Cola, carrying the good news of the all-American beverage to the uttermost corners of the earth. Venus finds most of her acolytes among Italian corporations—Ferrari, Farina, Ferragamo—with their emphasis on elegance and beauty. Juno, mother of the gods, looks after the family with good things and a sense of service—Boots and Sainsbury's, and Federated Department Stores, for instance. Apollo, god of the muses, represents quality and status—Harrod's, the Rover car company, Caterpillar Tractor and the Swiss watch companies. Vulcan is for those who concentrate on manufacturing skill, like the Plessey corporation, and Athene, goddess of wisdom, for the highly research-oriented corporation like ICI, Xerox and Bell Telephone. Jupiter, the father of the gods, is of course General Motors: corporate management at its most Olympian. But, different as they are, none of them are in opposition; there is room for them all in the corporate Pantheon.

The central faith is so strongly held and so deeply felt in most good corporations that it is wise to accept it as effectively unchangeable. This might seem to be a grave obstacle in times of rapid change, a force for reaction and a danger to survival. So it can be, if change is represented as abandoning the faith and going over to the devil, and of course there will always be those who do try and resist change on that pretext. But the great advantage of the central faith is its vagueness, and with the sort of skill that the Jesuits have refined over the centuries there is very little, apart from deliberate confrontation, that cannot be shown to be in accordance with orthodox belief.

This brings us to another of the elements of a tribe's cultural tradition: doctrine. Doctrine is applied faith; it is the way in which the central belief is interpreted in practical situations. Formulation and revision of doctrine is one of the most constant and important of tribal tasks. Faith is beyond argument and challenge: you accept it or you get out. But doctrine can be argued about, and the body of agreed, accepted, shared doctrine is one of a tribe's most valuable invisible assets. That news should be impartial is an article of faith. But if a paper receives pictures from the North Vietnamese of the aftermath of an air raid by the U.S., should it show them as news or reject them as propaganda? Should it show them, but say they came from the North Vietnamese? If so, should it also say that the American pictures were supplied by the Americans? Or take our restaurant chain: We guarantee that meals in our restaurant do not cost more than five dollars. The best value for the money is an article of faith. But when prices rise, should we raise it to six-fifty, or reduce the size of portions, or get the extra money from a surcharge on wine, or introduce a two-tier menu, or what?

All these are doctrinal points. Doctrine grows up around every activity; accounting, personnel relations, marketing policy, manufacturing standards, salary scales—there is no recurring activity in the corporation without a body of guiding doctrine shared among a ten-group or subtribe or tribe.

Part of the central doctrine of the corporation concerns the nature of its business. What business are we in? We make cars and trucks: Should we make motor bikes? Hovercraft? Tanks? Should we move up to the luxury end of the market? Down to the economy end? Should we start our own electrical subsidiary? Ought we have fewer dealers? The questions are endless, the answers promote the question "Why?" and eventually the "Why" leads you back to the central faith, and the doctrine is established. It is, however, never permanently established, and new facts or considerations can always reopen a doctrinal discussion. The danger point comes when doctrine fossilizes, and people regard it as religion: "We must never put on a 60 percent markup," rather than "We must not make an excessive profit." The latter is an article of faith, and agreeably vague, whereas the former is a precise doctrinal application which must be susceptible of revision. In a changing situation, the constant questioning and reexamining of tribal doctrine becomes a survival necessity. New experience and new information are the food and drink which nourish the body of corporate doctrine. They are sifted and assimilated by a process of conversation, argument, and discussion, as if in a collective mental digestive system. Much is expelled as waste matter, but the important elements are extracted and circulated to renew and revitalize the cells.

Distinct from doctrine, though related to it, is ritual. Most corporate tribes are rich in ritual—it is (and always has been) a good way of ensuring that things get done in the right way time and time again, even if people do not know why they are doing them. All over the tribe, every day, ritual forms are filled in, ritual procedures are followed, ritual meetings are attended, ritual maintenance is carried out, ritual safety precautions are observed. Ritual grows most luxuriantly out of priestly staff departments at headquarters. Lacking direct authority over people, they seek power by working on the vague and irrational fears of those who possess that power. When the ruler's chief fear is of labor unrest, the personnel priest has power. When it is lack of control over expenditure, the financial priest tightens his grip. When he is troubled by the poor shape of the corporate image, the priest of publicity and public relations extends his domination. Sometimes the ranks of the established church are swelled by the mendicant friars with their begging bowls—the firms of management consultants selling indulgences with names like "discounted cash flow program" and "long-range planning," which tempt the fearful sinner to buy his way to salvation. All the priests and friars operate by cornering a part of the ruler's authority to institute ritual observances for all time; expense forms, budget proposal forms, capital appropriation forms, holiday application forms, fire alarm tests, weekly safety inspections, daily maintenance schedules, daily clocking-in routines—these are a part of every tribe's existence. Some are useful and even necessary, but they are a constant danger; they always go on long after the need for them has passed, and no one ever questions them. When I was at the depot regiment in the army, one of the clerks in my office spent his entire working life at an ancient ritual: for every soldier being released from the army a small form was sent from the War Office, and he typed certain details from that form onto the man's record card. My only long-term contribution to the army was to buy him a stapling machine from petty cash and let him staple the form to the record card. His week's work was thereafter accomplished in an hour and a half. It could have been done anytime in the previous ten years, but the ritual predated cheap stapling machines, and no one had ever considered it as needing critical thought and evaluation. The real trouble with rituals is that people come to depend on them: they give a sense of work well done, a useful contribution made to the general good, while being totally undemanding once they have been mastered, and even if contributing nothing at all to the reality of survival and profit. They are a source of comfort and security, stable points in a confusing world. When Marks and Spencer had their blitz on paper work, some store managers could not bear to part with their sales record forms and went on completing them secretly at home.

The seventh element of the tribal culture is a shared concept of the right and wrong way to behave. This is not particularly related to the social code of the world outside, though this comes into it in a marginal way: do you call your superior "sir" or "Harry"? Whichever it is, you will soon find out if you choose the wrong one and be put right for next time. But it covers nearly all the working details of the tribe: what sort of omission deserves a telling-off, what sort merits the sack, what represents fair behavior by a foreman, and what is unfair, and what is exceptionally friendly or unfriendly, and what happens to you if three jobs in a row all fail inspection, and whether it's the supervisor's job to bring around the next drawings or the operator's job to go and get them from his office, and whether it was right to make Jean type the whole page again because of two little mistakes, and an endless series of tiny moral judgments which make up an agreed code of conduct. A sudden expansion or influx of new people, particularly into the management level, can radically upset those who have been used to the security of a moral code that everyone subscribed to (even though individuals frequently deviated from it). It is not necessarily a question of the discipline becoming more strict—it is just as disturbing if it becomes less strict: the details of the code of behavior are not important and they vary greatly from tribe to tribe, but the code itself is an important force in holding the tribe together.

Another vitally important element that grows up within a tribe is its internal communication system. At the tribal level this is nothing to do with memos and circulars and bulletin boards and house magazines, and owes nothing to presentation techniques. Most of it springs from some of the other elements—all communication is based on shared assumption about behavior and doctrine and faith and a shared understanding of how the tribe functions. "Jack had a word with George this morning" is a neutral and empty sentence in itself, but in the context of a tribal system it can mean a great deal. This body of shared knowledge and assumptions gives a speed and precision to communication within the tribe that is not possible outside it. Communication and community are derived from the same root because they are expressions of the same thing, and those who talk about failures of communication would do well to reflect that communication can only happen in communities. I certainly found that as film producer on *Tonight* I could brief a *Tonight* director or reporter on the treatment of a film story in a few minutes, whereas with an equally skilled professional who had never worked with us it would have taken an hour's discussion and been far less clear at the end. The reason was that within the community of *Tonight* we had argued out the right and wrong ways in hours of doctrinal discussions based on hundreds of films, and so we all knew the pitfalls too well to have to talk about them. With someone outside the community, I would have to point them out in advance—and I could never foresee them all.

The communication network, if it is working properly, is as powerful an instrument for fending off disaster as the informal organization. In an established and integrated community, it ensures that information gets quickly to the person who needs it. It means that as soon as the office boy sees the factory inspector's car, he rings Bill to tell him to put the safety hood over the chain drive in no. 3 shop. It means that when the chief accountant has finally gotten through the traffic holdup he warns the shipping manager to send the day's consignment down the A40 instead of the M4. It means the incoming stores checking clerk warns the turning foreman that the two-inch mild steel bar still hasn't arrived, instead of letting him find out for himself when he needs it next week. It means that people know everyone else's jobs and needs as well as their own, and are collectively using the communication network to facilitate the operation. A great part of this network is visual, which is why it works so badly in most office tribes: the majority of office blocks are designed to stop anybody from seeing who is talking to whom, who is in and who is out, who is frantically charging around and who is relaxed, how long that meeting has been going on, and all those tiny details which add up to a valuable store of current information. This is not an argument for vast open-plan ballrooms—office workers need territory, too—but for windows looking not just out onto the unchanging, uneventful world but also in onto the busy tribal encampment. The village spinster behind her net curtains amasses a huge amount of information in the course of the year without ever having to ask a direct question. This sort of information is invaluable for the internal self-regulation of a tribe, but most office blocks are at present designed to prohibit it.

A communication system seems to imply the use of language, but in fact it is much older than language and remarkably independent of it. There is no need to prove this —every motorist knows it from experience. A car has only the most limited communication equipment, much inferior to that of most animals, but any motorist who pulls out of his lane suddenly without warning, or drives at thirty miles per hour in the fast lane, or commits any of the offenses which endanger or frustrate other members of the motoring community, soon finds that the communication system is sufficient to bring him into line. Flashing lights, sounding horns, driving too close behind, overtaking inside and cutting across—the vocabulary of the car is primitive and restricted, but it serves its purpose. It also has its clear status-display with fine gradations of age and cost, speed and luxury, which are well understood throughout the community. The new motorist may study the law and the highway code, but only when he joins the community does he really learn the communication system and become a part of it.

The most important function of the tribal communication system is to act as an internal self-regulation system, and its essentially animal nature makes it impossible to achieve simply by memos and circulars. But it is also invaluable in helping the community to adapt collectively to innovation. A new machine, procedure, manager, or product is busily discussed by the network, ways of coping are passed on, judgments are ventured, circulated and revised, improvements are suggested, and a complete body of practice and opinion is built up and shared by all those affected. Since the network also transmits the status-ranking, it knows whose opinion counts for much and whose for little, who knows what he is talking about and who keeps changing his mind, and adds or discounts significance accordingly. However ingenious the innovation, it is in the tribes and through the tribes that it succeeds or fails; and it is the communication network that makes sure that the best pooled experience and ideas and judgments are brought to bear on it to give it the best chance. The formal committee meetings and operational discussions are of course a part of this communication system—but only a small part.

Finally, there is the tribal memory and folklore. All sorts of events and experiences and stories from the past are handed down, often as jokes. There are many such jokes in the film business—a location scene with three thousand mounted tribesmen charging into a river, and at the end of it the cameraman discovers that he forgot to load the camera with film. The picture of the cameraman's awful emotion on discovering his omission may bring a laugh, but it also brings home a lesson. Sometimes the stories are heroic narratives—"The time of the electricity strike when we had to quadruple our production of flashlights in three days and nobody got more than two hours' sleep at a stretch," and so on. Few of them retain much factual accuracy, but accuracy is not the point: like the apocryphal wartime stories about Churchill, they express an admiration of actions and qualities that are valued by the tribe, or (like the Hitler jokes) a derision and contempt of those that are not, and their purpose is to communicate and share common values and standards of behavior.

These then are the chief elements which grow up in the corporate tribe and, given time, are passed on as part of its informal tradition. They are what remained in my school after the people and buildings had all changed; they are the elements which, at every level from the board to the shop floor, constitute a good little firm or a good company, or a good corporation; and they are also the elements which constitute a bad one. Their mere existence does not guarantee success, but their absence is a guarantee of failure. However, with a tribe of the right size they are bound to grow up as the months and years go by, and they outlast individuals; whether they adapt to change or fossilize, whether they make for harmony or discord, whether they further the corporation's aims or frustrate them, is the measure by which the management of the corporation is judged. There is no way of reflecting them on the balance sheet, but there is a perfectly sound way of putting a valuation on them; they are the difference between the book value of a company's assets and the value the stock market puts on the company. In the case of Marks and Spencer, book value of the equity is about a hundred and twenty million pounds but the market capitalization is six hundred and thirty million, a difference of over five hundred million. In the case of Woolworth's, the book value is one hundred and sixty-five million and the market capitalization is two hundred and sixty million, a difference of ninety-five million. In other words Marks and Spencer's tribal structure and tradition are worth four hundred million pounds more than Woolworth's. Perhaps when the chairman says in his annual report, "Our staff are our greatest asset," he is, in some corporations, speaking the literal truth.

XV

Boom and Slump:
The Expendable Generation

T H E hunting band, the camp, and the tribe. I have already
suggested that these are the only units of organization apart
from the family which we have brought with us out of our
prehistory, the only groups we form by instinct. But ever
since we stopped hunting and began farming we have been
stumbling toward the formation and preservation of larger
units: the town, the city, the nation; the cohort, the legion,
the army; the small firm, the company, the corporation. I
say "stumbling" because there is nothing natural or instinctive about units of this size: the understanding of them and
the devices for regulating them are part of a cultural tradition and continuity which we have built up and passed
down during a mere ten thousand years.

But if the history of these larger groupings is short, this is
only because they were, presumably, not a practical possibility for a hunting species which had to keep on the move.

There was no question of building stable and permanent organizations; the tribe lived in constant danger of extinction, not only from predators, disease, and starvation, but also from annihilation by marauding tribes whose own source of food had disappeared. Perhaps if the food supply had remained stable and our method of controlling our numbers had worked adequately, we should all still be happily hunting the antelopes on the African grasslands; but we know it did not. Until we discovered farming, we had no answer. We had to live with insecurity—though insecurity is a retrospective value judgment which would have been meaningless to the tribes that had never known security. But with farming, it became possible for us to organize and control and regulate, to take thought for the morrow, to build towns and cities, nations and civilizations, to believe in our own permanence and act on that belief. You do not devote energy and resources to planting olive trees or building great temples and harbors if you expect to have to pull up stakes and be off tomorrow, or next month, or next year. Nor do you set up a long-range planning department and invest millions of dollars for a return in ten or fifteen years' time: a corporation, like a civilization, rests on the assumption of continuing for as long as anyone can forsee. What makes Corporation Man such a novelty, even though Industrial Man has been with us for two hundred years, is that only recently have corporations come to believe in their own permanence and organize for it.

However, the fact that we did not evolve these larger groupings does not mean that we lacked any mechanism for dealing with boom and slump, or dearth and plenty, in our hunting days. Stability is not one of the laws of nature, and all species have to find a way of adapting to a changing environment if they are to survive. I believe we can trace some part of that mechanism, or at least discover intriguing parallels, in the behavior of Corporation Man today; and so before we move on to the larger units of industry, let us think back once again to the hunting tribe and how it adapted to a changing environment.

It is inevitably the times of hunger that come to mind first. The effect of food shortage must have been to tighten the group structure and group discipline, and to increase the fighting as groups and tribes hunted into each other's territory. In times of severe hunger, selection pressures operate more rapidly in favor of the best-adapted groups, and the best adaptation for us was group discipline, with the prize going to the strongest, fiercest, and swiftest group. For gene-pool reasons, as well as fighting strength, we can assume that selection also favored those who maintained tribal unity as well, who fought as a whole tribe and wiped out those who tried to fight as simple ten-groups. It is noticeable that even today Corporation Man shows the same instincts in a business recession; all the individuals and groups who have been talking about breaking away and starting up on their own quickly forget the attractions of independence and stay close to the tribe, while all the corporate disciplines become stricter. Equally, the competitive struggle between corporations becomes fiercer and nastier when defeat means not just a blow to the pride and the pocket but the threat of extinction.

No one in the corporation welcomes a recession, but in fact it can be as valuable today as it used to be millions of years ago, and still is to animal populations. Times of prosperity are times of danger, to species and to corporations. For a species, it can mean the preservation of genetically deformed or inferior individuals who would not have survived normal conditions, but who in times of exceptional ease can breed and so dilute the gene pool which replicates the whole population. A drop in food supply sorts them out very quickly and leaves only the genetically superior to fill up the gaps and carry on the species. Of course we have not yet experienced a business boom that has continued long enough to have any genetic effect on Corporation Man, but it certainly affects his behavior. When money becomes more plentiful, it is all too easy to use it to take the pressure off the tribes and ten-groups: create extra posts, put difficult work out to small firms instead of doing it yourself, lessen the demands and ease up on the penalties, and enjoy the fruits of prosperity in lunches and dinners and country-house seminars and golfing conferences, and all the other instruments of enlightened managerial welfare. If this goes on long enough, the corporation can weigh itself down with people (especially around headquarters, not often in the front-line tribes) who become unfit for a genuinely competitive industrial life. I hesitate to draw too close a parallel, but I encountered a paragraph on a quite different subject that applies so beautifully to this kind of sheltered Corporation Man that I have to quote it. It comes from Dobzhansky's *Mankind Evolving:*

> Norway rats (*Rattus norvegicus*) have been kept in laboratories since sometime between 1840 and 1850. The modern laboratory rat belongs to a well-defined variety that differs from its wild progenitor in many ways. The laboratory rat is entirely dependent on the protected state of the laboratory where food, water, mates and shelter are provided, and the struggle for survival no longer exists. Among other differences, laboratory rats have smaller adrenal glands and less resistance to stress, fatigue, and disease than wild rats. Thyroid glands have also become less active in laboratory rats, while, on the contrary, sex glands develop earlier and permit a greater fertility. They have smaller brains and are tamer and more tractable than the active and aggressive wild rats. The genetic changes which occurred in the laboratory rat would, undeniably, make them unable to compete successfully with wild rats in the environment in which the latter normally live.

A corporation that lets *Homo norvegicus* establish itself in the years of prosperity will find itself in trouble when the depression draws in. Some people outside industry assume that it is pure greed which makes corporations compete aggressively for higher and higher profits and growth, but greed hardly comes into it at all. Status, of course, is an important incentive, but so is the need to preserve the integrity of the stock, to set difficult targets and keep all the ten-groups hard at work, so that when the bad times come they will be lean, muscular, and disciplined enough to survive in the wild rat race.

There is, however, another danger in prosperity, and it concerns a special group in the tribe and the corporation: the newly matured young males who have not yet acquired families or territory. In many primate species—and, I suggest, quite clearly in our own—they are recognized as a distinct sub-community. The fact that they are only just entering maturity makes them particularly competitive for status among themselves. As we have seen, status-striving and status-battles are always the product of an unsureness about your own status-ranking. Once you know it, and know that everyone else knows it, you do not have to assert or prove anything, but at the onset of maturity it has yet to be established, or rather it has to be established in a new way. It is the time when the simple animal dominance of the playground first starts to be modified by proficiency at adult, hunting skills: modified, but not replaced—physical animal dominance remains significant, but it is no longer the only or ultimate status-measurement. In a few years the new status-ranking will have been established and tacitly accepted by everyone, and the pressure is taken off the struggle: in a stable tribe the rankings change very little after the first shakedown, but the shakedown can be clamorous and even convulsive while it lasts.

The absence of territory and family has a different consequence: it means that this group is not tied to the camp with so tight a bond as the rest. They are no longer so young as to need it for protection, nor so established as to be an important part of its social structure and hierarchy, nor do they have children to look after and defend and teach. They are more free now than at any other time in their lives to wander and explore, which has historically served a useful function: it prevents excessive genetic isolation. By wandering from camp to camp in the tribe and choosing a wife from any one of them, they prevent excessive inbreeding; and the ones who occasionally venture into the camps of other tribes promote a cross-flow between separate gene pools which is an additional survival factor. I do not suggest that this happens in any literal way in the corporation (nor do I suggest that it does not), but the fact that this period of maximum exploration and minimum group loyalty has had evolutionary value suggests that we must still expect to encounter it among the young men of the corporation.

There is, however, another consequence which has a great deal of practical application: they are an instrument of social unity between the ten-groups. Tribal unity and identity are greatly strengthened if the males during this period of their lives form ten-groups of their own which cut across the boundaries between the hunting bands. It means that when they grow up and take their place in the hunt and the camp, they have memories of former ten-group comradeship with other hunters throughout the tribe, and this must inhibit damaging conflict between mature ten-groups within the tribe, as well as help to foster a sense of tribal solidarity and weld the single genetic group into a single fighting group when necessary. I myself had an exceptionally interesting experience of this principle in 1958. A survey of television had criticized the BBC for neglecting the adolescent audience, and the BBC committee which was discussing this discovered that no one around the table was ever going to see forty again, and thus were perhaps not ideally constituted to pass judgment. So they set up a subcommittee of people in their twenties: there were ten of us, from documentaries, current affairs, drama, light entertainment, design department, and the regions. Since we were not taken off our normal jobs, we worked fairly hard for a month or so, going out in the evenings to talk to teenagers about their viewing habits and opinions and attitudes, and meeting once a week during the lunch hour to pool our findings and discuss our next area of inquiry and research. After six weeks we produced a fairly comprehensive report (it had become clear that except for pop music there was no such thing as an adolescent audience—teen-agers liked good programs and disliked bad ones, like everyone else), and that was that. But the value to all of us, we agreed, was enormous. It gave us an insight which none of us could have achieved otherwise into the standards and beliefs and doctrine of all the other departments represented; it gave us a much clearer sense of what the BBC as a whole stood for, as opposed to just our own departments; and it left us with an informal network of friends in other departments whom we could ring up for advice and information and recommendations whenever we had to go beyond our own specialist expertise. It is clear to me now, as I look back on it, that these side effects were at least as valuable to the BBC as the report itself, and I suspect that in any corporate tribe with rather watertight internal partitions it would be worthwhile giving a lot of thought to devising research-and-recommendation projects of this nature simply in order to bring young tengroups of this type together and construct informal, lateralcommunication networks for the future.

The danger that prosperity brings is that this group of young males can become too large. Excessive numbers in a group that is young, healthy, energetic, and highly statuscompetitive, and that is also at its lifetime's lowest level of tribal loyalty, can build up a dangerous head of aggression. What happens? I have my own theory about this, which I cannot resist putting forward even though it has no scientific backing: I believe it is related to the phenomenon of mass hysteria. Mass hysteria has never, as far as I know, been explained, although it has often been observed and described: I have done more than observe it—I have experienced it myself.

It was a strange episode, and a trivial one in many ways, but it is still printed sharply on my memory. It happened one day in the spring of 1939 in my school playground. The current craze was playing soldiers, and various groups of us were drilling and marching and firing imaginary rifles. Then somehow these isolated groups started to coalesce and first march, and then run, around and around the playground. Someone started to chant a slogan from a current recruiting poster in a crude, basic rhythm, and we all picked it up: "Join the modern army, join the modern army!" More and more people followed us and took up the chant, until the entire school was charging around and around roaring the same mindless, meaningless chant in a rhythm—tum ti tum ti tum tum, tum ti tum ti tum tum—which I can still hear in my mind more than thirty years later. The bell rang for the end of break, but we were past taking any notice of it. I remember a part of my mind wondering if I would get into trouble—I was a circumspect and conformist child— but I realized that among so many I would probably not be recognized and certainly not singled out: if I was punished, the whole school would be punished, in which case the only humiliation would be to be one of the tiny handful of goody-goodies. For a few ecstatic minutes I experienced the exhilarating liberation that accompanies loss of identity, and then somehow—I still do not know how—the Gadarene rush was halted, the exhilaration died away, and we trooped off sheepishly into our classrooms.

We have witnessed this sort of mindless mass behavior many times: football crowds and student demonstrations and political rallies, the Hitler youth movement and the Moseleyites and the storming of the Bastille. No one doubts that it is a single phenomenon common to the whole of our species, and it seems to be totally destructive; and yet if it is a continuing part of human nature then it must have had some survival value. My belief is that it is the means by which we used to limit the size of tribal populations.

The normal method of regulation in a fairly static state

would perhaps have been for small parties to go off and start new hunting bands, or even new tribes: to find an unoccupied area with a supply of game, and establish a sort of colonial settlement. But in time of continuing population growth when all the land that could support life was annexed as tribal territory, simple colonization was impossible. The numbers of the new generation would start to build up inside all the tribes, beyond five hundred and even beyond a thousand; danger of overcropping the herds would become acute, and the entire population would risk extinction. I suggest that in this situation there were tribal gatherings at which mass hysteria started to operate, the young men began chanting, and finally they all hurtled off to annihilate a neighboring tribe and occupy their hunting territory. Perhaps they would succeed, and solve their problem. Perhaps they would be defeated, and solve the other tribe's problem. Either way, nature would win; the population would stabilize again, and overcropping would be averted.

There is no direct evidence that this involved only, or principally, the young males without territory or family, but there are grounds for supposing it may have been so. They are the most expendable group in many communities: the famous suicide emigration of the lemmings has the same function of relieving population pressure, and it is entirely composed of the young of the year—the males, and the females who are not pregnant; and there are many other species whose young adult males (and sometimes young adult females, too) are driven out to make room for the next generation and reduce the number of mouths to feed. Moreover, it is through the swelling number of young adults that a tribe first realizes it is getting too large. Smaller children are vulnerable to disease and predators in a hundred ways, but the mature young males and females are clearly here to stay. Certainly, it seems to have been the young males of our species who have always gone off to the wars. Even when I was in the army, the marriage allowance was kept uncomfortably low for officers and soldiers in their teens and early twenties: the explanation for this official discouragement of matrimony was that this was the time when the army wanted men to give undivided dedication to the service and be free to travel the world or stay away late, without causing domestic dissension and disruption; but it is hard not to suspect that at the back of it lay a desire to minimize the number of widows and orphans left by this vulnerable and expendable group. Any company that takes on large concentrations of these young males in times when there is plenty of work is obviously laying down a powder keg for the troublemakers to ignite when the recession comes. The universities, too, are at present suffering from concentrations of these young males, in groups that are beyond acceptable tribal size, and without adequate tribal structure. I would have thought that—on the principle of the foreman and the subaltern—a university would need one young member of staff almost full time looking after every forty or fifty undergraduates, and that there should be self-contained college or faculty units of not more than five hundred each, however large the total university, to give even a reasonable chance of avoiding aggressive outbreaks. But even when there are no aggressive and volatile concentrations, there is still a problem for a corporation which recruits a lot of young men during the fat years and is then left with too many on its hands when the lean years come. My observations suggest that the corporations who do best are the ones which stay lean and muscular even in the fat years, and use the young men to start up new hunting bands and new tribes around new products and services, rather than have them stay around in the established tribes and make life easier for everyone else. Some of them will want to leave and go to other corporations, some will want to start up on their own: this is what the young males are for, and it is a misunderstanding of their role to apply the standards of territoried older males and call them restless and unstable. It also means that when the climate gets colder and the recession settles in, the established tribes will be protected, and if some of the new enterprises fail and leave the young males out in the cold, at least they can fend for themselves and not have the problem of supporting wives and families. Nevertheless, they do have an abundance of energy and dedication, and a great desire to establish the highest possible status in the shortest possible time—a desire which time gradually commutes into the defense of existing status. This, and their exploring instinct, together with their minimal attachment to any established tribal group, makes a tengroup of them a very powerful force for developing new products, processes, services, and markets: in new growth areas, experience and judgment matter less—they can even be a disadvantage—and energy and enterprise matter more. In the old areas the clash of the two can cause friction, heat, and explosion.

There is an interesting parallel here with the animal world. Wynne-Edwards points out that in harsh and unstable climates there is frequent emigration and rapid interchange and new formation of populations, which means that populations throughout the whole area show a remarkable genetic uniformity, whereas in stable and serene conditions with much less cross-flow there is far greater distinctiveness and genetic variation between populations. I have noticed a close cultural parallel in the corporations: the older established and stable industries preserve a great deal of individuality, but the new unstable ones—television, advertising, publishing, journalism, films—have so much interchange that the separate competing companies might almost be branches of a single firm, since so many beliefs and assumptions and practices are the same right across the board.

In general, however, the effect of instability on the corporation is to produce a sort of long-term pulsating response. Boom is centrifugal, slump is centripetal. During the fat years, people—especially the young males—want to move out and explore and do better for themselves faster than they can within the tribal system. Discipline is a restriction; they chafe at delay and deliberation; the old men are missing all the opportunities because they are out of touch. In a slump, everything changes: it is cold outside, the tribal solidarity is secure and attractive, the old men may come up with a job if treated with the proper respect, and obedient conformity is a small price to pay for the security of belonging. Several people have noticed how the argument between centralization and decentralization, though it never ends, goes in phases: that there is no correct state to be achieved— even for a single corporation, let alone as an absolute rule for everyone. There is simply a central mark, and the needle moves from one side to the other. My guess is that the needle follows the movement from boom to slump and back. In the fat years, all the restrictions are questioned; the disciplines and rules all seem like restrictions on the initiative and enterprise that are getting competitors ahead faster; the ambitious young men are setting up on their own and making a fortune; and all the talk is of removing central controls and giving everyone more independent authority. Then the lean years come, and the danger is suddenly not of missing the boat but of running it onto the rocks. Proposals are carefully checked, budgets are rigidly enforced, everyone makes sure no one under him is wasting money or taking unacceptable risks, and the central control that was the millstone around everyone's neck now looks much more like a lifebelt.

XVI

The Gathering
of the Tribes

F O R millions of years the tribe was the largest unit we
know of, and, as I have suggested, it found a way of adapting
to the cycle of scarcity and plenty, and of controlling surplus
population. It was not, however, a particularly comfortable
or agreeable way, and no one could be blamed for trying to
find a more satisfactory arrangement. That arrangement, as
we know, was found some ten thousand years ago with the
development of farming, when it became possible to increase
the supply of food by agriculture, instead of reducing the
demand for it by warfare. Of course, the system did not
suddenly click into operation, particularly in the short term,
and it does not require a long or deep study of our history
to observe that we have continued to operate the two systems
in parallel; but for the first time we have at least devised an
alternative system, and I regard it as a notable improvement.

The new system, however, brought with it a problem. For

a number of reasons, the chief of which must have been the need to defend the agricultural settlement against marauding tribesmen, the single tribe was too small a unit. It became necessary to bring a number of tribes together for collective security, and—on the principle that if the enemy has a battleship, then you have to have one too—there were competitive advantages in bringing together the largest congregation of tribes in the district. Moreover, once a number of tribes became villages and then congregated into a township, they began to discover all the ways in which specialization and division of labor can increase the supply of food and improve the quality of life: a town can have a doctor, but a village cannot have a quarter of a doctor. The problem, however, is that we had and have no innate instinct for the formation of those larger groupings; we have had to work it out for ourselves or take it over as a working system from our parents and grandparents, or else do a bit of both. To trace the story of our trials and errors in this task throughout the course of recorded history would be beyond the scope of this book—and fortunately so, since it would also be beyond the capacity of its author—but it is not necessary. Since the process has to be passed on or discovered anew it still happens all the time: in every expanding corporation the mistakes are still being made and the answers are still being discovered every day. Many corporate executives are at this moment perpetrating errors of human organization which would be seen as elementary boners by the chiefs of what they would call "primitive" African tribes.

The most obvious and most common mistake, which has already been touched on, is to try and control the larger grouping within the framework of a single tribe. This is the most likely mistake if the increase in size is the result of organic growth rather than alliance or acquisition, because there is no particular point when subdivision has to occur; consequently, the pressure rises gradually as numbers go up in two's and three's, and it is easier to explain difficulties away by blaming people or circumstances than by looking at the system of organization that has lasted so well for so long. Instructions are not transmitted, or are misunderstood; salesmen offer impossible delivery dates because they did not see the revised schedule; a machining error goes on unchecked for three weeks; deliveries go to the wrong customers; parts are not ordered; there are delays with men idle followed by bursts of frenzied overtime; the accounts get in a mess because there is no time to do anything about it; and the boss who ought to be around more than ever is in fact seen less and less because he is sorting out rows between departments, soothing ruffled customers, sweating through the books with the accountants, or trying to reach an agreement with the unions. It does not occur to him that all this springs from the fairly quick growth from five hundred to sixteen hundred: he sees it as new young lads who don't give a damn about anything except the pay check, or as the loss of pride in work, or as a general decay of national moral fiber afflicting everyone except himself.

When a firm reaches this stage, it suffers from just about every corporate disease in microcosm, and everyone can produce his own diagnosis: lack of proper financial control, unclear lines of authority, a need for management accounting, insufficient personnel motivation, inadequate stock control and production control techniques, absence of grievance committees, failure to make a long-range plan, no management development program, or just a "breakdown in communication." There is hardly a single management technique that cannot be prescribed with some justification, though there is none that will solve the problem. Once a tribe outgrows its natural maximum size it creates all the problems in the book, and usually simultaneously. The term "breakdown in communication" is the currently fashionable way of avoiding saying what is wrong; but it is worth repeating that communication only happens in communities, and if the community has broken down there is no way of preserving communication.

The irony is that communication could not possibly break

down if it were not for communication techniques. It is only
the availability of documentation, drawings, lists, schedules,
memos, notices, instructions, and of course the telephone,
that gives people the illusion that they can operate more
than a thousand people as a single unit; without these, sheer
practicalities would force a subdivision into separate tribes
long before. All these devices and techniques are, of course,
invaluable: but not as a substitute for talking to people. I
sometimes believe that a manufacturing plant where no one
could read or write would have a much better than average
chance of profitability. If that meant that the designer had
to explain in person to the setter and operator how to
machine each new part, it would not necessarily be a great
loss. The loss would be in the area of recording, and certainly
it would do no harm to go through every piece of paper
circulating in the company and ask of each one if it is an
extension of memory (good) or a substitute for dialogue
(bad). When Simon Marks instituted his famous "Good
Housekeeping" revolution at Marks and Spencer, it began
simply as a blitz on unnecessary paper work; and since they
saved a hundred and twenty tons a year (the equivalent of
twenty-six million forms) and a quarter of a million pounds
on printing, it may be said to have succeeded. But in fact it
revealed something even more profound. People throughout
the organization were using paper as a poor substitute for
personal contact. Merchandisers would endlessly discuss the
figures revealed by sales charts—why was this cardigan selling
so much faster than that?—when any girl at the woolens
counter could have told them it was the neckline that all the
customers went for. As a result, Marks instituted the practice
of every headquarters manager and executive and director
visiting at least one store a week to talk to the staff in the
front line and encounter the reality of the business, instead
of seeing it through a chart darkly.

The other most common fault occurs at the opposite end
of the scale, and is the result not of unstructured organic
growth but of an inadequately integrated merger or takeover

or acquisition. I am not talking here of conglomerate-building or asset-stripping operations, but of a genuine attempt to integrate operations. There is presumably a convincing initial reason for entering into this kind of alliance, even if it bears little relation to the ultimate reality, and my guess would be that the underlying motive is not often, if ever, the simple desire for growth and profits. Nearly always it is a sense of danger, an apprehension that bigger and fiercer competitors will mop us up unless we become bigger ourselves. But whatever the reason, there is an assumption that the coming together can create a whole that is greater than the sum of its parts, and this is where the trouble begins. Whatever the commercial, industrial, or financial advantages ("savings on duplicated research . . . rationalizing marketing operations . . . comprehensive service to customers . . . export drive . . ."), the genuine integration of two independent tribes into a larger unit means a shattering convulsion of their separate cultural systems. The single overgrown tribe may have plenty of difficulties in splitting up into two or three separate tribes, but at least it is spared this one: it can preserve its territories and status system and doctrine and leadership style and the rest of its cultural tradition more or less intact. But two tribes that have developed separately, however great their respect for each other, have to put all these in the melting pot if they are to emerge as a strong single unit. Indeed, mutual respect may be a barrier: a tribe that feels it is just as good as the other will find it harder to see reasons for change; a clear sense of who is the master is essential for any real integration. But integration is very easy to block: each tribe simply continues as it was. It finds itself unable to divert any people or resources to joint ventures, explains that this is the wrong time to institute the common accounting procedures, insists on taking decisions on its own authority as it did before, never seems to have gotten the facts and figures out yet, and reduces the game to stalemate around the table of the policy coordination committee. None of the advantages is gained, time and effort are wasted, initiative is inhibited, everyone plays politics, and the last state is worse than the first.

How do you overcome the resistance, and integrate two self-contained tribes? I would suggest that, whatever announcements may be made for the sake of appearances, you do not even attempt the operation unless both parties are clear that one of them is leader, and the other is becoming a part of an existing organization. This is often the hardest condition to accept, but unless it is accepted there is very little else that can be done: two separate status systems and command structures cannot exist side by side and be described as integrated, nor is it sensible or possible to destroy them both and start building a new structure on the rubble of two shattered businesses. One must be preserved and strengthened, and the other must be assimilated to it.

This, of course, is all very fine in theory, but a great deal harder in practice, and one of the things that makes it so poorly understood is the shortage of people with a long record of success at achieving it. There has, however, been one quite outstanding example in recent years: between 1958 and 1969 Joe Hyman carried out a spectacular series of acquisitions which took him from the proprietorship of an East Anglia warp knitting company worth one hundred and eighty thousand pounds to the chairmanship of the Viyella International Federation comprising ninety companies, and with a stock-exchange valuation of close to fifty million pounds. In a depressed textile industry it stood out as the one shining beacon of consistent growth and profitability until the famous 1969 palace revolution when he was voted out of the chairmanship and the company joined the ICI empire. The combination of some twenty or more acquisitions (some of the companies were acquired as groups) with highly successful results suggests that his methods are worth recording.

Hyman's first principle was never to make a hostile take-over: every one was with the agreement of the taken-over company. The next was to move into the company himself:

he did not believe that integration by proxy was possible, so he took a house or flat in the district and lived with the business. In the initial stages this might take several days a week, shading off as time went by. He reckoned that it had to be a part of his own job for the first year, then watched closely by him for the next two, and then monitored for two more; after five years it could stand on its own. The third principle was to find the leader: one of his rules was that every chief executive must name his successor on the day that he took up his appointment, and he would not start integrating the company unless he had the man who was going to run it sitting next to him. To find the leader, he held seminars of from a dozen to twenty top executives, and before long he would identify the man he wanted, and they would start work.

Very few directors survived—there were four hundred fewer when he finished, mostly members of the families that used to own the business—but in principle he worked with the existing executives, though some of those fell by the wayside too. But another principle was never to leave a man in the job he had before. By turning narrow, functional managers into genuine directors, he was able to make them start looking at the merger as an expansion of horizons instead of a defeat. Also, of course, a manager in the same job is defensive about his way of doing it—reeducation is a form of personal criticism.

The first reaction was always hostility and fear, but there were a number of factors on his side. The businesses were mostly family businesses, and once the family directors had gone the executives were not implicated in the wrong decisions, or lack of decisions, in the past: they could change direction without losing face. Then, Hyman kept the central faith intact: they believed in high-quality, up-market textiles, and so did he. He was not asking them to change over to the cheap and tatty end of the business. And as the seminars went on, all sorts of privately held information about the company became public as the executives pooled their in-

formation about the business. Also—another principle—
Hyman always lunched with the executives, and if there was
no dining room he had one installed. Gradually, a ten-group
started to emerge and grow together, socially as well as operationally; hostility turned to reluctant admiration and then,
in a surprising number of cases, to hero worship. It was clear
that Hyman understood the business and its finances better
than any of them, and a lot of what he was saying was confirmation and extension of what the younger managers had
been muttering to each other over their coffee for years.
Now they were offered a glorious vision of a new, thrusting,
successful textile industry, with all the latest capital equipment, carrying out all the operations—spinning, weaving,
dyeing, finishing—on all the fibers—nylon, terylene, cotton,
cotton-and-wool—to replace the out-of-date, fragmented little
family businesses employing too little capital and too much
labor on a single fiber and a single process.

This vision, however, could only be realized through
Viyella, and Viyella was Joe Hyman. He was never in any
doubt that allegiance to Viyella had to begin, and continue
for some years, as allegiance to him. Nor was he satisfied
until the members of a new firm had a sense of belonging,
until being a part of Viyella was an aspect of their personal
identity. "I have to become a myth," he used to say. "People
must believe I'm here even when I'm not." He was acutely
conscious of the need to foster and encourage this myth. He
used to work in his house next door to the factory through
the night alongside the night shift, and stroll around now
and then to stretch his legs—and also to show the shift
workers that he was there too. On one of these occasions the
night watchman saw his door open and the light on, and
locked him out. He had to summon help to break into his
own house at four in the morning. This, to him, was an
invaluable addition to the myth, a story that would go on
being told and referred to down the ages.

It is unfashionable management theory, but nevertheless
I can think of few cases of successful and lasting integration

in industry or history that did not have a hero and a task, a great leader and a promised land. Usually, too, the starting point was a fear of extinction, a need for an ally to face the danger alongside you. Given these prerequisites, the task is then to achieve cultural integration through doctrinal alignment. The central faith must be shown to be the same, but the means of preserving it have to be changed. Hyman's commercial and industrial logic entailed a big doctrinal shake-up—carrying far fewer lines in far greater bulk, not supplying customers who ordered less than a certain volume a year, shift working, giving big management jobs to men in their twenties, and so forth—but this in fact was the key to unity: when so many techniques and procedures were in the melting pot, it was fairly easy to put certain aspects of the old culture—command system, status-ranking standards of judgment—into the pot with them. The new ideas were part of a total package, and the package had Viyella on the label and Joe Hyman inside.

Successful integration is harder and rarer than the subdivision of an overgrown tribe: there is nothing natural about the welding together of two culturally distinct units, whereas subdivision of a large tribe is quite natural and, as we have seen, still happens among the Australian hunting tribes. But whichever way the larger grouping is now formed, if it is to be held together as a single unity then something has to do the holding, and that something, as I have suggested, is a discovery we are still making and not an innate or instinctive formation. But if we are not to live all our lives with the constant anxieties and insecurities of tribal life, then the tribes must be combined into a more powerful unit, and that means taking the first step toward the foundation of a kingdom. And the kingdom is the unit with which we are now concerned.

Kingdom is perhaps an exaggeration: two or three tribes linked together would perhaps be more aptly described as a barony, and even ten or a dozen are closer to a duchy, or at most a principality; and of course all these can exist either independently or within corporate empires. But they all have this in common: there is a central group whose job is to direct, control, and regulate the tribes who do the work, and this is the point at which government, management, and politics all begin. To be a good tribal chieftain is a big job, and the tribal chiefs are the backbone of the corporation; but they are not the brain. They need an unusual combination of qualities and qualifications—authority, experience, judgment, the respect of the tribe, knowledge of the business, sense of priorities—but familiarity with sophisticated management technique is not one of them. Once a central group is formed, however, direct personal contact with everyone becomes impossible, and you cannot run the business by the seat of your pants any more. The instinctive has to become explicit.

Yet some things cannot be changed, and among them are the basic building blocks: the ten-group, the camp, and the tribe. Consequently, the central organization itself has to develop around the king's ten-group, the council of state. Experience suggests that the council of elders which guides the whole kingdom is at its best when it is fairly small, perhaps numbering only four or five including the king and the prime minister, the chairman and the managing director. But in every large corporate state, it is necessary to form a number of ten-groups to look after certain aspects of the king's job—a financial ten-group, a legal ten-group, an administrative ten-group—and it is not difficult for the headquarters operation to grow into a tribe in its own right, or even to become several tribes.

It is in fact all too easy, and for a reason well known to anyone who has worked in a large organization. Once you have a headquarters tribe, or even subtribe, it is almost impossible to avoid having a permanent residence; and the permanent residence, the headquarters, the central office (call it what you like), becomes the palace. And throughout history, and around every corporation and state, the palace has exerted an almost irresistible attraction on the ambitious

and the status-hungry. It looks like a quick route to the top
—a place where a bright young man can be noticed early and
promoted rapidly, or an older one can demonstrate his fitness
for high office. The fact that in every kingdom and corporation there unquestionably has to be some kind of court leads
to pressures to increase its size, and it can all too easily
become a monster which consumes the wealth of the state.
Perhaps the king only needs one financial adviser to start
with: soon the adviser needs a group around him—an internal accounts specialist, a tax specialist, an investment
specialist—and in time each of them needs a group, and a
subtribe is formed. The same is happening to the legal
department, the central buying department, the architect's
department, the publicity and public relations department,
the personnel department: all of them have unanswerable
arguments for having their offices in the palace. Everything
that annoys or worries the king or his prime minister can be
solved by a new man or a new group in someone's department, to see that it doesn't happen again. The northern
regional manager failed to depreciate his equipment fast
enough? We will create a post in the finance department for a
man to keep a permanent check on depreciation rates in all
the regions—he will save five times his salary in profits tax;
all regional managers will submit their depreciation proposals to him six months before the end of the accounting
year. Sales executives are changing their cars too quickly?
A man in central purchasing will keep an inventory of all
company cars with their cost and mileage, and permanently
monitor the secondhand rates and instruct each executive
when to trade his vehicle in; he will save five times his salary
in transportation costs. And so it goes on. Parkinson put
forward the theory that the day a firm moves into its own
new building is the day it starts to die: like most of his
breath-taking exaggerations, there is a disturbing truth at
the root of it. The new building gives permanence to the
size of the court it can contain, and since a desire for
external status prompts kings and chairmen to have the

largest possible building, they are saddled with a huge permanent court as well. If the corporate headquarters can be divided up into self-contained tribes of not more than five hundred or so, with a clear role, an evolved leader, and an objective measurement of success and failure, the corporation may still survive and prosper; but if it tries to operate a headquarters of five thousand as a single unit, then the malignant cells will be almost impossible to check.

It is also desperately easy for the people around the court to become the focus of the king's attention, so that he spends nearly all his time running his palace instead of his kingdom. They are, after all, the people he sees every day, and it is easy for him to accept the role as leader of the palace tribe and look to the palace as the instrument through which he and the prime minister achieve their aims. This of course means delegating to the priests and courtiers little corners of authority over the outlying dukes and barons and tribal chieftains—it is so much easier if you can put something right or get something done by sending for someone in the same building, and what is more it is natural tribal behavior. But as the palace becomes more and more a self-contained tribe, so it drifts away from the rest of the kingdom, and the outlying dukes and barons and chieftains see in its carpeted warmth, its bars and cinemas and squash courts and swimming pool, its vast army of parasites and sycophants, not the heart and brain and nerve center of their kingdom but an alien institution which soon becomes their prime aggression focus.

The palace tribe is the central problem for any leader who wants to run a kingdom. It is no answer to fix a limit—the operations may absolutely demand a large number of people at the center. Marks and Spencer, with its highly centralized purchasing and marketing organization, finds it needs close to three thousand people at headquarters, and since it has virtually no regional organization—just the two hundred and fifty stores—many people wonder how it can manage with so few. On the other hand Viyella, with Hyman's belief in decentralized operations, ran the same number of people —about thirty thousand—with a headquarters staff of forty, including secretaries and switchboard operators and the stock boys. There is no universal rule that can be numerically expressed. Nor is the evolutionary nature of our species any help; on the contrary, our nature inclines us to split up into totally self-contained tribes, and it is our nature that leads us toward a palace tribe that loses touch with the kingdom. Nevertheless, there is a way of holding together a group which is larger than the tribe, and our history is (among other things) a record of how this unity is forged, sustained, and dissolved. We are now discovering and adapting the techniques of the Roman and Islamic empires, the British raj and the Catholic Church, to the needs of IBM and Unilever and General Motors. With all the vast differences that divide them, they are united by certain enduring features which, if we can isolate them, will give us a most valuable insight into the nature of Corporation Man.

XVII

The Dispersed Tribe and
the Unity of the Kingdom

A corporation, as we understand it today, is a far more recent notion than a manufacturing business; it is also very different. Manufacturing businesses, of the sort that began to dominate our lives about two centuries ago, were defined by their product: if it was yarn they were a spinning business, if it was cloth they were weaving businesses, if it was steel they were in the steelmaking business, and that was that. Few employees were asked to do much more than learn a process and then keep on applying it. If demand rose, more machines and people carried out the same process; and, while everybody hoped the business would grow and prosper, it nevertheless had a slightly temporary feeling about it. The business existed for as long as people wanted the product, but if they stopped wanting it then presumably the business would cease to exist. If you invested in it, you were basically investing in the product as if it were an extension of the commodity market, and your chief concern was the same as with any other commodity—how strong was the demand and how great was the supply? A manufacturing business of that sort required very little in the way of management: it chiefly depended on capital, entrepreneurial flair, a pool of cheap labor, a source of power, strict industrial and financial disciplines, access to raw materials, and access to markets.

The corporation did not begin until a new idea started to grow: the idea of permanence and, even more important, confidence in and commitment to permanence. This is not to say that some Victorian mill-owners did not believe their business would go on and on, without any foreseeable end to the world-wide demand for Lancashire cotton; but that is simply blind optimism. The commitment to permanence says, in effect, that whatever may happen to the market, the technology, the raw materials, the processes or any other variable, we shall still be in business; our aim is not to produce a particular product, or carry out a particular process, or provide a particular service: our aim is corporate survival, whatever internal changes or convulsions it may entail. The investor is invited to invest not in the corporation's product, but in its ability to survive and grow. Donald Schon pointed out in the 1970 Reith lectures that it is no longer any good simply thinking of "the laundry business": housewives buy their own washing machines, chemists come up with drip-dry cotton and permanent-crease terylene, manufacturers develop throwaway paper clothes, retailers open Laundromats and start diaper services, and what has happened to your laundry business after all that? The only constant is that people like to wear clean clothes, and if you are committed to permanence you have to be in the forefront of as many of these developments as you can. If you are exclusively committed to a steam laundry, you are committed to obsolescence. It is clear that this process is accelerating, not so much because there are no longer any simple processes that have to be carried out year after year, but because it is now economic to build machines to carry out those processes;

and now that the computer is taking over the simple clerical processes in the same way that automated equipment and transfer machines are taking over the mechanical ones, more and more people are spending more and more time creating, or adapting to, change and innovation. And what is a corporation then?

It is, of course, still a manufacturing business; but the emphasis has been shifting steadily away from what the corporation *does,* and onto what it *is.* A few years ago there was a bright future for a firm that published school textbooks: in a few years' time it will only have a future as a part of an integrated corporation producing complete science and arts courses on slides, transparencies, cassette films, discs, tape, wall charts, and teaching machines, with a comprehensive system of liaison with schools and universities to keep the content up to date and to keep improving the techniques; instead of the solitary author there will be production teams comprising film directors, writers, professors, schoolteachers, photographers, animators, graphic artists, and learning programmers. They will be supplying every age group from three to twenty-five and on into adult education and industrial training, and covering every branch of every subject that enough people want to learn. It will be no use trying to judge that corporation by a single product: its success will depend on the continuing value of a whole range of learning systems which are constantly being revised and improved and extended. From being a single entrepreneurial act, like weaving bales of cloth or publishing a textbook, the corporation has evolved into a place of continuing entrepreneurial activity.

It is this, of course, that creates the central problem of organizing the corporate kingdom. So long as all the employees are only following simple instructions and carrying out routine procedures, there is no great problem in organizing a large number of tribes: it is not hard to tell a mill to produce ten percent more of one quality cloth next month and ten percent less of another. But even in the oldest and simplest businesses, more and more change and complexity have crept in over the years; in the newer ones they have been there from the start. And the problem is this: how do you incorporate such a wealth of innovation, creativity, and enterprise, with all the attendant administrative complications, within a single corporate kingdom? How do you free people from the shackles of bureaucracy without losing all power to deploy the resources of your kingdom as a single unit? In military terms, how do you avoid such a vast and inflexible concentration of troops that you can never adapt in time to shifts in the battle, or such a loose assembly of independent units that you never know where they are, what their strength is, or what they think they are doing?

If we wanted to strangle our learning-systems corporation at birth with red tape, we now know how to do it. We bring all twelve thousand employees into a single building, and set up departments by function: separate departments of writers, of film directors, of graphic artists, of photographers, of learning programmers, of film cameramen, of sound recordists; separate technical departments for slide projectors, for tape recorders, for film cassettes, for printing, for film editing, for programmed-learning machines; an advertising department, a sales department, a market research department; a department for schools liaison, and another for university liaison; and, interwoven with these, an accounts department, personnel department, stationery department, accommodation department. We would then appoint an editor without authority over any of them to produce a geography course, and make sure the medical department had a bed ready for him.

If, however, we want to survive and grow, we create ten-groups: we bring together the sort of team I outlined earlier —film director, schoolteacher, writer, artist, professor, etc.— and ask them to design and produce a first-year physics course. We then build them into a tribe; perhaps the tribe is called "first-year courses" and has ten-groups for each first-year subject, but it is much more likely to be called "physics" and take the subject right through from the first beginnings up to degree standard. We have other tribes for all the other subjects. We have technical tribes responsible for all the different types of equipment, but they have to sell their services on their merits, as do our printing tribes and film-developing tribes. Every tribe, of course, is treated financially as an independent firm, with its own budget and accounts and profits target, and it has its own separate building.

A tribal organization like this should prevent the bureaucratic stagnation and paralysis that results from size without structure. It does not, however, solve the problem of deploying the resources of the kingdom as a single unit. The separate tribes can be so separate that they might just as well be independent firms: they derive no benefit from their association since they do not fit into a master plan, nor do they have access to a wider network of information, and they can call on no wider human or financial resources for equipment purchase, advertising, research, etc., than if they were in business on their own account. They have to make the same mistakes all over again instead of learning from the others, they have to pioneer new markets and products and techniques themselves instead of sharing the experience of their fellow tribes, and they can only offer their customers the solution to a small part of their problem instead of being a part of the total solution which the corporation supplies. Somehow they have to keep their tribal independence and yet be welded into the corporate kingdom.

You can make the problem sound insoluble, but in fact a number of our great corporations have found a way of uniting these apparently conflicting requirements. They would all explain it in different ways—in terms of organization structures or liaison committees or information procedures or some other management device—but behind them all there is the same instrument of unity: it is the king's tribe. In almost every way it operates like other corporate tribes, but it has one great difference: it is a dispersed tribe. The members do not leave their own tribes to join it—they remain in them, scattered throughout different buildings, or different cities, or different parts of the world, and what holds them together is not charts or memos or procedures, but tribal membership and tribal unity. No one appoints them or tells them they have joined, and there is no formal membership. Even the existence of the king's tribe is seldom consciously realized or acknowledged; but in every large corporation it is very much of a reality, and it is the force which enables all the other tribes to operate independently and yet work together.

In Chapter IV I touched on the question of dispersal when describing how a member of a ten-group can spend months away from the group and still be a part of it. Perhaps the classic case of ten-group dispersal in business was when the five sons of the Rothschild family founder settled in London, Paris, Vienna, Naples, and Frankfurt, and by their total mutual trust and understanding founded Europe's greatest private banking dynasty, which is still flourishing one hundred and sixty years later. A dispersed tribe is too large to have quite the same tight unity of a dispersed ten-group, but the Jesuits, for instance, were able to disperse around the world and still remain very much a part of their order after many years on the other side of the globe. The king's dispersed tribe comprises the five hundred to a thousand members of the corporation who know that the king—the chairman—knows them: almost all of them are the people he would invite if in an hour of corporate crisis he had to address the top executives and managers in a hall that would hold only five hundred or so. They may not see him very often, but they expect him to know them and acknowledge them; whereas other tribesmen are pleased if the king recognizes them, they are bitterly hurt if he fails to.

In a small corporate kingdom of ten or a dozen tribes, something under ten thousand people altogether, the king's dispersed tribe will presumably include everyone of seniority; the tribal chieftains as the leading ten-group of warriors will be among the most significant members of it, next to the king's council of elders; but there is a place in it for even the most junior manager. It is as the kingdom grows larger, however, that the composition of the king's tribe becomes critically significant, and for an obvious reason: the strength and unity of the kingdom depend on the degree to which the tribal chieftains feel identified with it. So long as the chieftain knows the old man, so long as the chairman says "Morning, Jack, how's Betty feeling?" on the one or two occasions in the year when they meet, the tribe is welded to the kingdom. If, however, the chieftain's name is Albert and his wife was called Mabel and left him twelve years ago, that weld becomes very insecure. It is personal loyalty that unites a tribe, and if it is missing no amount of organizational procedures and financial controls can replace it; but every loyal tribal chieftain ensures that five hundred or so tribesmen can be in personal contact with a loyal member of the kingdom, and that the whole tribe's operation will be directed in a spirit of loyalty. But, of course, the difficulty of maintaining this personal loyalty and identity rises with the number of tribes: when there are two or three hundred of them—especially if they are geographically dispersed—it becomes critical. Of course, it is possible for a cluster of them to remain loyal to a baron or duke, but then their loyalty to the kingdom is in his gift and if he becomes disaffected or recalcitrant he is dangerously powerful. It is for this reason that ambitious corporate barons and dukes are often anxious to keep their subordinate chieftains out of the king's tribe. Equally, as the kingdom grows, it becomes more and more important for the king to make a conscious and deliberate effort to ensure enough contact with the tribal chieftains to weld them all into his tribe.

It would be fascinating to analyze the constitution of the king's dispersed tribe in a number of our great corporations, but extremely hard to get at the real truth since several thousand would claim membership and the chairman would publicly acknowledge them all: only in the deepest private confidence would he admit his inability to put names to faces or faces to names. But I suspect that if the truth could be established, we would find three main ways in which the king's tribe goes wrong; all three result in the alienation of tribal chieftains and other important but distant executives, but the reasons are different. The first is most common in times of adversity: it is the dominance of the palace tribe which we have already touched on. The king spends far too much time with comparatively unimportant palace officials, usually because he prefers their reassurances to the harsh truths that come from tribal chieftains. The second is the stagnant tribe, when very few new people join each year. This often goes in parallel with powerful dukes and barons, who block the membership of new candidates, and a king who spends too much of his time away from the kingdom so that the new people he meets are not members of the corporation. The third is the sectarian tribe: most corporate kings have risen up through their success in one branch of the kingdom, one region or product or division in which they had conspicuous success, and it is natural for them to give senior posts to members of their earlier ten-group whom they know they can trust; but as time goes on, unless they make the effort, it is very easy for more and more people from that single area to join the tribe and influence the climate in which the king moves in a way that builds up irritation and resentment among less favored divisions.

All these forms of imbalance in the king's tribe are dangerous for the same reason: they create a shortcut to the top. Membership in the king's tribe in an honor, and all the members of that tribe believe they have earned it through the objective value of their service to the kingdom. Once a whole lot of people whose service to the kingdom is small start to join the tribe, the value of their own membership is debased. They will not all agree about who should be admitted, but they will all agree about who should be excluded. So long as continued success and high corporate status are the criteria, the kingdom is healthy; when subjective favor replaces objective achievement as the qualification for membership, this is the start of tribal alienation and loss of central control. And although these unhealthy tribal formations have separate causes, they have a central fault in common: the king is not meeting enough of his subjects. "Queen Elizabeth slept here" is one of the indicators of a good monarch who knew her duty in times of national division when unity was of prime importance; "England" was a difficult concept for people to be loyal to, but a real live Queen who waved from her carriage and stopped in your town and talked to the mayor and the squire and the rector and spent the night up at the manor house, that was another matter. She, of course, had the great advantage that the telephone and telex had not been invented, that written communication was laborious and slow, and that there were no planes or cars or trains to let her feel she could always get there in a few hours if there were a crisis: she knew she had to go in person, and plan the visit well in advance and irrespective of any operational requirement. Technical progress has not altered that necessity; it has merely provided a variety of excuses and delusions for chairmen who start to feel uncomfortable west of the Hudson. The royal progress is just as necessary for the corporate chairman as for the Tudor monarch if the king's tribe is to be a healthy, living community; it is also a more productive activity than sitting behind a desk at the top of a New York skyscraper setting up committees to investigate the breakdown in communication.

The chief purpose of this royal progress, or chairman's visit, is to keep the tribes welded into the kingdom, and to update the king's dispersed tribe by ensuring that the rising young men come to his notice; but it does have certain more immediately practical advantages as well. One of them is cross-fertilization: by going around every part of the business at the highest level, the chairman can often give one tribe some surprisingly useful information about what another tribe is working on or thinking about—new techniques, new potential customers, new sources of supply, new activities that qualify for government grants or tax rebates, opportunities to economize by working together or stimulus to beat the other to it by competing; there is really no one in the corporation except the chairman who has access to so much high-level and perhaps confidential information about every aspect of the business combined with the opportunity to circulate and discuss it among the top people in every outpost. The prime minister—the chief executive officer—is too closely focused on immediate operational needs to have much time for this sort of visit or to exchange this sort of almost accidental information; it is a part of the chairman's job that no one else can discharge so effectively.

The chairman's progress is also one of the fastest ways of getting things done. No amount of memos and directives from palace officials can achieve as much, as quickly, as a personal word of reproof or commendation from the king. There are many Marks and Spencer stories about Simon Marks's royal visits (on one of them, to Scotland, he could only call on the Paisley store after it had closed for the day, and the whole staff asked if they could be allowed to stay on in order to see him), and many of them illustrate this principle. Once, on a west country progress, he visited the Exeter store and reprimanded the manager for displaying some folding bags by stuffing them out with newspaper. By the time he got to the Torquay store after lunch, all folding bags were displayed flat and empty. (Such was the force of his command, and the speed of the tribal communication network, that probably every bag in every store in the land would have been flat and empty by teatime.) However, on this occasion he sent for the manager and asked why the bags were not padded out. The manager mumbled something in total confusion about understanding that Sir Simon preferred them flat, at which Marks—with a twinkle in his eye according to some accounts—replied, "Listen, lad, just because I like them flat in Exeter, it doesn't mean I like them flat in Torquay." This illustrates an almost equally important point: any number of corporate practices become enshrined in unchangeable ritual because "the old man likes it that way" or "the old man can't bear it," when the only authority is a chance remark in a special context. If the old man actually travels around, he can loosen up some of the rigidity by his presence and his questions. Rigidity is the product of insecurity; if people get a chance to see the king themselves, to talk to him and listen to him, much of that insecurity will disperse. Instead of having their actions and decisions constricted by a host of mysterious injunctions and prohibitions from some unknown but terrible figure hundreds or thousands of miles away, they will be much happier to use their own judgment and initiative so long as they feel they could creditably explain the reason for their action to the man they have actually met. The image of the boss stands behind every executive's shoulder: by coming around in person, he makes that image much more distinct and accurate, and greatly increases the chances that the executive will act as the boss would wish, that he will follow the spirit of the corporation and not just obey the letter of the law.

There is one other reason why the chairman has to keep in personal contact with his tribe, and it is perhaps the most important of all. Long-term survival demands that the right man or group shall be in the right job. In an ideal stable situation leaders evolve through their ten-groups and tribes, and there is not often a problem; but where there is rapid change and growth the correct selection and placing of leaders assumes overriding importance. In nearly all corporations this is one of those cases where the present is the enemy of the future: if a man is making a great success of his job, it is all too tempting to let him go on doing it year after year. If a new company has to be started, it is all too tempting to find someone who can be spared. The managing director has to think of this year's results and next year's forecasts; the chairman must think of who ought to be at the head of the corporation's affairs in ten or fifteen years' time, and what experience they ought to be gaining now. There is no personnel inventory or management development program that can make this sort of judgment for him: it may only be drawn from a chance remark which shows that a good executive has begun to start thinking like a director; or by a couple of minutes' conversation with a man who was stimulated and extended by his job a year or two ago but who is now starting to outgrow it and be bored by it; or by a feeling that another man who would have rejected an offer of an early retirement last year would accept it gratefully this year. These feelings cannot be measured or tabulated, and you do not discover them by poring over personnel files, nor can any less senior official make these judgments; only the chairman has the necessary knowledge of where men are needed, what qualities they require, and who within his kingdom is the best man for the job. Putting the right man and the right task together can be a creative act, just as putting the wrong ones together can be a destructive one. Only by personally welding his dispersed tribe into a unity of all the best men in the kingdom, only by progressing around often enough to keep making the adjustments in this constantly changing equation of men and tasks, can he be in a position to go on making his unique creative contribution to corporate renewal.

XVIII

Evolution and the Committee

T H E R E is a story that Alekhine, when he was world chess champion during the 1930's, stopped for a drink in a Paris boulevard café and an old man shuffled up to him with a chessboard and asked if he would like a game. Alekhine said he would, and the old man—who clearly had not the slightest idea who his opponent was—began to lay out the pieces. When the board was set, Alekhine removed his king's rook. "But, Monsieur," protested the old man, "why do you believe you can afford to give me a rook? You do not even know me." "Monsieur," replied Alekhine, "if I could not afford to give you a rook, I would know you." The story is a good illustration of one of the principles of a dispersed tribe (in this case the tribe of international chess players) : that if it is functioning properly, you can know negatives. You trust the network so completely that you can be sure something is not so, or has not happened, because you just know you would have been told if it had.

A corporation gains enormous strength if the king's dispersed tribe constitutes a network of this nature, but it cannot be achieved by royal progresses alone; their great contribution is in binding the periphery to the center, whereas this network is built of lateral as well as radial links. It cannot operate unless people with no direct operational relationship are in the habit of calling each other up whenever they come across a piece of information, or meet a person, or hear of a development, or have an idea, which is of no use to them but might be of value to the other chap. It may sound easy and obvious, but it is not. To start with, you have to know enough about the other chap's job to realize that it might be of use to him: and that means not just knowing the post he occupies, but also knowing what he is trying to do and how he is trying to do it and what are his main hopes and fears. Then you need to be sure that he respects your judgment and accuracy and reliability, so that he will give proper weight to the information or recommendation. Thirdly, you need the incentive to take the trouble over something which does not help your job or get you any credit. For all these reasons, this sort of lateral communication hardly ever happens between people who do not know each other, or have only met occasionally and socially, and it happens best between people who have at some time been part of the same ten-group. If they have ever been in the same subtribe or tribe, that is a help. But if they only know of each other as functions or job titles, this most valuable communication just will not take place.

The ideal network in a king's tribe would operate like the Midwich Cuckoos in John Wyndham's science fiction story—those strange children who seemed to share a collective brain, so that, however far apart they were, the moment one of them learned something the others all knew it too. A village or a small, self-contained firm of tribal size can come very close to this, but of course it is the constant physical proximity that makes it possible. The dispersed tribes which work best have certain things in common, of which the most important is continuity: the members have grown up together in the corporation, and have moved around enough over the past fifteen or twenty or thirty years to have worked fairly closely with a large proportion of the dispersed tribe. Usually, too, they have moved about quite a lot in their earlier years (this can, of course, be done while staying based in the same local tribe and even the same ten-group), so that when they graduate to the king's dispersed tribe they already have quite a rich network within it. And then they make sure there is frequent contact across the formal operational boundaries within the king's tribe: in a compact operation this can be informal—like the weekly visits to stores by all the Marks and Spencer directors, executives, and senior managers—but in more diffuse and decentralized businesses it has to be specially arranged, so that 3M, for instance, nicknames itself the Minnesota Manufacturing and Meeting Corporation. However it is achieved, they have in common a regular bringing together of people who would not necessarily meet in the course of their immediate operational duties.

If you asked any Corporation Man the purpose of the meeting he was just off to, he would usually be able to give an answer: to review next year's budget proposals, to plan the new product range, to discuss advertising policy, to brief sales managers on the new bonus scheme, or any of a thousand other objectives. I am writing this page at ten past ten on a Monday morning, and the effort to visualize how many meetings are taking place at this moment stretches the imagination beyond its breaking point. And yet the sheer volume itself is significant: this activity could not go on in such volume with such frequency if it were unnatural. In fact, so far from being unnatural, meetings serve an underlying need of our species; they are an integral part of Corporation Man's behavior as they are of every human community—civilized or uncivilized, modern or primitive—

of which we have knowledge or record. This does not mean that we are wrong to describe them, as Corporation Man describes them, by their operational purpose; but it does mean that we would be foolish to ignore their underlying compulsion. Foolish because, if we accept only the operational purpose, we are in danger of assuming that the meeting will result in the furthering of corporation objectives, whereas those who habitually attend meetings are well aware that in practice no such consequence can be assumed. This will not, however, leave all those who were there frustrated at the waste of time, nor will it stop the same meeting from taking place at ten o'clock next Monday morning, and the Monday after, and the Monday after that.

All the same, the fact that it serves no operational need does not mean that it has no value to the corporation or to individual Corporation Men. On the contrary, the species we belong to, and from which we have descended, survived by keeping together, and irrespective of the demands of the job Corporation Man needs to come together regularly with other members of the species; operational objectives can always be found to justify this deeper need. I have a strong impression, though I know of no evidence, that meetings are most frequent and most enjoyed by men whose work keeps them solitary or in very small groups for most of the week, and who do not serve on any committee in their neighborhood either, just as they are most resented by members of tightly-knit ten-groups. There is a need to feel the security of the ten-group around you, even if you do not belong to a real or effective one. In addition, there is status-satisfaction in being able to summon people to your presence and look around the office at the group which acknowledges your leadership. Because of this, and particularly in large office blocks full of small offices, it is all too easy for meetings which start with sound operational objectives to fossilize into ritual assemblies whose only value is to treat cases of social deprivation by regular group therapy.

In practice, even the most apparently futile of meetings

usually serves some wider corporate purpose than simply preserving the mental health of those who attend: it builds and maintains the communication network, it gives a feeling of security, it helps to sort out status and quasi-territory, and it reaffirms identity and the sense of belonging. No corporation could survive, or be described as a corporation, if every member traveled in from his private house by his private car to his private office, met no one during the day, and traveled back in the evening. Any Corporation Man who found himself in that position for a few weeks would start to wonder how long it would be before he got the sack. A certain amount of factory work is in fact very like this, since the noise or the demands of the operation make each man into an island: it is hardly surprising that if the corporation does not bring them together for regular meetings, they seek assembly and association through the union. But at the higher and more comfortable levels, most corporations have found ways of channeling this need for association into useful and productive purposes, and in fact the more visibly effective and valuable the meeting the more it fulfills all the social and therapeutic needs as well.

These purposes are, of course, tremendously varied; but the kinds of meetings are much fewer, and a look at them may enlarge our understanding of corporate communication. There are in practice only three kinds, although there are subdivisions: the small meeting—or committee—of ten-group size, the larger meeting of something around fifty or sixty, and the large assembly of two hundred or more. All the intermediate sizes are, of course, possible, and there is no firm boundary at which the meeting is declared to be in a different category; nevertheless, the three kinds are distinct in operational and social function and have to be treated quite separately.

The meeting of ten or so is the most common. The unique feature which distinguishes it from the larger meetings is that everyone present can contribute to every part of the discussion. Once this becomes impossible, the meeting stops serving its purpose, or becomes a small version of the next size. It can stagger along, however, if some people never open their mouths and become in effect spectators, or if some people only contribute on some points and some only on others, so that the meeting is in practice several different meetings held consecutively. In a sense this meeting is impossible to generalize about: the actual committee meetings that take place in corporations vary in size from two or three people to twenty or thirty; the agenda can have anything from one to over a hundred items; they may be high- or low-level, hostile or friendly; and they can change their entire nature halfway through with a new item on the agenda. But from all the meetings I have attended and read about—among military or political or business corporations, in the present day or in historical times or among primitive communities—I believe it is possible to isolate four or five recurring types of meetings of ten or so people which have to take place in any integrated community as soon as it reaches tribal size, and which may go back many thousands of years into our prehistory.

The obvious one is the meeting of the hunting band, the ten-group. It can, of course, be the meeting of a permanent ten-group, like our morning meetings to plan the day's program on *Tonight,* but it does not have to be. Any gathering of ten-group size with a joint task in which they succeed or fail together, even if they only meet each other once a month, comes under this heading. Out of this meeting comes a decision, a report, a recommendation, a plan of action, which usually (though not necessarily) is put into effect by that same group. The decision is made by the leader, and the purpose of the meeting is to bring everyone's special knowledge, experience, and ideas together to enable him to come to the best decision. It may also include the allocation of duties among the group when the plan has been decided on. At the end of it every member knows his task, and everyone else's, and how they all fit into the overall objective, and they go off to carry out what they have determined.

The other necessary meeting of this ten-group takes place at the end of the hunt: in practice this may be the beginning of the next planning meeting, but in any case it is the first occasion when the hunting band reconvenes. This is where they talk over the events of the hunt and see if there are any lessons to be drawn. It is the first stage in the corporate digestive process referred to in Chapter XIV; they chew over the raw experience and information to see if there is anything nourishing to be extracted from it. Later on, when it has been digested, it can be circulated through the body of the corporation by other ten-groups, and at the meetings of forty or fifty and the large assemblies of over two hundred which we will meet in Chapter XIX.

Then there is the meeting of the king and his council of elders. In a sense this is a ten-group meeting, but it differs from a hunting band in enough ways to be considered separately. Hunting bands decide among themselves how the job shall be done, but the king and his elders have to decide what the job is, and in which direction lies the best hope of survival and success for the whole community. Moreover, the king and his elders do not take action themselves as a result of their meeting, nor is any one of them individually responsible for any specific success or failure in the past; they have nothing to defend or excuse, no hope of individual glory or fear of individual shame. This, above all, is where the modern corporate king goes wrong: he fills his "board" with divisional heads, the corporate princes and dukes from production and marketing, or product ranges, or geographical regions, and then finds he cannot really get impartial expert counsel. Each nobleman is grinding his own ax, and even when he is not, the king cannot be sure he is not. So he turns to his accountant and legal adviser and company secretary and head of public relations, and the court starts to dominate the nation.

A good council of elders normally seems to be small—

about four or five including the king—though it also has
frequent discussions, formal or informal, with all sorts of
people from inside and outside who may contribute to
their deliberations. Its basic concern is with the tribe in
relation to the wider world: the world of prey and predators,
scarcity and plenty, allies and enemies—the world outside
its jurisdiction and beyond its control. For the corporate
kingdom this means capital markets and government policies, investment and taxation, competition and acquisition,
new technologies and new markets—everything which im-
pinges on the external identity of the tribe and the kingdom,
and may affect the direction in which it will have to move.
The elders are also concerned with the internal health and
fitness of the kingdom, with its strength, its freedom from
internal strife, its ability to respond instantly and move
rapidly when situations change. In earlier political communities, the result of the deliberations of the king and his
council was called lawgiving when applied to these internal
affairs as they affected the permanent identity of the kingdom; today it is called "corporation policy" or "the way we
do things here," but the effect is the same.

When specific action has to be taken, this leads to a third
kind of ten-size meeting, when one or more of the king's
group discuss with one or more leading princes or dukes
the action that must be taken to achieve the objectives the
king and his elders have fixed. For any corporate organization, this meeting is the crunch. Sometimes it is an easy,
happy meeting—but all too often it is not. When the policy
of the elders is unwelcome there is a sequence of standard
responses from the divisional head, all of which can cause
friction and resentment. The first is to criticize the objective itself: "Why the hell do we cut home expenditure
anyway?" The elders can easily take offense at this, but in
fact it is a useful opportunity to educate executives in the
wider issues which may one day confront them. And if that
question is answered, the next standard response is to
criticize the application: "Why don't you get the south

region to cut back? They spend far more than I do." This section may well produce, under powerful emotional pressure, a better solution than the elders had seen, and if so they would be foolish not to adopt it. This is easier for them if they have raised the matter as a discussion ("The least damaging way we can see is for you to cut your expenditure—but you may think of some other course") rather than a briefing session ("This is what we have decided you must do"). If the executive sees he has to admit defeat at both these arguments, the third course is to prove that it is impossible. But the elders, by insisting that it must be done, can quickly force him into the position of saying it is impossible for him, leaving them free to suggest they should try and see if one of his subordinate barons could do it for him. Since he knows they would all leap at the chance whether they could do it or not, his fourth and final response is to resort to salvage: to see what he can pick up to replace the loss ("Well, I shall need direct authority over the regional personnel officer, and six extra posts in overseas operations, and an increase in the European budget . . ."), and it is only at this stage that the elders counter by making it clear that his personal status is unchanged and can be enhanced by a successful conclusion of the operation ("We hate having to do this to you of all people, because morale is so high in your division. On the other hand, we believe you can achieve it with as little damage to corporate morale as anyone we know").

This meeting happens in modified form all the way down the corporation, and it should not be rushed: it is an important instrument of vertical communication. Under the pressure of argument, the resentful junior learns, even if traumatically, a number of new and important facts about the wider environment in which he works and the higher considerations which affect his labors. He goes away realizing that to win the next argument by countering with better alternatives, he must think about them from his superior's point of view and not his own—a valuable preparation for succeeding to his senior's job. Equally, it educates the elders, or whichever other corporate superiors have to pass on the bad tidings: by having to meet every objection, they are forced to make sure that their decision is based on solid factual and logical ground, while the facts and the arguments brought forward give them valuable understanding of their subordinate's job and its problems. When this meeting is reduced to brief unexplained directives or replaced by written instructions, one of the prime instruments of corporate communication is removed. In a corporation where everyone has grown up together it is much easier, because on the whole everyone knows how the other will react and takes account of the likely objections while formulating the decision, but in a newly formed or newly merged operation there is no getting away from this meeting if a proper community is to be formed.

The fourth and last small meeting is the one referred to earlier when the king and his elders meet all the divisional heads or departmental managers who make up the ten-group of operational leaders. This is the meeting most often by-passed, since unlike the others there is rarely any immediate operational need for it; but in a dispersed tribe it is of great importance. Its prime function is to make the individual generals look at the whole war, and to give the cabinet of elders an insight into the feelings of the whole army. In corporate terms, the executives go away with a better understanding of their place in the whole enterprise, and the board go away with a fuller and more accurate sense of the feeling of the whole body of the corporation. If all the executives together say the new system of forecasting does not work, it is more forceful than if each one mentions it separately. If half say it does and half say it doesn't, the snags can be argued out here. This is where the elders get the feedback from previous decisions in the most reliable form, and where they get the best guidance on how to achieve in practice the objectives they have determined: "We need to expand our dollar income from synthetics—but should we increase our home production, or start up new plant in dollar areas, or acquire overseas companies, or what?" This is the place where the best practical solutions are likely to appear—not the best view of what needs to be done, but the best view of how to do it.

In a changing situation, this meeting has another significant function: the revision of doctrine. It is the place to question practices which are the result of decisions made long ago when circumstances were different, but which have rigidified into unchanging ritual—the place where everyone should be encouraged to ask "Why?" about any and every time-hallowed and unquestioned assumption and procedure. Often this will result in useful simplification and sometimes considerable money-saving; the Marks and Spencer revolution is the most outstanding example, but many Marks and Spencer men think that the greatest value was not the initial saving but the permanent change of attitude, the continuing revolution, so that every form and document and regular committee meeting and routine procedure comes under constant scrutiny. And even if the answer to the question "Why?" produces a very good reason, the act of uncovering that reason is a valuable piece of education.

There is one other permanent need in every corporate community which this meeting serves: the regulating of boundaries between the separate areas of quasi-territory. A specific dispute between two neighboring executives will normally be sorted out separately; it will only be discussed here if it starts to threaten the unity of the realm, but this is the place to establish and revise the relationship between the executives and the boss, and the principles which regulate the internal boundaries between executives. The less this has to happen, the healthier the state of the corporation. But to keep this sort of discussion low the tribal structure has to be very good: tribes and tribal groupings must have clear objectives with little or no overlap, they must have all the necessary authority and resources to do their job on their own, and there must be no court officials with little enclaves of authority in their gift. When tribal structure is undefined, when functional authorities multiply and the palace grows larger and larger, these sources of uncertainty and dispute spread into every activity, and this meeting has time for little else. The consequence is that it delegates the less pressing topics to a lower level and sets up that bane of corporate life, and prime indicator of structural deficiency: the permanent committee; in other political institutions it is usually called a law court.

The permanent committee is not inherently wrong: it could, for instance, be a good ten-group systematically scrutinizing all aspects of the business and reporting to the board. But nearly always it is a law court, and often gives itself away by terms like "liaison committee" and "coordinating committee," indicating that everyone arrives in a spirit of competition and hostility, briefed to gain the maximum possible advantage for his tribe and to make the fewest possible concessions, and usually with considerable powers to delay or frustrate the reaching of any binding decision. From time to time a subject crops up which unites the whole committee, and it produces a useful decision or recommendation, but then, of course, the committee is no longer a law court: it has become a working ten-group. The more cumbersome and detribalized a corporate organization becomes, the more these law courts multiply and the busier they become. They have a fatal, seductive fascination for underemployed managers and officials: they offer a morning or afternoon of invigorating competitive activity or pleasant somnolent ease, according to choice and the agenda, and give the illusion of achievement without effort or risk. There is no product by which any committee member's performance can be measured, and no outcome for which he can have the responsibility pinned on him. The permanent committees which exist for litigation and negotiation are malignant growths which endlessly consume managerial and executive time without nourishing the body of the corporation, and surgery is the only cure.

XIX

The Tribal Assembly

T H E small meetings of ten-group size take place all the time, and besides serving the needs of corporate digestion and communication they are the instrument through which Corporation Man achieves his daily and monthly and yearly objectives. They are operational necessities, whereas the other two larger kinds are not. But in a dispersed tribe, the other two take on a special importance which is almost entirely connected with digestion and communication, and has little if any operational value. The problem they can solve is the problem of passing it on: however good the communication within ten-groups, the report the divisional executive brings back to his ten-group of regional heads is not the unblemished reflection of the real event, and by the time the regional heads talk to their area managers another selecting and distorting lens has been interposed. Even if the instruction of what they have to do is faithfully preserved and accurately transmitted, the reason why they are doing it has probably taken a bashing on the way down, and the image of the chairman and the board which they piece together is bound to be a grotesque caricature of the reality. Even the most loyal, honest, and devoted executives will—indeed must—carry back a violently distorted selection of events; the less loyal or honest can play havoc with them to their own advantage. And the same applies in reverse: at each level the members of the ten-group will tell their leader about the feelings of their tribes, and this too is bound to be selected, even if unconsciously, to help their own cases. It is this defect in the two-way repeater chain which is responsible for much of the failure of the corporate transmission system.

This defect can only be remedied by the king and his elders going and explaining the reasons for decisions to far more people than is practicable in ten-groups, and by that same large number of people being given the opportunity of asking the questions that are on their minds and getting grievances off their chests. This need seems to be best served by a meeting that can comfortably reach a size of forty or fifty, and perhaps go up to a hundred. It is large enough for everyone to realize that it cannot be conducted as a general discussion, but not so large as to inhibit questions from anyone who wants to ask. Once numbers rise above a hundred or so, people feel it is assertive to claim the privilege of asking one of the few questions there is time for, so nobody asks any, or only the top people do; there are deep inhibitions about asking questions when you feel that your status in the group is low. For this reason the status-spread should not be too great either. And finally, but most important, it is vital to the success of this meeting that there should be a fair amount of dialogue, so once the numbers reach the point where anyone has to raise their voice above normal conversational level, the success of the meeting is threatened. As I have said, my own experience suggests forty or fifty as the size which most satisfactorily meets all these requirements, with a hundred as the upper limit; there is, of course, no lower limit until the point where it changes to a ten-group discussion.

If these meetings are held regularly, they do not need to be held frequently; the royal progress is usually one good occasion for them, and if every member of the king's dispersed tribe takes part in one of these sessions a year with the king, that should serve admirably. Its effect, of course, is to correct the distortion. If you can match the executive's account of the meeting against your memory of the man you listened to and questioned and even argued with, you are much more likely to deduce the reason behind the decision even if it is inaccurately relayed to you; equally, if you felt any warmth toward the king (and I believe there is built into us an instinct to do so if we possibly can), you will be inclined to choose the more charitable of two possible explanations. And, of course, the simple act of saying what you wanted to say to the man you wanted to say it to can relieve pent-up frustrations wonderfully.

There is a further value to these meetings if the king is wise and reasonably secure. Two of the major disqualifications for a leader are to be deaf to the warning signals from the pack and to fail to learn from past experience. At these meetings the king can remove fears that he may suffer from either. Candid admission of past errors usually works marvelously in these gatherings: "Yes, the 450 model was a ghastly failure, wasn't it? I'll tell you what we did wrong . . ." The audience is not worried by the failure one-tenth as much as by the fear that the board might still be pretending to themselves that it was a success. The other necessity is to take all reasonable suggestions and criticisms seriously by really arguing them out ("I think you're right about the demand, but how would we produce them that cheaply?"), rather than crushing them with authority ("Sorry, it wouldn't work—Next?") or patronizing by too easy acceptance ("Good idea, we'll certainly discuss it"). If the purpose of one of these meetings is to give early advice of new plans or products or procedures, it is a good occasion for the king to get guidance on specific applications and practical difficulties which may be seen more clearly by people closer to the tribesmen who will have to put them into effect: for that reason they should be presented before that sort of detail is fixed beyond revision.

Everyone in the king's dispersed tribe should attend at least one of these meetings with the king a year; but they may well need to attend several others where he is not present, either within their own tribe or with people doing similar work in other tribes: the fifty-group meeting of area sales managers, of production engineers, of plant accountants, of research managers. The larger the corporation, the more often these meetings need to be held. It is all too easy for valuable ideas, information, and experience to be locked up in a lot of isolated ten-groups dotted around the corporation. These larger meetings can turn these little pools of valuable folk wisdom from a scattering of stagnant ponds into a chain of linked reservoirs. It is no good hoping to do it by circulars and memoranda—it must be by personal contact. This is because—to revert to an earlier parallel— the fifty-group meeting is another chain in the digestive process. Anything brought to this meeting will have already been chewed over by a ten-group, but it needs a further stage of argument and discussion and collective rumination before it can be circulated right through the corporation.

Obviously, the small tribal firm hardly needs to arrange this sort of meeting: if they are all in the same geographical location, exchanges of this kind will take place informally without prearrangement. But in larger companies and corporations it is all too easy for outlying tribes to become narrow and isolated. They are cut off from the process of learning and adapting which is constant at the center, and they make mistakes and miss opportunities in a way which seems incredible to anyone who has kept up to date. The royal progress alone cannot remedy this: a good network needs lateral as well as radial links, and these occasional meetings of fifty or so people from different tribes are the best means of constructing and maintaining them.

The last of the three kinds of meeting is the assembly of the whole tribe, the gathering together of five hundred to a thousand people. There is no possibility here of dialogue and not much point in inviting questions; the assembly is an audience. And whereas anybody can chip in to a ten-group discussion, and most executives can handle a group of fifty to a hundred of their subordinates, a full assembly is daunting to those who have never addressed one before. It requires experience, confidence, and a certain amount of technique: ordinary conversational voice levels and ordinary small movements of the facial muscles and hands will not carry beyond the twelfth row, and if a microphone is used as a substitute for technique it only makes a flat and dull performance audible at the back. Perhaps this is why the full assembly is the most disastrously under-used management instrument in the modern corporation; firms with large numbers of salesmen or agents usually realize the value of it, but the corporate need is not restricted to salesmen.

What happens to a group of individuals when they become an audience? I have worked in television since 1955, and so could claim at this moment some sixteen years' experience of audiences; but in fact the television audience watches in groups of two or three, and the broadcaster does not perceive any instant and continuing reaction from it. Until 1963 I had no more real experience of audiences than anyone else who has been to the theater and cinema, football matches, church services, speeches and lectures and school prize-givings, and all the other events where two or three hundred are gathered together; but in the autumn of 1963 I had to produce a television program in front of a studio audience, and I have been involved in audience programs ever since. In recent years I have also had to address audiences myself from time to time. When I began, I searched for guidance on the general nature and principles of audiences, and found

none at all that was of any use except for a most interesting
theory about laughter from the French philosopher Bergson,
which I will come to in a moment. So I plugged into the
folklore network and went to the nerve center of audience
expertise, the executives of the popular entertainment business: they were as mystified as everyone else. Sometimes you
had good audiences and sometimes you had bad audiences,
and that was that. And so in the absence of any general
theory I had to work it out for myself in practice by trial
and error; this was interesting enough on its own, but as I
thought more and more about evolutionary theory in terms
of population genetics and cultural anthropology it became
more than interesting—it started to look extremely significant. All the same I have to issue a warning that what follows
is my own theory and lacks any scientific backing: but even
if the theoretical explanation is wrong, the practical observations are still true to my personal experience. An incorrect
explanation can still be an illuminating metaphor.

The first question to ask is "When is an audience not an
audience?" In theory the question is unanswerable: the
number can be quite small if they all know each other and
the speaker, and if they are closely packed in a tight space
in the dark. If they are all total strangers and have never
seen the speaker before and are scattered thinly around a
huge, high, light auditorium, then twenty times the first
number may still fail to become an audience. But in practice,
for the purposes of studio television programs when every
seat is filled, we set a minimum of two hundred to two
hundred and fifty, though we would like more. The crucial
measuring instrument is laughter; the point at which a joke
gets an immediate solid laugh instead of a scattering of smiles
and sniggers and titters is the point at which a group of
single individuals has become an audience. Once that point
has been reached, you are in communication not with a wide
range of diverse intellects, but with a single collective entity:
after a while you do not hope a joke will get a laugh, you

know it will, and that knowledge itself is a guarantee that you will deliver it with such confidence that it does get the laugh.

Laughter is central to the understanding of audience behavior. Bergson explains it as an act of collective aggression, on the grounds that it is rare for individuals to laugh when they are on their own and that the baring of the teeth and shortening of the breath are physical expressions of aggression. At first sight this is ridiculous: laughter is warm and friendly, not aggressive at all. On reflection, however, it is less ridiculous: the warmth and friendliness are within the laughing group. If you are the only person not laughing in a roomful of laughing people, and even more if they are all laughing at you and against you, the friendliness vanishes and you realize the exclusion and aggression it implies. The comedian who makes us laugh is identifying an aggression focus, a kind of behavior or attitude or person we reject or exclude, often (according to Bergson) for ancient survival reasons—it is behavior which can lead the hunting band or the tribe into danger. (Compare the hooting of cars at the motorist whose road behavior endangers everyone's survival.) Even the man who treads on a banana skin represents this in a basic way: he is too inflated with his own importance to notice small danger signals, the high-dominance, low-intelligence leader who spells extinction for the group. Most broad humor depends on someone's unawareness of what the rest of us know. This is too complex a theory to pursue any further here, but the important point is clear: laughter is a collective activity which affirms and defines group membership and identity and standards by what it excludes and whom it includes.

Queen Victoria's diaries revealed to me a significant aspect of laughter. I had dipped into them once or twice in the library, and smiled quietly at the naïve charm of the early entries. Then I went to a performance of *The Hollow Crown*, an anthology of the literary efforts of English monarchs, and in a crowded theater I listened to Peggy Ashcroft reading some of the same extracts. The whole audience fell about with almost painful laughter, and I was doubled up with as much ecstatic anguish as anyone. Why? I had already read those passages. I had been interested and mildly amused. Now, without any alterations, those same passages were making tears stream from my eyes and causing acute discomfort in the diaphragm.

What had happened was that when I read the diaries in the library they generated a small private amusement, but with Peggy Ashcroft's art in a packed theater they generated a collective discovery for all of us in the audience, a discovery of unity and identity precipitated by our realization that Queen Victoria was not one of us. In the library I discovered that the diaries amused me; in the theater I discovered that they were funny, and the fat man next to me dabbing his eyes and gasping for breath as if for mercy was as much an instrument of that discovery as Peggy Ashcroft's technical mastery. And the same can happen in reverse: film sequences which made me sob with laughter in a crowded cinema raise no more than a slight smile when rerun on television a few years later. Often the discovery is simple reaffirmation of a uniting emotion, but sometimes it can have national importance; we shall never know how many people were privately amused before 1961 by Macmillan and the rest of the British politicians, but *Beyond the Fringe* and *That Was the Week* transformed the private amusement into a collective realization that they were funny, and the British national attitude toward politics has never returned to the solemn respectfulness of the 1950's.

Laughter is the key to understanding the nature of audiences, but there are other indicators too: applause, cheers, booing, restless movement and withdrawal of attention, extreme stillness and silence—all these, even if they start with one person, can quickly generalize into a collective reaction. And together they add up to a language: it is a very primitive and limited language, closer to the baying and grunting and barking of animals than to human speech, but it is sufficient for its purpose—and the purpose is a collective tribal communication with the speaker. I have said that "community" and "communication" come from the same root; so does "communion." If the speaker is in communion with the community, they communicate, and the audience's expressions of collective response tell him at each stage how the community is accepting him. Lloyd George, who understood audiences as well as most people, used to go to large public meetings with half a dozen topics in his head which would each have done for a speech. He would start on one of them, and if it aroused no response he would move on to the next, and so on until he felt more reaction. Then he would develop that topic, and at each stage thereafter the audience reaction would guide him toward the areas in which he could best express the emotions, the aspirations, and the aggressions in which they found their strongest unity. He was sometimes accused of inventing government policy while he was speaking; perhaps there are worse times to invent it. I have seen something similar myself. In the autumn of 1965 a Labour MP on the Frost program defended the government's record on the grounds that it was still coping with the results of thirteen years of Tory misrule. This had been said by many MP's on many television programs for the past eighteen months; but the Frost program had a studio audience of two hundred, and they broke into a spontaneous groan. For the first time, the community had a chance to communicate its views on that line of defense, and it was never heard again.

For the corporate tribe, and above all for the dispersed tribe, the full assembly is a unique and irreplaceable instrument of communication. It enables the leader—king or elder, duke or courtier or tribal chieftain—to sense the true collective feeling with a certainty that is beyond flattery or politeness or misrepresentation. It enables the whole tribe to decide if the leader is leading them in the right way, and to warn or encourage him collectively without risking personal careers or reputations. Above all, it enables the tribe to make a collective discovery of its identity—what it stands for and what it stands against, what it believes in and is proud of, what it rejects and despises. There is a deep need to know this tribal feeling. With the decline of large political meetings, which told us very well, has come the rise of the opinion poll; the decline of other large gatherings has generated the top-ten lists for records, books, films, and television programs: all of these attempt to remedy the loss of this ancient method of reflecting the collective tribal reaction, but none of them provides the sensitive living interaction between all the assembled individuals which gives such power and truth to the instantaneous response of an audience.

I am sure this need to congregate in groups of five hundred or so is a primitive one; how primitive is another matter. It might be a part of the mechanism for regulating the population of the tribe, the coming together to see how many of us there are this year and to update our ability to recognize the separate individuals from other camps and hunting bands; and as I suggested earlier, if there was a dangerous surplus of young people it might be at this gathering that emotions rose beyond the normal to the hysterical, with violent consequences. But does it go back to our ancestral species, or is it tied up with language and the enlargement of the brain and the emergence a few hundred thousand years ago of our own species? Did the speaker emerge and give a focus to an existing unstructured assembly, or did the assembly grow from speakers and small gatherings? I am now in the region of pure guesswork, but I would plump for the former, and the reason is song. There is still some strange irrational compulsion for a tightly-knit group to have its song: schools, regiments, football teams, religious groups, political parties, revolutionary movements—it expresses and affirms unity at a depth that is beyond words. It is a primitive ritual chant which could have grown out of a group before the development of language, or at least alongside it. The singing of its song by a group can draw out collective emotion and express solidarity in a way that nothing else can, though the time and place and mood must be right. When they are wrong, it sticks in your throat: how shall we sing the Lord's song in a strange land?

I do not know of any systematic research into the songs of the modern corporations, but I know they have them— or had them. IBM in its earlier days had a book of IBM songs which they sang to familiar tunes, though if you confront the suave and sophisticated modern IBM executives with their memories of it you encounter the slightly sheepish evasions of emotion recollected in embarrassment. NCR had a song, and so did (does?) Hoover, and I am sure there are many others. I would dearly like to know when the songs started, when they stopped, how those events related to the growth and profitability of the company and the number of staff employed. The great place for corporation songs today is Japan ("Grow, industry, grow, grow, grow! Harmony and sincerity! Matsushita Electric!"), and in some companies it is sung before work every day, almost as if it were part of the morning service.

I do not suggest that the route to corporate success lies in teaching all staff a song and making them sing it together in groups of five hundred: song expresses a unity that already exists, it does not create it when it is not there. I do, however, suggest that everyone in the corporation needs to attend at least one meeting of five hundred people—one tribal assembly—each year, and that if the meeting bursts into community singing at the end of it the sense of belonging to the corporation will, to say the least, not be damaged. But it is the coming together that matters, even in the comfortable, easy, prosperous, centrifugal fat years—though it is in the centripetal lean years when the cold winds blow that Corporation Man most needs to affirm his membership of the tribe and have the tribe confirm it. In times of danger, insecurity, and threat to collective survival—powerful enemies at hand, the loss of a trusted leader, profound and disturbing changes, terrible disasters which threaten livelihood—the need becomes so strong that the assembly is likely to take place anyway, even if it is held by the union leader outside the factory gates. The question then becomes not "Shall we hold a meeting?" but "Who is the real leader of the tribe?" I suspect that even in the most primitive times, the tribal assembly was the occasion where the tribal leader proved his leadership by public acclamation. It does not have to be a formal gathering: an annual dinner or cocktail party with a speech from the king or chieftain may be enough for some tribes, whereas others, if they are more geographically isolated and dispersed during the year, may want to take over a theater or cinema and devote a day or more to the occasion and build other small- or medium-sized meetings into it as well. But the leader's speech to the whole tribe is the climax.

Apart from collective acclamation and confirmation of the leader, this assembly contributes to corporate unity in a number of different ways which are perhaps worth listing:

It permits the tribe to see itself as a group and discover basic facts about themselves: "We're mostly over 50." "We're a young bunch." "There's only two women among the lot of us." "A lot of people look less prosperous than last year." These facts may be important when deciding how much weight to give to various group reactions.

As mentioned earlier, it allows the group to make statements and discoveries about its collective identity through its reactions to speeches by the leader and others.

It gives the leader an opportunity to demonstrate his fitness to lead the tribe by showing them that he is in touch with their feelings, that he is hearing the signals from within. ("I guess we've all had our bellyful of economy drives that start out as fundamental reappraisals of policy and end up as thinner carbon paper and thicker toilet paper. Though I suppose the toilet paper is fundamental in its way.")

In the same way it lets the leader show he is aware of the tribe's environment, the competition and the customers and all the marketing considerations. ("We have to face the fact that the days when we could blind our customers with science are over.")

It is a proving ground for new aspirants to high office. Speeches by elders, dukes, and courtiers give the tribe a chance to make collective judgments about leaders other than the king, which may among other things sort out the succession.

It is an opportunity to keep status in line with achievement, and bestow status on those who have earned it in the ways that best serve the survival needs of the group. ("A special mention for the appliances division, who in a tough situation brought out four new models and have moved up from fifth to second place in market share. The 480 model only took seven months from the go-ahead to the launch.")

It is the place to confirm old aggression focuses and identify new ones ("There's a firm around—I'm not mentioning any names—who don't seem to care very much about the safety of the consumer. In fact I hear that with their latest dishwasher they're throwing in an offer of free funeral expenses.")

The standards of group behavior can be confirmed and clarified by judicious apportioning of praise and blame. (". . . been too prissy and uptight with the press. But we're improving. I saw a statement from Harry Ferguson, the southwest regional manager, last month. A couple of years ago, the manager would have said, 'No comment,' but Harry said, 'If any customer's unhappy, you can take it from me that the corporation's unhappy.' That's what we have to aim for . . .")

In a changing situation, this is the best time for the king to make sense out of recent experience, to show the pattern it fits into and indicate what general collective lessons should be drawn from the experience, what doctrinal points must be reviewed or changed, what new doctrines are being developed.

Following on the above: This is a unique opportunity to point new directions, to start moving away from established practices and long-standing assumptions, to prepare the tribe for a change in its internal arrangements or external identity.

Whatever else happens, this is a time to reaffirm the faith (". . . quality of our products, and our service to the community by enabling our fellow citizens to lead an easier and richer life . . .") and show that it remains unchanged and unchangeable.

In a self-contained tribal community—a village, a little one-man firm of a few hundred—all these objectives will be achieved by the informal network that grows up over the years among people who spend all their working lives together, who grow up and grow old side by side. They will gather together from time to time when they need to, but it can happen spontaneously and without arrangement. This informal network, however, cannot exist naturally in a dispersed tribe: it has to be built up, and the three kinds of meeting described in these chapters are the frame it is built on. In a corporation that has grown organically and not too rapidly there is likely to be a fairly good informal network anyway, and probably enough of these meetings will take place for operational purposes to keep it working. But in a new corporation, or one that has grown rapidly, or one that has acquired or merged with others—indeed wherever the natural organic community does not exist but has to be manufactured—these meetings become more and more important whether operations demand them or not. Under heat and pressure and with the exhilaration of success, a ten-group can be formed in a few weeks: intensity of experience is a fair substitute for simple duration in the forming of human communities, though the links formed so quickly need to be constantly maintained to hold the group together, in a way that is not necessary in a community with deeper roots. But the larger meetings do not happen with the natural spontaneity of the hunting band; they have to be convened as a deliberate act of policy.

If a corporation is to adapt to change, to be flexible in its operations, then a flourishing healthy community with frequent contact in every kind of grouping and cross-grouping is the only real way; so long as everyone in the dispersed tribe understands what the whole job is, where the tribe is going, where he fits into it and what everyone else is up to, so long as there is a rich informal network with people thinking with or ahead of each other and confident of each other's loyalty, then there are insurances and safety nets at every point. Without this sort of community you have to fall back on authority: operations have to be controlled by detailed and explicit instructions, by regulations, memos, edicts, rulings, standing orders, and ritual observances, and the driving power is supplied by sticks and carrots. Then the instructions are misunderstood, the rulings are wrongly worded and half the people do not hear about the alterations, the memos are countermanded, the edicts are not sent to European operations because someone was off with the flu, the ritual observances are continued long after they stop serving a useful purpose, the sticks do not hurt and nobody likes the taste of the carrots; and we say we have a breakdown in communication. That breakdown is the result of trying to extend the old system of functionaries carrying out unchanging procedures on standard products into a world where no procedures are unchanging and no products are standard and the only functionaries are machines. The answer, as we all know, is to decentralize operations; but decentralized operations are chaos and anarchy unless all the people responsible for them are strongly centralized in their minds and their hearts, so that however scattered they are, they all belong to a true community, a strong and united king's tribe.

X X

Authority, Doctrine, and Ritual

T H E tribe is a very ancient unit; the kingdom, formed and held together by the king's tribe, is much more recent—perhaps only a few thousand years old. We have seen how the king's tribe, the dispersed tribe, is kept together as a genuine tribe by a formal or informal system of meetings and assemblies; it remains to look at the corporate kingdom as a whole and examine those elements in it which are inseparable from any grouping that has to hold a number of tribes together in a permanent relationship. Some have already been dealt with or touched on in previous chapters, but I feel it is worth mentioning them again to give completeness to this summary and to show how they fit into the framework of the corporate state.

It is only recently that the nature of the corporate state, as distinct from its management, has become so important. In the days when the product was the dominant idea, the

company was bound up with the act of producing something: its responsibility stretched into the heart of every
tribe, issuing designs, ordering machinery, controlling production processes, as if it were the manager of every factory.
Only one ten-group, the board of the company, had any
need of initiative or creativeness or enterprise; the rest were
asked to contribute only skill, efficiency, honesty, and compliance with instructions. But over the last fifty years or
more there has been a wider and wider extension of the
functions of the creative entrepreneur throughout the corporation. Today's tribal chieftain is measured no longer simply
by the efficiency with which his tribe executes orders and
carries out prescribed functions, but more and more by his
flexible and enterprising response to changes in the technology and the market. Tomorrow's prizes are reserved for
the corporations that are made up of networks of enterprising and profitable small companies, tribal in size, and almost
self-contained, left as far as possible to their own devices.

But how far is "as far as possible"? Or to put the question
another way, where do we stop on the road from bureaucracy
to anarchy? Bureaucracy is the first response to complexity:
coordinate at the center, have specialist departments at the
center, refer queries and anomalies to the center, issue instructions from the center, hold information at the center,
keep power at the center. As we have seen, the end of this
process has been delayed by the apparatus of typewriters,
duplicators and copiers, telex and telephone, which have
given the center the illusion of control long after the reality
has departed. But the bureaucratic, highly centralized approach to the running of the corporate kingdom has been
losing ground for some years, and in its place we see the
development of the multiplicity of "profit centers," the
development of a larger and larger number of these virtually
separate businesses within a single corporate kingdom. The
greatest and hardest change is an emotional one: the change
from controlling people to trusting them; the change from
giving them functions and procedures and checking that they

have performed the functions and carried out the procedures, to giving them power, resources, and a target, and letting them use the first two to hit the third by whatever functions and procedures they choose.

It is, of course, a much better system in survival terms. A number of discrete cells are in less danger than a single vast cell. The succession is far better secured if there are many heads of businesses to choose from than if all senior men except the chairman and chief executive are specialists in production or research or sales or accountancy, with no experience of priority balancing for overall profitability. It is also much more satisfying in human terms—far more people are given the chance to grow and expand to the limit of their ability, to use with greater freedom their instincts to explore and compete and create, if every tribe has the liberty to try out its own ideas in its own way. But as this process accelerates it raises in the most acute form the question "What is the corporation?" How far can you go on and on decentralizing operations and delegating authority and still remain in effect rather than just in name the unit to which all the others belong? What are the basic elements of sovereignty which must be kept at the center, in an African kingdom or a medieval state, in the Roman Empire or the British navy or General Motors, however much independent power is allowed to the men whose provinces or territories or baronies or operating divisions combine to form the corporate kingdom? What has to be lost before the unity is broken, the center loses control, and the kingdom degenerates from a living reality into an empty name?

To answer these questions with specific reference to the modern corporation, we have to ignore the tremendous diversity of operations which make up the daily and monthly and yearly tasks of the hunting bands, and examine the part that does not change—the apparatus of permanence which has been growing up inside corporations under pressure of necessity, as it grows up in all large human organizations that intend to endure. And when we look closer, we see that

it is composed of four elements, and that they are responses
to the four ways in which the corporation can be destroyed:
conquest by outside enemies, tearing apart by internal strife,
loss of strength and skill and vigor until it decays and wastes
away, and loss of cohesion until the grouping falls apart into
single tribes. These four dangers are ever-present—all but
the last threatened even the primitive hunting tribe—but
they are a much more powerful threat to a less natural,
larger grouping like a state or a corporation. The larger
grouping is a response to the first danger, the threat from
outside, but it makes the next two much more acute, and
creates the fourth. Together these four elements determine
the role of the king—the corporate chairman—since they are
all central to the survival of the kingdom; but as corporations decentralize, every duke and baron (or profit-responsible executive) encounters them in a lesser degree and every
member of the king's tribe needs to be aware of them.

To be strong in defense and dangerous in attack, the king
needs a powerful army and the chairman needs large profits.
They are much closer to each other than they appear at
first sight. An early agricultural community living off poor
soil may have to keep everyone at work all the time to scrape
a subsistence; there will be no one to spare for training and
weapon manufacture and maneuvers, while eating the food
produced by the others, since the others are flat out producing enough for themselves. But as the community finds new
crops and learns better farming methods, it has some produce to spare, some surplus over running costs, in fact some
profits. It can use these to feed its own young men while
they build fortifications or train for the army, or to pay
mercenaries. In the public corporation it works in a surprisingly similar way: the best defense against takeover is a
share price high above the asset value, and this is achieved
by a long and strong profit record or a high expectation of
future profit. There is little point in paying five hundred
million for a company whose net worth is only one hundred
million, unless they will go on working as willingly and

successfully for you as for the previous owner: you either rule them with their consent and approval, or risk losing a fortune. On the other hand a company with a disastrous profit record, valued by the market at seventy million and whose assets can be sold off for a hundred million is asking for a hostile takeover. And, of course, it works in attack as well as defense—a highly valued company can buy up others with its own shares at a far lower real cost than the cash equivalent.

For this reason the chairman more than anyone else in the corporation is pressing for profits to distribute, and he often has to press against considerable resistance. The tribal chieftains look upon them as taxes: they would much rather have all the money back again for next year's budget, to build up their tribe's power and status—and their own status within the tribe—by putting the profit to new buildings and plant, more staff and higher salaries, or perhaps a higher standard of tribal hospitality. If a chairman has a proper organization of profit-responsible tribes, there will for this reason be tremendous pressure from the chieftains to close down loss-making areas of the business when they see their hard-won profits being poured away into them. It is painful enough to see profit distributed; to see it dissipated is unbearable. Just like taxes, profits can always be a source of tension between the king and his chieftains, and the tension is increased or relaxed depending on their judgment of how wisely the profits are being employed; but the discipline of profit is at the root of corporate existence. When Durant was running General Motors, the separate divisions had their own bank accounts and the chairman had to go around almost with a begging bowl to get the money for central operations. With such an arrangement it is questionable whether General Motors could have been properly called a corporation at all. I suspect that even in a communist state, the low-cost, high-efficiency industry is very strong and much harder to meddle with than the weaker ones: the state has too much need of it to take risks.

Strength in attack and defense is the first requirement of any corporation or state or tribe, but not the only one. As the competing kingdoms establish their external identity, as each carves out its niche, there are many differences which can be resolved without war. For states, this heralds the growth of diplomacy; for the corporation, it means the growth of new or greatly enlarged departments at the court of the corporate king. To protect the strength and external identity of the corporation may mean protracted lawsuits, sensitive negotiations with the government, ingenious arrangements with overseas capital markets, major rearrangements for taxation purposes, or swift action on vehicle safety or pollution control. There may be licensing or joint trading agreements with other corporations; new companies may have to be taken over and incorporated. To enable the best decisions to be taken, masses of facts will have to be compiled about what is happening in the world outside. No important decisions of this nature can be delegated, because only the king combines in one person the understanding of the corporation, the understanding of the world beyond it, the responsibility for its future identity, and the power to make things happen; but a large number of people can be employed to collect and digest the information on which his decision will be based.

There is one further significant point about the corporation's external identity: if the corporation is a large and important one, that identity will be a factor in many outside people's attitudes and decisions; how foreign governments, members of congress, civil servants, graduates, and local government bodies make up their minds about the corporation and what decision they come to may significantly affect that corporation's future. Is it a tough, money-grabbing, polluting, hire-and-fire industrial juggernaut with nothing but contempt for the community, or is it a creative, enlightened, public-spirited group of intelligent and civilized human beings dedicated to improving the quality of life? One reputation or the other may have a profound effect on

permissions, concessions, recruitment and government legislation, and it usually depends not so much on facts learned
from experience as on impressions picked up from television,
newspapers, advertisements, and hearsay. Moreover, this
reputation is endangered whenever even the most junior
official talks to the press. An assistant manager of a small
and remote upcountry factory of a vast corporation has only
to say to a reporter, "Frankly, our company's policy is to
maximize profits and let the community sweep up the mess,"
to have the chairman bursting blood vessels. It is often this
sensitive and passionate concern with reputation (or "image") that gives a chairman a name for interfering with
detail: but that sort of detail is no detail. Any branch executive of Coca-Cola may perhaps choose his own advertising
agency without referring the decision higher; but if the ad
is a couple of half-naked hippies sipping Cokes on an anti-
Vietnam protest march, he is damaging the image of the
good clean fresh healthy patriotic American beverage in a
way that is very much the chairman's concern. Consequently,
more new departments of state grow up around the chairman in his capacity as custodian of the corporate image:
press relations, public relations, prestige advertising, pam-
phlets, films, lecture services, community relations, and even
a college of heralds (now called design consultants) to devise
heraldic badges, crests, symbols, colors, and livery which will
suggest "modern technology" or "friendly and intimate"
or "reliable," and carry them blazoned on products, con-
tainers, vans, and airplanes to the furthest corners of the
globe.

It is, however, not sufficient to preserve the corporation
from its enemies and strengthen its bonds with its friends if
rebellion and civil war are destroying the corporation from
within. To prevent this, every kingdom has had to evolve
the second element in the apparatus of permanence, and for
this the essential instrument is the king's authority. Just
how far that authority extends in practice is something every
kingdom and corporation must work out for itself: what

some executives would think an intolerable intrusion into their division's operations would be unquestionably accepted as normal practice by their counterparts in another firm. In the best corporations the informal understanding within the king's dispersed tribe usually ensures that the question never has to be raised. But even in the loosest and most utterly decentralized organization, three absolutes remain. The first is the acceptance of the king's authority. However much freedom of operation is allowed to executive dukes and managerial chieftains, there are times when the wider interests of collective survival demand actions which, from the point of view of their dukedom or tribe alone, look misguided or damaging. The history tribe of our learning-systems kingdom may think it crazy to postpone the modern history course, with its wealth of film and photographic material and a strong interest expressed by California and Texas, in favor of the less promising medieval history series; but if the corporation is closing a deal with the governments of New Zealand and Australia for a complete secondary course in all subjects for every school in the land, then if they want medieval history they must have it. If the history chieftain tells the king he must wait till the modern course is complete and so loses the deal, most of the point of belonging to the kingdom is destroyed—it has degenerated into a sales agency. If the king cannot enforce obedience in such a case, he has no kingdom.

Even in the absence of this sort of defiance, the king may still have to exercise his authority over the internal affairs of a tribe. If a frontier province is so incompetently governed that the enemy can easily overrun it, then the whole kingdom is in danger. If the science division has such a bad reputation for the quality of its scholarship that we keep losing contracts to provide entire courses for whole schools in all subjects, then our corporate survival is threatened. In both cases the king has no alternative: the frontier or the division must be strengthened even if it means removing the responsible governor or executive; and, of course, the corollary of this is the king's authority to remove any man from his office if the safety of the kingdom requires it.

The second absolute is the acceptance of the king's jurisdiction, his verdict on matters of internal disagreement. Internal disputes are inevitable in any tribe or kingdom, especially when areas of quasi-territory overlap. Who should authorize advertisements in the national press—marketing or advertising? When marketing takes the responsibility, advertising says the ads put their image in Washington back to where it was ten years ago. When advertising takes over, marketing says they lose fifty thousand dollars' worth of business with every shot. Only the king can resolve this dispute, and once he has given his ruling there can be no further argument. If he says advertising must have the final say, and the chief marketing executive then puts in an ad without submitting it, then he must be banished. If he is not, most of the corporation's energy will soon be consumed in civil war.

The third absolute is allegiance. Kings may vary in the tolerance they show to vices such as incompetence or laziness, but there can be no tolerance of treason. Giving damaging information to the press or betraying plans to a rival are the actions of an enemy, and anyone who does so declares himself an enemy of the king; these are unpardonable offenses. Probably the most acute moral discomfort that the modern manager or executive suffers in his relationship with the corporation is when he applies for a job with its rival; even approaching a friend in another part of the corporation to suggest a transfer to his division can provoke furtive and guilty behavior.

These are the two prime duties of any king or chieftain or chairman, of any man who embodies the unity of a number of groups who band together for collective survival: he must secure the organization or state against destruction from without, whether by enemies or the forces of nature or circumstance, and he must preserve it from destruction from within, whether by treason, rebellion, or civil war. If he fails

in either of these tasks, the failure is immediately visible
and the consequences are likely to be sudden and dramatic.
But the fact that the kingdom or corporation exists at all as
an independent unit is proof that these tasks are being
discharged, even if only precariously and with minimal
efficiency. But when we move on to the other two requirements of collective survival, this is not so; failure in these
can go on for a long time with no sudden surge of alarm
or resentment and no sense of crisis. It is a much slower
process, but it is also far more common among our large
corporations. If they also lack a clear structure of ten-groups
and tribes and chieftains, their situation is enormously
worsened: but even with a good and clear structure they can
fail through this gradual diminution of efficiency and alienation of people. When corporations complain about the
problems of size, and envy the flexibility and dynamism (not
to mention the profits) of smaller companies, they have
fallen down on the first of these tasks. When they complain
about lack of loyalty and people concerned only with their
pay checks and the loss of the old sense of belonging to the
corporation, then they have fallen down on the second.

The first concerns corporate health and vitality and mus-
cularity, fitness in the sense of "survival of the fittest." In
the simplest terms of a primitive hunting tribe, if the game
keeps getting away from the hunting bands then the tribe
is on the road to extinction. The failure of a single hunt
may be a mistake in the planning or carrying out of tasks;
in corporate terms, a disappointing result for the year may
be traced to a misjudgment of market or production capacity.
If so, it is the fault of the chief executive, and the kingdom
may still be sound. But the hunt may fail because the
hunters are getting fat and slow, there is confusion about
roles, no one trusts the man in charge, the only hunter who
could read the signs was off visiting another tribe, or someone forgot to mention about the lions who were hunting in
the same area the night before. If the corporate parallels
of that kind of failure keep happening, it is beyond the

power of any chief executive to put things right: like physical fitness, corporate fitness takes time to build and it requires constant effort and attention to maintain it. It is a part of the total corporate identity, and since the king's job is to ensure the long-term survival of his kingdom whatever changes and challenges it meets in the world outside, its fitness to meet those challenges in the long term is his constant responsibility.

The seat of a corporation's fitness is its doctrine, the great volume of tribal wisdom built up over the years to guide it in all its dealings with the outside world and keep it constantly adapting to its environment. Doctrine, as we have seen, is a body of principles and general lessons argued out by a group of people on the basis of their experience, and then proved in practice and accepted by everyone. Every ten-group and tribe has its own doctrine, but the king is the fountainhead and all other doctrine is a more and more detailed application of the doctrine of the king and his elders. Every corporate activity—product design, pricing policy, advertising methods, process planning, bonus schemes, the lot—is a product of doctrine: policy made or action taken on the basis of shared and rationalized experience. Ask the question "Why?" about any established practice in a good corporation and you will encounter an expression of doctrine.

If the corporation is to survive, it must constantly keep doctrine renewed and keep it circulating. The communication network, above all within the king's tribe, is vital to this: any significant new information or experience encountered by anyone in the corporation should come quickly to a member of the king's tribe, and through him into the central pool of tribal knowledge by means of the communication network; it will then be tried out, and finally processed by argument and discussion into an addition to doctrine. Suppose the purchasing manager of a distant factory happens on a new way of bonding metals: he could just keep it to himself, but in a healthy corporation he will mention it to his head of department, who will pass it on to the heads of engineering factories. They give it to their appropriate ten-groups in production engineering; it gets tried out and talked over, and finally passes into manufacturing doctrine as, say, "good for nonferrous metals except at high temperatures." How quickly it gets around to all the people who need to know is one measure of the health and fitness of the corporation.

That is a tiny instance, but hundreds of tiny instances are happening all the time, and if they remain locked up in the isolated ten-groups and tribes where they were discovered the corporation will start to die. It is for this reason that the corporate king has a special responsibility for keeping the communication system alive, for making sure that different groups from his dispersed tribe keep meeting each other, as well as personally visiting as many tribes as possible.

Even if information does circulate, there is another danger: that instead of passing into the living body of corporate doctrine, the information will bounce off solid rock. It is all too easy to accept doctrine as final once it has been formulated, to let it become hard and rigid so that it cannot adapt to a changing world. Even the doctrine of a small ten-group can grow rigid, but the higher up the corporation the rigidity sets in, the more it threatens corporate survival. If the king and elders let their doctrine fossilize, the whole enterprise is in peril, because their doctrine expresses the identity of the whole corporation; all other doctrine is founded on it. For this reason it is the king more than anyone else who has the responsibility for keeping doctrine from becoming fossilized. Once a point of king's doctrine has been established, most people are happy to accept it forever, and the longer it is established the more blasphemous it will seem to question it. But if the king himself brings it out into the open, everyone can discuss it freely—indeed, many of them may have discussed it privately already, but were afraid to risk their reputations by raising it publicly. It is natural to imagine that there must be a good reason for anything a lot of people have assumed for a long time, and it sounds like criticism of one's superiors to suggest they have been acting for years on a false assumption. The king has no superiors to affront: he can establish as doctrine that all questioning of doctrine is good—but only he, as king, can establish it.

Fossilized ritual is almost as dangerous an enemy to corporate fitness as fossilized doctrine. Whole departments can grow around unnecessary ritual. I have heard of (but cannot vouch for) one corporation which developed a sizable department to deal with the purchase and distribution of stationery and office equipment. The purchasing side held endless discussions and negotiations with suppliers; they had a large storage warehouse with a vast inventory and catalog to be updated, a reordering system, annual stocktaking, and expensive fire insurance; every secretary in the corporation had a copy of the catalog with stock numbers, and a variety of order forms; and even so they were always running out or unable to get what they wanted. I am not sure of the amount they saved the day they told the manager to let his secretary go out and buy what she wanted from the local stationer out of petty cash, though it was a startling sum. But the purchasing and indenting ritual had been going on for years without a thought. All ritual should be deemed useless unless it is proved useful; but it cannot be stamped out unless this attitude to corporate rituals is made explicit by the chairman himself, unless he is regularly discovering and pillorying useless pieces of ritual, and unless he publicly commends everyone else who finds and destroys a choice example. There is, of course, far too much for the chairman to eradicate on his own, but it is his concern more than anyone else's. His first survival preoccupation is to keep adapting the corporation to the changes in the world outside, and fossilized ritual combined with fossilized doctrine (and doctrine is only ritualized thought) is the great obstacle to corporate adaptation.

There is one other aspect of fitness which is uniquely the

king's preoccupation: the danger that the tribesmen may grow soft and flabby, and that the young men may not learn the disciplines and skills needed to turn them into good hunters in the years to come. The setting of annual targets is, of course, the province of the prime minister, the chief executive and his line managers, and, of course, they bear much responsibility for keeping the people under them fully stretched; but in fat years they may be able to secure good results even if they relax over costs and time taken. It is in the fat years that the chairman has to worry most, to make sure that the disciplines of cost and quality and time are maintained: it is not just that they are hard to recover when the lean years come—if new people learn the softer ways they may find it physically impossible to tighten up later. If he sees signs of this kind of deterioration, he must step in, however satisfied the chief executive might have been with the results.

But even if the young men do not grow up in the easier and softer ways, they may still be trained to chase the wrong kind of game—the kind that is abundant now but rapidly dying out. This is why the chairman-king has special interest in the recruitment and training of the year's new intake. The managers can only see them as a dead weight to be turned into a useful pair of hands as fast as possible; the king's mind is on the situation fifteen years ahead, when the graduates in their early twenties will be pushing forty. Will the corporation be bursting with research engineers when it needs an army of technical salesmen who speak fluent Japanese? Should every potential tribal chieftain have six months in the tax accountant's department and six months in community relations? Is the whole training program a waste of time—should they learn the job on the job? Will they grow up remote from the men who do the work—is there a horizontal gap being built into the corporation? In the same way he may form a ten-group to study and prepare for a new market or a new technology long before it becomes operationally justifiable simply because he sees that the corporation will have to move in that direction in the years to come. Long-term survival means regeneration and renewal, but these are often a tax on the time and effort of people with enough to do to secure this year's survival—a tax that only the king can impose.

It is also the king who has to watch for the dangerous rise in tribal numbers when times are easy. Everyone can make a good case for recruitment, and if the money is there it is an attractive way to spend it. If the result is new ten-groups all hunting hard, growth of numbers may be no bad thing, so long as new territories are being opened up. The danger arises when the purpose of recruitment is to take some of the load off the existing ten-groups: it may be easy to feed them all in the days of summer sunshine, but the consequence may be the most clamorous and convulsive strife when winter comes. To survive the cycle of dearth and plenty the whole body of the corporation, not just the bodies of its individuals, must remain lean and muscular.

XXI

The Instruments of
Corporate Identity

T H E fourth ingredient in corporate survival is the most
personal of all. External strength, internal order, the general
fitness and flexibility of the corporation—these are primarily
the concern of the king's dispersed tribe and the various
levels of management. But cohesion, the sense of belonging
to the whole corporation, of being a citizen of no mean city—
this is something that grows (or fails to grow) inside every
single employee. On his first day at work a man is conscious
of little more than just doing a job, and he encounters only
the foreman and a few other men and women; after a while
he may be accepted on probation as part of a ten-group;
later still he may be a full member of the ten-group and
begin to feel part of the whole tribe; but even if he becomes a foreman or a manager there is no need for him
ever to go further. Tribal membership is enough for any
tribesman. It is not, however, enough for the corporation:

if it is composed of tribes that are totally self-sufficient, it is on the edge of anarchy, of falling back into its component parts, of being utterly at the mercy of its tribal chieftains, of totally losing control over its external identity. If it wants to operate as a single corporate unit and not a holding company, it has to find ways of making every individual feel he belongs not only to his tribe, but to the corporation as well. And, of course, it succeeds: it is undeniable that two men who have spent their working lives in the same corporation, but have never previously met, experience a kind of fellowship at their first encounter which they would never feel toward any other kind of stranger. But how does the individual encounter and begin to feel part of the wider corporation beyond his ten-group and his tribe? What is "the corporation" to the employee, over and above the place where he earns a living and the few people he meets there, and distinct from the external identity by which the general public recognizes it?

The first necessity is a good communication system, which as we have seen is not dependent on paper or wires. "The corporation" has a certain number of physical expressions, but at root it is an idea—a complex and many-sided idea—which is the entire cultural tradition of the king's tribe. The more clearly and fully the individual members of the king's tribe perceive and share in that cultural tradition by frequent contact and discussion, and the more fully the managers and foremen of the tribe are taken into the confidence of their tribal chieftain who belongs to the king's tribe, the more the idea of "the corporation" will get through to the individual members. If there are occasional larger meetings, especially an assembly of the whole tribe, this will greatly increase the speed and certainty with which the idea takes root. (Even if the meetings are union meetings, those too will transmit a view of the corporation, even if it is not the one the corporation would choose.) And almost equally important is continuity: the longer the members of the working tribe have been in the corporation, the more folk wisdom they will have to pass on, and the more they will come to embody in their attitudes, behavior, judgments, and assumptions the corporation's cultural values.

Most corporations now take direct action as well. They issue house magazines and newspapers to all employees, they pin notices and news sheets to bulletin boards, they show films made for internal consumption, and some even mail to their employees at home to make sure the wife sees the good news, too. In addition a great deal of prestige corporate advertising is drafted with the employee very much in mind. It is easy to dismiss it all as paternalistic brainwashing propaganda, and certainly the corporation's motives are not altruistic: but in practice it seems to be most effective where there is already a strong sense of community, and to work not as a substitute for nonexistent communication but as an enhancement of a system that is already there.

The communication system, however, is only the means by which the picture is transmitted; what are the elements of which that picture is composed? The first, I suppose, is the simple addition to one's identity: "You're in the army now," as I and several million others were endlessly told in our first few weeks after conscription. The army was in a hurry to turn us into soldiers, and could not let us wait to discover its identity gradually: within a few hours we were all in full uniform, blazoning to the world that we belonged to the British army and the Royal Signals, however deep the doubts and misgivings inside the tunics. All the same, it was proof that the army accepted and acknowledged us—the army, not just the lance corporal in the stores who issued the battle dress. No one outside the army was allowed to wear it. In fact, some visible display of corporate membership is a symbol of much greater potency than most corporate executives realize: their refined and sophisticated gradations of status make simple membership a trivial thing to parade. But some badge or button or pin or tie can be a powerful magic, as it is for all of us if it represents a level of status we would be proud to reach. If the badge is not issued until the end of a probationary period—even if only a fortnight—it takes on even greater power. It is the first step on the status ladder, and the higher you climb the more carefully you think before you jump off. It also makes you look out for the other badges of the honors system, and thereby grow further in understanding of, and identity with, the corporation.

Most corporations extend this offer of identity through membership of subgroups—the many social and sporting clubs which offer further group membership and opportunities to climb other status ladders. The league and knock-out matches they play against other tribes create valuable lateral links at the lowest level. And by getting onto the football team or organizing the Easter outing, the employee gains further points of distinctive identity within his tribe, besides being entitled to wear the club tie as a further badge of status and membership.

I recently encountered surprising evidence of the power that badges of conformity can exert. A friend of mine was with IBM in the days when everyone from the lowest management or salesman level up had to wear a white shirt. It was never a written instruction, but everybody obeyed it nevertheless. Then, in their liberalizing era, it was made clear that the instruction no longer applied, and no one's promotion would be affected by the color of shirt he wore. But it was no good: everybody went on wearing white. A few tried to break the habit, but it was too strongly embedded in the tribal culture. They felt they were rebelling, or at least that everyone would think they were rebelling. My friend left IBM seven years ago, and is not very fond of white shirts, but he still wears one to work every day: the compulsion is too deeply ingrained to resist. In the same way there was an IBM taboo on pipes, and—at least in the presence of the Watsons—he and the other pipe-smokers never smoked them; it was held that pipe-smokers were complacent. He smokes his pipe freely now, but still feels, though he knows it is irrational nonsense, that all other pipe-smokers are complacent.

If the corporation does have any badges or other outward signs to show that it has bestowed its identity on an employee and accepted him into the community, that is the first strand in the cord that binds him to it. It takes a little longer to find out the second: the way it treats individuals, the way it exercises its authority, its system of personal justice. Does it give days off for compassionate reasons? Willingly or reluctantly? Does it trust your word, or keep checking up on you? Does it always want proof of every penny you pay out for it? Are they interested if you propose an idea? If you're off work, do they go on paying you? For how long? If a man is injured, does someone visit his wife? Will they help you out of a tight spot? How much holiday do you get? Do they give you a say in things, or just tell you to shut up and get on with it? If business turns down, do they just hand you your notice, or are they sympathetic and reluctant to lay off? If you retire after forty years, do you get a party and a gold watch and a speech from the boss, or do they just put the notice in with your last pay check? When you've retired, do they still invite you on outings and to Christmas parties? Is the tribal consensus "They look after you" or "They just chuck you on the scrap heap"?

There are hundreds of events in the tribal year which give the employee an answer to these questions; some he finds by his own experience, many more by the experiences of his friends and through the tribal communication network. Together they add up to the most powerful single factor in determining whether the corporate employees are integrated into the corporation or alienated from it. If the consensus is that they just chuck you on the scrap heap, the victims of the system will turn to the union in much the same way, and for much the same reason, as their forefathers turned from the parson and the established church to the preacher and the nonconformist chapel in the eighteenth and nineteenth centuries. And once that has happened, once the battle lines have been drawn, it is appallingly difficult to make peace and create unity ever again. Once the cultural tradition of the tribe includes the assumption that all managers are enemies, that they don't give a damn about you, that they're all looking after number one and lining the stockholders' pockets, and the only way to survive is to grab every penny you can while you can, then virtually every action of management can be shown to confirm it. And because of the enduring nature of this cultural tradition, the assumption becomes self-proving and self-perpetuating: by far the easiest way to lead is to fill the mold created by your predecessor, and if that mold is shaped like a battle-ax, if the tribe is shaped to accept and deal with a battle-ax, the easiest thing is to turn yourself into one. Everyone will understand, they will all know what to do, and it will all go on as before. Lord Robens, when he was chairman of the National Coal Board from 1960 to 1971, said you could still tell from the attitude of the men at any pit whether the original owner had been a good employer or a bad one. One lot would look at an offer in a fair and reasonable spirit, the other lot would be full of truculence, suspicion, and mistrust. I sometimes wonder how far Stalin and his successors imposed a new tyrannical system on a suffering nation, and how far they simply fell into a mold left vacant by Nicholas II and formed long before by Peter the Great, Ivan the Terrible, and Genghis Khan.

If, however, the tribal verdict is "They look after you," the chances are that the congregation will not desert to the chapels but remain with the state religion. In corporate terms, the state religion springs from the central faith, and ties individual behavior and moral standards to the external identity and long-term objectives of the corporation. For example, if the central faith of the corporation is tied to high-quality craftsmanship, a man whose shoddy work fails inspection will, in a nonconformist tribe, just be thought unlucky to have been caught out; in a religious tribe he will be held to have let the tribe down. Since the central faith is so close to corporate survival, the link between it and the personal morality of every employee is of inestimable value: but it has to be earned. If it is there, in the cultural tradition of every tribe, then not even the king can change it; if he deviates from it he will be harshly judged, and the moral standard will remain unaltered. This sort of moral condemnation rises in exact proportion to the degree in which it threatens survival: for instance, a head of a university science faculty who in a scientific paper omitted some inconvenient facts and embellished some more promising ones would be finished; the reputation of the university would be irreparably damaged. But exactly the same treatment of facts in a paper listing the hours worked by his staff, to show the grants committee that he needed two more lecturers, would be viewed somewhat more indulgently.

There is one special constraint on the corporate religion: it cannot be in conflict with the standards of the wider community in which the employees live, and the more it appears to be in harmony with it the better. Sometimes the corporation makes this connection in tribal assemblies, sometimes by word of mouth. I have even seen it done during sales training, on a Metropolitan Life Insurance film strip on how to close a sale. After going through the various forms of resistance and the ways of overcoming them, it finished by reminding the salesman that it was a grave disservice to a fellow American to let him risk leaving his wife and children penniless: overcoming his ignorant and irrational resistance was an act of kindness and virtue.

The new corporate employee will have far less to do with the corporate doctrine and rituals than with the religion. There will be, as we have seen, any amount of tribal doctrine and rituals, and some of them may be general to the corporation; but by their nature they are detailed, specific, and local. Much more significant in showing him the approved standards of behavior are the systems of payment, promotion, seniority, and special reward. These show in fine gradation the kinds of people, qualities, and behavior which the corporation is looking for: Does it go for ability at all costs? Seniority at all costs? Does it reward the loyal and patient, or the pushers? Are you promoted for performance or sycophancy? There is plenty of evidence generated by a year or two in a corporate tribe, and it is much more significant and trustworthy than information culled from the house magazine. This understanding of the corporation is broadened when great men from outside the employee's own tribe come and visit. Are they treated with genial informality or respectful deference? Are they large bearded men with shaggy jackets, or small and spruce with rimless spectacles? No single piece of evidence is worth much on its own, but as the pieces accumulate the common elements begin to stand out and the picture of the corporation, as distinct from his own tribe, becomes clearer.

Then there is the corporate folklore. I talked about the tribal folklore in Chapter XIV, the word-of-mouth tradition of stories and legends and anecdotes from the history of the tribe; in a tightly knit corporation the employee will encounter not just his own tribe's folklore, but the corporation's. There is a deep and ancient need in us to make sense out of important events, and to record the words and deeds of great men, as a part of the process of survival. This goes right back to our tribal hunting past; the story helps us to identify friends and enemies, safety and danger, courage and cowardice. It gives us a wider understanding of the world about us than we can gain from personal experience. It shows through its heroes the behavior we should aspire to. The Homeric legends were just such stories; the strict verse-meter is a help to memory—it is harder to get the wrong word when you have a strict meter or rhyme scheme. They were sung by minstrels going from tribe to tribe in the days before the written word, and they give sense and shape and morality to what was probably a squalid little conflict over trading rights in the northeast Mediterranean. The arrival of print has not diminished the demand for this kind of verbal narrative, nor the supply of it. The corporation is full of stories about great triumphs, great disasters, and great men. Especially disasters: since great efforts are made to keep the truth out of print (the Edsel was a rare exception), the stories circulate with rich embroidery; the Rolls-Royce crash produced a flood of apocryphal anecdotes. Almost everyone has a version of how and why any great disaster happened— you have only to look at the newspapers after a flood or fire or crash or any other great catastrophe to see the process in operation at a national level. We desperately need to know the answers so as to keep it from happening again, and if we can discover it was one person's fault we can secure our future safety by removing him. It is through this anecdotal folklore that a large part of the more nebulous idea of the corporation comes through to every corporate citizen: names of great heroes with their oddities of behavior or appearance, a vague idea of the corporate geography of divisions and regions and headquarters, a smattering of its history, a picture of its main rivals, and the beginnings of insight into its standards, its central purpose and its survival needs. Many of the stories are told over and over again—it needs only the excuse that someone has not heard it before, and the rest of the listening group enjoy it just as much every time.

The corporate folklore provides a part if the bond by which people from different parts of the kingdom, even if they have never met, can recognize each other as fellow citizens. If this bond is strong it is a sure indication of the strength of corporate unity. But folklore is only one of the strands; the central faith is another, and so are doctrine, rituals, and shared awareness of the quasi-territorial geography and the delicate gradations of the status system. There is even a shared corporation dialect: the pronunciation of the word "shibboleth" was enough to tell Jephthah who were his own Gileadites and who were Ephraimite outsiders, and in the same way to refer to "Our Marble Arch store" in Marks and Spencer (instead of "the Arch") would be a complete giveaway. Indeed, the U.S. army exploited this phenomenon during the war: German spies whose accent and papers were impeccable were caught out by questions such as "Who's the Brown Bomber?" and "Where's the Windy City?" All strong, united corporations have these small but significant variants of usage and pronunciation, though most of them are totally unconscious of it. I was quite unaware, until a journalist pointed it out to me, that you can tell television people by the fact that they never say "TV" and stress only the first syllable of "television"; once it was pointed out, I realized that I always subconsciously noted the stressing of the third syllable as a mark of someone outside the business.

And finally there is the king himself—the boss, the old man, the father figure, the subject of a hundred apocryphal stories, the focus of all unity and loyalty. The family business is an unfashionable idea at the moment—too many families traded for too long on family loyalty as an alternative to efficiency, competitiveness and fair wages—and we live in the age of management science and depersonalized interchangeable chairmen and chief executives. But if you ever happen on a corporation with a king who is prepared to risk abusive terms like "charisma" and "paternalism," who consciously and deliberately puts himself across to all his employees as the human personality at the head of the business, you can be in no real doubt of the holding power, the magnetic attraction, of personal monarchy. I remember General Sir John Hackett saying, "If you reach the rank of general without any personal oddities or idiosyncrasies, you'd better go out and get some damned quick." I suspect that none of us in our hearts really believe in organizations that do not have a single, personal leader at the head. All our experience of successful ten-groups and tribes teaches us that in the end it comes down to one man. Of course, he must have counselors, he must delegate authority, and there must be constraints on his power: but he must be there, and he must be one man, a single, clear-cut personality. And as with any leader, we have a great need to know that we can trust him, that he is strong and brave and wise and will protect us, so he starts at an advantage. Charisma is not manufactured by kings, but by their subjects; he has only to notice and speak to a man by name on one of his progresses to ensure at least another twelve months' loyal service. If he is good at the job of monarchy (and it is a skilled trade) he will have a vast card-index memory. And, unfashionable though it may be, his family is a part of it: people can identify with a family, and feel even more secure if there is a family up there at the top, even if it drives in a Rolls-Royce and has a yacht in the Caribbean. Walter Bagehot, the nineteenth-century British political commentator, was in no doubt about the appeal of a family: "A royal family sweetens politics by the seasonable addition of nice and pretty events. It introduces irrelevant facts into the business of government, but they are facts which speak to 'men's bosoms' and employ their thoughts." That passage came irresistibly to my mind when the Viyella switchboard operator described to me the excitement of the day Mr. Hyman's son was born and how she got through to all the other corporation switchboards around the country to tell the news. Life is earnest and business is business, but if there is a man with a wife and children at the head of it we can tell ourselves that, poor relations though we may be, we are still part of the family.

In these last two chapters we have put together the component parts of the corporate kingdom, the elements without which no corporation can survive: the means to defend itself against destruction from without, the means to preserve internal order, the means to ensure continuing health and vigor and skill, and the means of giving cohesion and unity despite geographical dispersal. Without them no human political institution can continue for long: not the primitive hunting tribe, nor the Roman Empire, nor modern Britain; not IBM, nor ICI, nor General Motors. And of them all, it is the last—this shared sense of all belonging together, this shared understanding and recognition of what it is we belong to—which is the hardest to build and the hardest to destroy: it can survive defeat and subjection, and yet be reborn. Poland was obliterated as a political unit, but the sense of cultural unity survived and was reincarnated. The Jaguar and Rover car companies were absorbed into the British Motor Corporation, but they are still there and could re-emerge tomorrow. We may discuss ailing corporations in terms of communication problems or poor personnel motivation or lack of corporate enterprise or growing too large—the corporate sickness has many symptoms and takes many forms—but there is only one form of corporate health: the continuity of the vigorous, successful, and united community. And that community finds its collective expression and its constant renewal in a loyal and united king's dispersed tribe.

XXII

The Empire

I T is the king's tribe that binds the kingdom together. So long as every tribal chieftain belongs to the king's tribe, then however many layers of hierarchy the organization chart may show, no one need in practice be more than one remove from the king; the king knows every chieftain, and the chieftain knows every tribesman. If the king's tribe is a thousand, and each member is chieftain of a thousand, this should give a theoretical maximum of a million: in practice, the maximum size for a kingdom is far lower. In the first place, the tribal maximum may be one thousand, but the optimum is five hundred, which reduces the figure to a quarter of a million. In the second place, many of the king's tribe are staff men with nothing like a full tribe under them, and others are senior executives with their own smaller staff, commanding the allegiance of several tribal factories or departments. In the third place, it is normal (and healthy)

for more than just one member of each tribe to belong to
the king's tribe. These three considerations combine to
reduce the actual size of an effective and practicable kingdom
to a much lower figure. How much lower? In a sense it is
pointless to try and fix the size of a corporate kingdom:
there are too many variables. Moreover, "kingdom" is a
somewhat arbitrary term anyway; unlike the tribe it is not
a self-contained biological unit—it is an interlocking arrangement of tribes around a central tribe, which each
corporation has to work out for itself. There is no reason
why a firm of five thousand should not call itself a kingdom
if it wants to. Having said all that, I still find the thirty
thousand size running around in my head. I cannot offer any
theoretical explanation, but having come to the figure it is
possible to make a case for it. For instance, the four most
efficient and successful chain stores in Britain's High Streets
—Boots (43,000), Sainsbury's (32,000), Tesco (25,000), and
Marks and Spencer (32,000)—are not too far from that
figure, and two of America's most successful and united
corporations, 3M and Coca-Cola, are in the same range. As
a size for a town, it has the right sort of feel to it: it can
have a single town center and an administrative and social
coherence that cannot be sustained at seventy thousand or
eighty thousand. Indeed, there were very few towns much
larger than forty thousand, except for the great national
centers, until the industrial revolution. And in military
terms it keeps cropping up throughout history as the largest
self-contained and integrated formation that can be controlled on the field. It is about the size of the modern division; with any larger number, you are commanding a
number of divisions. But illustration is not proof, and even
these illustrations offer a fairly wide latitude. Nevertheless,
even if the figure can range between twenty thousand and
sixty thousand, we still have to accept that corporations of
over a hundred thousand like duPont, Westinghouse, and
Bethlehem Steel, or over three hundred thousand like ITT,
G.E., and Sears, Roebuck, not to mention the even vaster cor-

porate giants right up to General Motors' seven hundred thousand and AT&T's million, must be regarded as being in a quite different category from the simple corporate kingdom. At that level we are not dealing with kingdoms any more: we are dealing with empires.

Since "empire" is an even more arbitrary term than "kingdom," it is even harder to state the point at which a small empire might start, but it is less hard to list an empire's identification marks. First, of course, is size: when numbers are so large that it is impossible for every tribal chieftain to belong to the king's tribe, it becomes difficult to run an integrated corporate kingdom. When it contains a large number of provinces the size of kingdoms, geographically separated and perhaps with different languages, when its asset value and market price are so high that a takeover is a practical impossibility, then it is unmistakably of imperial proportions. But to deserve the name "empire" it must have something else: the same cultural unity, the same shared body of doctrine, the same central faith and folklore, collectively held and renewed, as a corporate kingdom; the only difference is that the dispersed tribe which holds it and passes it out to the provinces and on to the new generation is the emperor's tribe. Without that unity it may be a single unit legally and financially, but it can fall apart as quickly as it was put together. This, of course, has been the trouble of the conglomerates: it is easy enough to become a star growth stock by buying up undervalued companies and maximizing their assets, but what do you do then? To become a true united corporate kingdom with such diverse tribes is a mammoth task that has proved too much for any conglomerate so far; most of them end up as an amalgam of company doctors, management consultants, holding companies, and investment banks. The separate companies lack that central community of experience and standards and cultural tradition that make up a true corporate identity; it is this identity that distinguishes both kingdoms and empires from looser and more temporary political federations.

For this reason, virtually everything that has been said so far about the corporate kingdom is true of the corporate empire: it is just a group of kingdoms united as provinces under the emperor in the same ways that the dukedoms and baronies are united under the king. The sheer size and diversity, however, make the government of an empire into a different kind of operation in a number of important ways.

The first and most obvious consequence of size is that conquest by an enemy is virtually out of the question. A kingdom can never lose sight of the possibility of a hostile attack by a dangerous competitor, which in a year or two could so reduce its sales, lower its profits, and bring down its share price that a takeover bid might be welcomed by the stockholders. The narrower the kingdom's range of products and the more limited its market, the more acute this danger becomes. But an empire is too large to be toppled by a sudden twist of fate or turn of the market, and it has the additional protection of diversity. The best illustration I can think of is the peppered moth. It flourished in the Midlands, and two hundred years ago it used to be nearly white in color: it rested on the bark of plane trees, where it was almost invisible to the birds who lived off it. There was, however, a darker gene in the gene pool, and so darker moths cropped up from time to time and were quickly seen and devoured. But with the grime of the industrial revolution the plane trees went nearly black, and the white moths stood out a mile. Had there not been the diversity, that population would have been extinguished like a one-product kingdom. But the darker variety now had the camouflage; they filled up the population gap, and survived. The product pool and market pool of a corporate empire are likewise so varied that it can survive, and perhaps even profit from, the sort of calamity that can destroy a kingdom.

This same variety makes it possible for the empire to smooth the decline of a product or market without the convulsions that a kingdom might have to endure. The traumatic decline of the British cotton industry and the long agony of Lancashire went in parallel with the boom in synthetic fibers and the desperate hunger for trained management. An empire of all the fibers could have smoothed the transition—as Viyella and Courtaulds later tried to do— so that cotton could have peacefully and happily contracted as synthetics expanded. And when this is possible, there is a rich harvest to be reaped. One of the greatest obstacles to corporate unity is the need to lay men off: it is hard to feel you belong to a family if they tell you from time to time that there is no room and no food for you, and they don't want to see your face for the next few months. But a kingdom is often so much at the mercy of outside forces that it simply cannot guarantee its own survival if it has to pay all its labor force even when there is no work for them. Of course, even an empire may have to do this—it is only a group of kingdoms; but by its diversity and wealth it can sustain a lower profit or a loss in one of them for longer than any kingdom which stands alone. This makes it possible to offer citizenship to everyone in the empire, at least once they have come of age by a certain length of continuous service: citizenship in the case of the corporation—sometimes called "staff status"— is a public declaration that you cannot be laid off, and an implicit undertaking that the corporation's affairs will be conducted with the maintenance of full employment as a part of all policy. When this happens, it is usually the end of strikes; there may still be union activity, but the whole climate changes. I have already suggested that a part of the strong sense of belonging in Japanese corporations stems from their refusal to lay off: IBM, which follows the same policy, has no unions at all in its United States factories. It is the same principle as universal suffrage: to give all citizens the chance to vote you out is to undertake to bear their welfare in mind while you govern, which means accepting the same sort of constraints as guaranteeing to see there is always work for them.

Size and diversity do not, of course, mean that the corporate empire can stop worrying about survival: only that as it grows the emphasis at the top shifts more and more from the short-term operation to the long-term realities, from the government to the state, from the hunting bands to the camp. A tribal factory of a few hundred is totally dominated by making and selling, and its continuing identity mostly has to take care of itself; by contrast, the government of a corporate empire is almost totally concerned with the continuing identity. If it is concerned with operational errors in the kingdoms, it is not for the errors in themselves, but as symptoms of a disease. I have noticed this in television: most bad programs were reasonable ideas that for one reason or other did not come off. You can see what they were trying to do, and having failed at it yourself from time to time you sympathize. But just occasionally there is a program that was doomed from the start, that could not possibly have succeeded: then you start to worry about the health of the whole body, because if anyone can reach the seniority needed to approve such a program without acquiring enough experience to know it is a nonstarter, then the whole system is suspect. It means that some central point of doctrine has not been passed down. One of the few inexorable destroyers of empires is this creeping decay from within. Almost always it is a consequence of poor communication (and therefore poor community maintenance): it means that the lifeblood of the organization, the shared corporate culture, is not being pumped out to the extremities any more. When he realizes this is happening, the corporate emperor is liable to fall for anyone who seems to offer a remedy—management consultant, computer expert, behavioral psychologist, astrologer, or practitioner in internal public relations. But if the community is healthy, if the doctrine and the rest of the culture are being properly transmitted and renewed, if the collective survival kit is in good working order, then the corporate emperor is free to look outward.

He does not, however, look at the world with the eyes of a corporate king. A corporate kingdom has to adapt itself to its environment—to competitors, suppliers, governments, technologies—but an empire is so large and powerful it can begin to adapt the environment to itself. It can never do so completely, and it can often try and fail: but for an emperor, some control of the environment becomes a real possibility. His provinces will have to go on playing the game as hard as ever, but he can try and arrange for them to play downhill with the wind behind them the whole time.

In corporate terms, any company under the size of a kingdom is a fighting unit. It is usually one among many within its industry. Some warlike small duchies are expanding and have to be vigorously resisted; some established principalities are encroaching on the sales and product territory of neighbors; some have their backs to the wall and are fighting with the fury of desperation, and with the disregard of conventions that accompanies fear of extinction. A kingdom has a little more breathing space, but it is constantly under pressure from rival kingdoms and aggressive smaller units: Marks and Spencer are surrounded by British Home Stores, Littlewood's and Woolworth's, and in special parts of their business by Sainsbury's, Mothercare, Burtons, Richard Shops, and many others, all of them waiting to snap up any customers they lose. Everyone knows that their field of operations is a battlefield.

Empires, however, are another matter. They are so large and well-established that a fight to the death is out of the question. It is not merely that it would be a long, costly, and vicious battle: it is that the rival empires need each other. The great empires of oil or heavy electricity or automobiles or steel do not want to conquer all their enemies—the dangers and worries of total monopoly would be a bitter reward for a devastating conflict, and the conflict would be very nasty. A frightened empire is an ugly enemy, as Ralph Nader discovered. The result is, of course, an exact parallel to Professor Wynne-Edwards's discovery referred to in Chapter X: conventional competition. A price war in the oil or automobile industries would mean ever-diminishing revenues for ever-increasing effort, as would a competitive auction of royalty offers to the Middle East sheikdoms: the classic over-fishing situation. So the competition is conventionalized. The Oxford ethologist Professor Niko Tinbergen has filmed herring gulls doing exactly the same thing: when defending the frontiers of their nesting territory they confront each other with fury, beaks wide open; but they do not attack each other—they furiously pull up clumps of grass. It is called "displacement activity" and is a form of ritualized aggression. There is much ritualized aggression between empires—in packaging, styling, quality of service, free offers, press and television advertising—and the tribesmen on the frontiers are kept on their toes; but a fight to the death would upset the delicate ecology of the industry, and it never happens.

Some observers have taken this to mean that the corporate empires can completely manipulate the consumer. This, of course, is not so; in the automobile industry, for example, the consumer still has a great deal of choice—conventional competition can still be vigorous within the conventions. And there are always the energetic and enterprising kingdoms and duchies threatening the frontier provinces of the empire; the Gillette empire on its own might never have offered the consumer a stainless-steel blade, but a tiny English barony, Wilkinson's, put one on the market with such electrifying success that the empire had to compete or risk the permanent loss of a province.

Nevertheless, an empire's survival is not threatened by its rivals: the smaller ones may goad it into unwelcome expense and activity, but cannot imperil existence; the other empires have an interest in collective survival and preserving the existing balance. The slow decay from within, the fossilization of doctrine and the relaxation of corporate fitness, are a far greater danger than any enemy activity.

And it is not only the competitive environment that the corporate emperor can hope to manipulate in ways not open to a single kingdom: he can influence the economic climate as well. If a king is thinking of exporting to a small developing country, he has to study the economic projections and calculate the amount it will be able to spend on his product and the market share he might capture. An emperor can actually influence the level of spending power by his investment decisions. This is not arbitrary and unfettered power —there will have to be sound financial reasons for the investment, and other empires will be investing too—but his decision will still influence events as well as respond to them. And not only in developing countries: Ford (and I expect most other empires as well) has an expert whose job is to give the corporation early warning of likely devaluation in countries where it has investments. If a number of corporate empires get the same early warning and all of them suddenly change to a stronger currency, the likely devaluation becomes the inevitable devaluation.

This sort of consideration, too, has led to a misunderstanding: because the corporate emperor is so far removed from the product and the customer, because he is looking toward and participating in the economic development of different countries in ten, fifteen, or twenty years' time, it is easy to think that any good banker-economist can run a corporate empire. It is certainly true that running a corporate empire demands all those skills, and that the activities at the very top are closer to those of an investment bank than a factory or a refinery; but an equally important ingredient in all decisions is a deep understanding of the business, born of long experience and endless reviewing and revising of doctrine, a long recollection of successes and failures, and the lessons drawn from them all. And even more important, the emperor is an emperor—the top of the status ladder, the focus of admiration and unity, the chief of the emperor's dispersed tribe, and the central figure of the entire corporate community. That great office cannot be filled with distinction and conviction by some economics expert who has just come over from a merchant bank.

The power to influence, and in part control, both the economic climate and its competitors' behavior gives a corporate empire a freedom, a stability, and a certainty of permanence beyond the dreams of kings. But the more those two variables come under control, or at least into the realm of confident prediction, the more sharply the third feature of the environmental landscape stands out, the last unpredictable obstacle on the road to imperial security: the government. And the story of how Corporation Man is overcoming that obstacle is one of the most absorbing of the untold stories of our time.

I hasten to say that I cannot tell the story: the facts are hard to come by and harder to verify. The occasional instance slips out: There was the case of Australia's balance of payments problem with Japan, which could have been solved by exporting cars to Japan, but was not so solved because General Motors had told their Australian company to export all their output to the United States. There was the American company which was forbidden by the U.S. Department of Defense to export a paper mill to Rumania, so their British subsidiary exported it for them. But reports like these are rare, and neither the corporations nor the governments have any desire to add to them; both have an interest in preserving the fiction of the sovereign state. Nevertheless, although the story cannot be told, the general pattern is becoming clear.

Until 1945, war was the dominant political issue in advanced industrial countries, and consequently national defense and foreign policy were the first concerns of government. In this climate a nation's industry was as important a resource as its army—the great national companies like Krupp and Skoda, Boeing and Vickers, were virtually an arm of government. But ever since 1945, world war has been receding as a political issue: this does not mean that we do not retain a lurking dread that some lunatic may blow us all to pieces, but it does mean that it is no longer the overriding political preoccupation. Its place at the top of the charts has been taken by unemployment and national prosperity; the thirties, not the forties, are the specter that haunts today's political leaders. But the thirties saw more than the slump: they also saw the birth of Keynesian economics, and of the idea that the elected government has the power and the duty to ensure the full employment and rising prosperity of the electorate.

As the immediate threat of war receded, so governments turned more and more of their attention to employment and prosperity, and, of course, the Western governments encountered a problem; they could not command corporations in the way they could command fleets and armies. They could manipulate the knobs on the Keynesian dial, but these were insensitive and unspecific: the point of balance between "inflation and balance of payments crisis" and "squeeze and unemployment crisis" was dangerously elusive. Nor did the instruments have a control for relieving local unemployment in electorally important areas, or for raising the level of productivity and increasing the total wealth of the country. Government's province is the distribution of wealth, not its creation. For these and many other reasons politicians needed some power over the actions of kingdoms and empires if they were to be reelected.

They were, in fact, rather slow to realize how well equipped they were with the instruments of persuasion. It was not only that the kings and emperors had to seek government permission for many activities, especially at the highest level of exchange controls, capital movements, and the like; they also increasingly needed government support in their dealings with foreign countries. And most of all, the purchasing power of the government as a customer with its massive taxation revenues gave it tremendous leverage when suggesting, for example, that a corporation would have more chance of a contract if the tender specified that a new plant would be opened in a depressed area to execute it. To say that the corporations resented this power might be an overstatement; they were glad of the business. But the gain in security of work was a loss of freedom of action. Government contracts are an addictive drug (as they are also sometimes

narcotic and even hallucinogenic), and prolonged depend-
ence can damage the corporation while being almost impossible to break; and—to change the metaphor—many firms
like Rolls-Royce and Lockheed who grabbed the rope the
government had thrown them because they thought it was
a lifeline discovered too late that it was a noose. The corporation's interests may overlap with the government's at many
points, but they are never identical: for example, the reelec-
tion of the present government for a further term rates
a good deal higher on the government's list of priorities than on the corporation's. Political logic and industrial logic rest on different premises and lead to different
conclusions.

But as the governments began to realize their power, so
Corporation Man found his defense: it was called "internationalism." Many corporations were already manufacturing and selling overseas for straightforward industrial and
commercial reasons, but the new political reasons gave these
activities a tremendous impetus. The logic is obvious: all
governments need the corporate empire's investment, especially if it means more jobs and more exports. Once the
corporations are truly international, with half or more of
their profit coming from overseas activity, they are no longer
at the mercy of their national governments. They do not
have to invest the money at home at all—many foreign countries will welcome them. If an American corporation had to
run down its home operation to a holding company, the
imperial capital could shift to London or Paris, as Constantine transferred the geographical location of his empire from
Rome to Byzantium. And, of course, their leverage on other
governments is enormous—Ford of America is Britain's third
largest exporting corporation, bringing her two hundred
million pounds of foreign exchange a year. The international empires also have tremendous scope to exploit the
differing national tax laws, exchange controls, and customs
regulations for maximum corporate benefit. Furthermore,
they can manufacture where labor is cheapest and sell where

profits are greatest. The logic of internationalism is inescapable.

All this, of course, is not so easy as it sounds: it means extending the corporate culture, and spreading its religion and doctrine, to many nations outside the national culture in which the corporation was born, most of whom speak different languages. But it can be done, and I speak from experience—brief experience, but significant. In 1967 I was one of a ten-group that mounted the first world-wide live television program—a two-hour hookup from fourteen countries. The ten-group, all senior television producers, included a Canadian, an American, a Frenchman, a Russian, a Japanese, an Italian, and three Englishmen; we mostly spoke English. The difficulties and pressures were considerable, but the project excited us all, and as the meetings went on the true ten-group spirit grew up as everyone's loyalty and professional skill and commitment to the group objective were progressively tested and proved true. The consequence was a warmth of fellow feeling and respect which still endures and has proved, at least to me, that in those terms an international community is a perfectly practicable possibility: and what I have discovered in a ten-group is equally possible, given a little more time, within an emperor's tribe, and within the various provincial governors' tribes that compose the empire. Governments find great difficulty in forming international communities, but under the stimulus of industrial, financial, and political advantage the corporate empires are building them all the time.

Many of the international corporations are now calling themselves "multinational." I suspect it is a public relations device to dissemble their national origins and deflect the charge of economic imperialism. "No, we're not an American corporation, we're multinational. Just happens we're all from Poughkeepsie." Up till now no great corporate empire has done a Constantine; the American international corporations are just that, and so are the Dutch, the French, the British, and all the others. Nevertheless, as they encompass more and more foreign nationals within the emperor's tribe and the governors' tribes, so they come more and more to deserve the title of, if not "multinational," then "international" in the very fullest sense.

Corporation Man, therefore, is an international man. Not, of course, at the lower levels of tribal operations; it is only in the high courts of the empire that he enters an international community. This does not mean surrendering his national identity, but it does mean belonging to a dispersed tribal community of many nationalities. And what is more, he is an international man at the highest level: at the heart of the corporate empire, his dealings are with financiers and economists, with statesmen and top civil servants, with presidents and prime ministers, as the representative of an international power at least as formidable as most of the world's national states.

XXIII

The Century of Corporation Man

U P till now we have been content simply to observe the behavior of the Corporation Man and try to deduce his essential nature from the way he works and the organizations he builds. We have followed him from the hunting band into the camp, and from the camp into the tribe. We have seen the tribes coming together into kingdoms, united by the king's dispersed tribe, and now we have looked at the growth of the empire. But the question we have never asked about Corporation Man is whether we like him. Is he a friend or an enemy?

In a sense it is too late to ask: he is here to stay. It seems almost inevitable that well before the end of this century most of the wealth of the Western world will be controlled by three to six hundred giant international corporations; the only argument now is about the exact number. If this century is the century of the common man, the next will just as certainly be the century of Corporation Man. The small private corporate kingdom controlled by its proprietor will be as rare an anachronism in the future as the landed aristocrat is today. All the same, the few landed aristocrats I have met seem to bear the affliction of unorthodoxy with remarkable cheerfulness: they have survived the common man's century without beating him and without joining him. We cannot beat Corporation Man, but we do not have to join him if we discover that we do not like his face. It is, of course, not very easy to discover anything at all. The corporations are experts at concealment, and employ further experts to burnish the corporate image, by selective disclosure of favorable information. Moreover, when we contrast their glowing self-portraits with their actual behavior as we encounter it directly as customers, employees, and members of the public, or vicariously through friends, hearsay, or the occasional scandal, we become aware that the benign smile is painted on a mask. We only see occasional shadowy glimpses of the face behind, but we cannot help wondering why, if the face is friendly, it should bother with a mask at all.

Besides, we see enough to know how unfriendly the face can be. There are too many accounts of oppressive, unjust, and despotic behavior to employees for us to sustain the myth of universal benevolence. It is not an answer to say that people can always leave: they are encouraged to become part of the corporate culture and to commit themselves to the organization for life, and if they discover too late that the loyalty flowed in one direction only, their simplicity does not justify the corporation's duplicity. It is too easy for a corporate executive to talk about freedom and democracy at home while running a repressive autocracy at work. Many of the battles for the rights of man that have been won in the nation's political arena are lost daily in the executive offices and board rooms of the corporation.

We also find out enough about the corporation as a neighbor to know that excessive trust in its neighborly instincts would be misplaced. Its concern with our rivers and coasts and atmosphere, like its concern with safety and fair prices, is concern that it should not be found out. It may be shamed into neighborly behavior, but since the instincts are not there it needs our constant vigilance to stop it from dumping its trash in our backyard. And when we try to influence its actions, we discover something else: it is ultimately answerable only to itself. It has to operate within the law, but beyond that it is free. The power of any government over it, as we have seen, is diminishing, and at best is only a bargaining power. The power of the community is only the power of restraint by shame, adverse publicity, and the fear of restrictive legislation. The power of the stockholder, except after years of disastrous results, is so dispersed among hundreds of thousands of people as to be impossible to mobilize. The power of the emperor's ten-group and his tribe is the real force; it is a significant force in any community, and yet not accountable to the community's elected representatives. And in the absence of any information we are bound to suspect that the private agreements and understandings between the "rival" corporate empires operate for their benefit and not for ours.

For all these reasons we remain deeply unimpressed by the corporate apologists who assure us that the corporation is the abject slave of its stockholders or an extension of the community welfare service. The true face of the corporation is the face of self-interest, a face (if we are honest) not widely different from our own. So if we want to know if Corporation Man is friend or foe, we have to ask how far his self-interest coincides or conflicts with ours.

Very simply, his interest is in the creation and distribution of wealth for his own advantage. Not necessarily for his own profit: he will certainly try and arrange for himself a comfortable present and a secure future, but profits as such are a local convention. Many of the vast Japanese corporations show a tiny return on assets: it is their growth rate and sales volume that are impressive. Corporation Man, once survival is assured, seeks challenging hunting activity and the tribal honor and status that rewards his success. If success is measured in profits he will seek profits; if the convention is growth, or production volume, or capital formation, he will compete for those. But whatever the convention, the corporation offers millions of people rewarding work, the chance of status, vigorous tribal activity, a channel for aggressive instincts, and an identity, while all the time increasing the wealth of the world. What other institution can say the same?

The only one that has tried to do so has been the national state. If it is by industry, it merely creates more corporations —the ownership, as we have seen, has very little effect on corporate behavior. The only other way it has found, as a state, has been by armies and war. War certainly provides employment, in the services and in armaments factories; it gives identity and status and competitive activity, and it channels aggression. As world population rises, war, as we have also seen, offers the solution by decreasing demand just as the corporation offers it by increasing supply.

We are all aware that national wars brought us to the edge of extinction a quarter of a century ago. When the national state was the only organization with real independent power, the final arbiter of status among nations was war. With the international corporation, we have evolved a displacement activity: we have ritualized aggression by changing the convention. We now look to the national state to order our communities, to protect our property, to maintain a just, free, stable, and prosperous society—but not to express our competitive aspirations and channel our aggressive impulses. The World Cup and the Olympic Games and the Space Race are the appropriate arena for national pride; for the more serious tribal contests, the international corporation, with all its faults, offers a far better hope of survival for the species. As Dr. Johnson said, there are few ways in which a man can be more innocently employed than in getting money.

The corporation is in business for a long time, and it needs peace and stability more than anything. The corporate emperor has to see further ahead than any presidents or prime ministers serving four- or five-year terms. Long-term investment demands prediction, and war is the great unpredictable: it may generate short-term business profits, but the long-term self-interest of more and more international corporations is on the side of peace as it is on the side of wealth. Moreover, the growing internationalism of the corporation makes national wars less and less of a practical possibility: how do you turn your nation's industry over to war production as its operations become more and more entwined with other countries who do not share your intentions, or who even oppose them? Could the government of an advanced industrial nation resist the combined pressures of all the corporate emperors and international banks, and prepare to go it alone? Could it guarantee its food and fuel and aircraft supplies against their wishes? It has to choose between the suicide pact of a nuclear strike, or peace. There is still the great divide of the iron curtain, but already the logic of prosperity is leading to closer and closer commercial and industrial connections; Corporation Man does not put ideology before profitability.

But almost more important than the dispersed operations of the international corporation is the dispersed tribe. The comradeship of international corporate tribes is a valuable counterweight to the chauvinism of national governments. It is this more than anything else that gives me hope. Of course, the hope is qualified—the menace of industrial pollution is now obvious, and the corporations are its chief cause —but all the same a mass of small companies is much harder to control than a few vast ones. Corporate emperors need status and acceptance too, and the condemnation of the wider national community in which they compete for honor and respect is a powerful deterrent. The dangers are still real enough to make confidence in our future a premature emotion, but for me at least the internationalism of Corporation Man outweighs it. Kenneth Clark observed in "Civilisation" that nearly all the steps upward in civilization have been made in periods of internationalism. The international corporations are forces for internationalism, and the nation-states and national governments are forces against it. If the balance is now tilting away from nationalism, we have much to be grateful for.

I know that it is foolhardy to look at history in three-hundred-year cycles, and yet the past nine hundred years have seen three great periods of internationalism, all of them three hundred years apart. There was the great twelfth-century renaissance, the age of the great Gothic cathedrals, which ended with the dynastic nationalism of the thirteenth century. Three centuries later there was another great period of civilized internationalism, the fifteenth century—the age of the Italian renaissance, the age of Erasmus—and that ended with the religious nationalism of the sixteenth century. Another three hundred years, and there comes the enlightenment of the eighteenth century, Gibbon and Voltaire, before the political nationalism of the nineteenth century put an end to it. It is tempting to think that we are once more emerging from nationalist darkness, and that the twenty-first century, the century of the Corporation Man, will continue the three-hundred-year cycle with another period of internationalism and another step upward for civilization. Certainly I find it hard to imagine what harm the international corporation can do to the human race in the twenty-first century that would be comparable with the harm done by the national states in the twentieth.

E D U C A T E D at Cambridge University, ANTONY JAY joined the British Broadcasting Corporation (BBC) in 1955 and rose to become executive producer of its most advanced programming, including the famous Talks Features Department. In 1965, he formed a management consulting firm regarded to be the most imaginative in Britain—with the BBC as one of its major clients. Mr. Jay is the author of *Management and Machiavelli,* which has sold over a quarter of a million copies worldwide since its publication in 1967. He was co-author with David Frost of *The English,* and this year the American Management Association is publishing his new book, *The New Oratory.*